Writing Thesis in English
A Course in Writing for English Majors

英语专业
毕业论文写作教程

(第2版修订本)

主编　张秀国

编著　张秀国　王　炜　焦立东

扫描二维码,
获取相关教学资源

清华大学出版社
北京交通大学出版社
·北京·

内 容 简 介

本书从切实培养和提高英语专业学生运用英语进行论文写作能力的目的出发来组织编写内容,共分为9章。第1章为序言,简要介绍研究与研究论文的定义。第2章介绍论文写作的一般过程与步骤。第3章介绍论文包含的各个主要部分及其结构。第4章介绍论文的语言特点和文体风格。第5章介绍英语写作的技巧,涉及英语论文写作者常常忽略和经常感到困惑、容易出错的地方。第6章专论标点符号,讨论常用标点符号在各种情况下的一般使用规则。第7~9章讨论引文和参考文献的三种常用格式。本书强化直观性,突出实用性,每个部分之后均编写了相关练习供学习者复习巩固之用。同时,本书还提供了许多格式实例,供学习者比较分析及写作时模仿。

本书内容丰富,资料性强,既可作为英语专业本科生的教材使用,也可供其他英语研究者写作论文时参考。

本书封面贴有清华大学出版社防伪标签,无标签者不得销售。
版权所有,侵权必究。侵权举报电话: 010 - 62782989 13501256678 13801310933

图书在版编目(CIP)数据

英语专业毕业论文写作教程/张秀国主编. — 2版. — 北京:北京交通大学出版社:清华大学出版社,2019.9(2025.1修订)
 ISBN 978-7-5121-4029-5

Ⅰ. ①英… Ⅱ. ①张… Ⅲ. ①英语-毕业论文-写作-高等学校-教材
Ⅳ. ①G642.477 ②H315

中国版本图书馆 CIP 数据核字(2019)第 186110 号

英语专业毕业论文写作教程
YINGYU ZHUANYE BIYE LUNWEN XIEZUO JIAOCHENG

责任编辑:张利军
出版发行:清 华 大 学 出 版 社　　邮编:100084　　电话:010-62776969
　　　　　北京交通大学出版社　　邮编:100044　　电话:010-51686414
印 刷 者:艺堂印刷(天津)有限公司
经　　销:全国新华书店
开　　本:170 mm×240 mm　　印张:16　　字数:340千字
版　　次:2019年9月第2版　2024年8月第2版第1次修订　2025年1月第5次印刷
书　　号:ISBN 978-7-5121-4029-5/G·1898
印　　数:8 501~10 500册　定价:49.00元

本书如有质量问题,请向北京交通大学出版社质监组反映。对您的意见和批评,我们表示欢迎和感谢。
投诉电话:010-51686043,51686008;传真:010-62225406;E-mail:press@bjtu.edu.cn。

前　言

论文写作（包括毕业论文写作）是综合检测学生学业能力、训练和培养学生创新思维能力的重要环节。《高等学校英语专业英语教学大纲》（2000年）指出，各个高校都应强化对毕业论文的指导，要求英语专业学生的毕业论文都应当用英文撰写。用英语撰写论文必须符合英文论文的格式规范，因此需要帮助学生提高论文写作能力、了解和掌握英语论文写作的格式。英语论文写作是高校英语专业的一门必修课程，其目的就是通过该课程的教学，使学生了解英语论文写作的一般过程和英语研究论文的格式，并掌握其写作规范。

本书从切实培养和提高英语专业学生运用英语进行论文写作能力的目的出发来组织编写内容，共分为9章。第1章为序言，简要介绍研究与研究论文的定义。第2章介绍论文写作的一般过程与步骤。第3章介绍论文包含的各个主要部分及其结构。第4章介绍论文的语言特点和文体风格。第5章介绍英语写作的技巧，其中涉及英语论文写作者常常忽略和经常感到困惑、容易出错的地方。第6章专论标点符号，讨论常用标点符号在各种情况下的一般使用规则。第7～9章讨论引文和参考文献的三种常用格式。其中，第7章介绍美国现代语言学会（MLA）格式，第8章介绍美国心理学协会（APA）格式，第9章介绍美国芝加哥大学出版社采用的芝加哥（CHCAGO）格式。

为改变目前英语论文写作能力训练的书籍大多用中文撰写、不适应英语专业高年级教学需求的现状，本书用英文撰写，以切合英语专业高年级教学的实际需求。本书既涉及选题、发掘材料、收集资料、提炼主题、确定写作提纲、撰写初稿、修改与定稿等具体写作过程，也涉及引文、注释、参考文献等写作规范；既介绍如何引用书籍、期刊等纸质文献，也介绍怎样引用网络文献；既介绍MLA格式的要求，也介绍APA格式和CHICAGO格式的要求。本书内容丰富，资料性强，既可作为英语专业本科生的教材使用，也可供其他英语研究者写作论文时参考。本书强化直观性，突出实用性，每个部分之后均编写了相关练习供学习者复习巩固之用。同时，本书在9章内容之后还设计了"综合练习"（Appendix A），为学习者提供了MLA、APA、CHICAGO三个常用写作规范的对比实例，供学习者比较分析和写作时模仿。本书习题内容丰富，形式多样，针对性强，答案简明准确，既便于个人自学使用，也便于课堂讨论和讲解使用。

本书自2007年出版以来颇受广大读者的欢迎，已重印十余次，被众多高校选作英语专业学生长期使用的教材。为更好地服务高校英语专业师生、服务广大英语爱好者，在北京交通大学出版社，特别是责任编辑张利军的鼓励和支持下，编者对原书内容进行了调整、修改与补充，推出第2版。

本次修订遵循保持原书风格与基本架构不变的原则，各章节的标题、各章的主要内容及第7、8、9章的整体内容均未作变动。本次修订的内容主要有以下3个方面。

（1）调整补充了部分章节的内容。第1~4章是本次修订的重点，在保持这些章节原有主要内容的基础上，删除了部分内容，同时也补充了部分内容，并对部分段落进行了重写。

（2）重新设计了练习项目与练习内容。本次重点修订了第1、2、3、4、6章所附的练习，有的增加了练习项目，有的变换了练习项目的类型，有的则增加了练习项目中的题量。绝大部分练习均配有参考答案，有需求者可发送邮件至cbszy@jg.bjtu.edu.cn索取。

（3）删繁就简，锤炼文字。本次修订对已发现的第1版中语言表达不够明晰的地方及讹误一一进行了修改或匡正。

经过本次修订，编者希望新版教材比第1版更加有利于提高读者的英语论文写作水平，更加方便教学，更加有利于提升高校英语专业学生撰写英语毕业论文的能力。

本书可供一个学期使用，建议安排20个学时左右完成学习任务，使用者可根据实际情况灵活挑选学习内容，掌握学习进度。

本书第1版由张秀国负责制定编写原则和全书的整体设计，编写第1~6章、第9章的9.2节及附录、参考文献、索引和"综合练习"（Appendix A）中APA、CHICAGO格式习题的解答，并通读全书；王炜负责编写第8章和第9章的9.1节；焦立东负责编写第7章、"综合练习"（Appendix A）的习题和MLA格式习题的解答。本书第2版的全部修订工作由张秀国负责。

在编写过程中，我们广泛参考了各种书籍，在此就各位专家、学者对本书的形成所做出的贡献致以崇高的敬意。本书的出版得到了江苏省教育厅和淮阴师范学院的资助，在此我们表示诚挚的谢意。同时，我们还应该感谢清华大学出版社、北京交通大学出版社的大力支持，特别要感谢张利军编辑，是他的鼓励与支持使本书能够在较短时间内与广大读者见面并发挥作用。

由于编者的水平有限，书中肯定存在不少疏漏和欠妥之处，欢迎广大读者和同行批评指正。

编　者

2024年7月

Contents

Chapter 1 Introduction: Research and Research Paper ·········· 1

  1.1 Research ·········· 1
  1.2 Research Paper ·········· 2
  Exercises ·········· 3

Chapter 2 The Process of Research and Research Writing ·········· 6

  2.1 Choosing a Topic ·········· 6
    2.1.1 Importance and Interest ·········· 7
    2.1.2 Manageability ·········· 7
      2.1.2.1 Avoid a Too Broad Topic ·········· 7
      2.1.2.2 Avoid a Too Narrow Topic ·········· 8
    2.1.3 Availability of Resources ·········· 8
    2.1.4 Where to Find a Topic for Research ·········· 8
  2.2 Exploring Data ·········· 9
    2.2.1 Reference Works ·········· 9
      2.2.1.1 Encyclopedia and Dictionary ·········· 10
      2.2.1.2 Biographical Dictionary and Index ·········· 10
      2.2.1.3 Book Index ·········· 10
      2.2.1.4 Periodical Index ·········· 10
      2.2.1.5 Computer Database ·········· 11
      2.2.1.6 Internet Sources ·········· 11
    2.2.2 Evaluating Sources ·········· 12
  2.3 Gathering Data ·········· 13
    2.3.1 Preparing a Working Bibliography ·········· 13
    2.3.2 Reading Sources with a Critical Eye ·········· 15
      2.3.2.1 Objectivity ·········· 15
      2.3.2.2 Qualifications of the Author ·········· 16
      2.3.2.3 Publication Background ·········· 16
      2.3.2.4 Level ·········· 16

  2.3.2.5 Primary Source and Secondary Source ············ 16
 2.3.3 Assessing the Author's Argument and Evidence ········ 17
 2.3.4 Taking Notes ··· 17
  2.3.4.1 Note-taking Methods ···························· 17
  2.3.4.2 Note Form ·· 18
 2.3.5 Avoiding Plagiarism ································· 22
  2.3.5.1 Materials Not Requiring Acknowledgment ········ 22
  2.3.5.2 Materials Requiring Acknowledgment ············ 23
  2.3.5.3 Recognizing and Avoiding Unintended Plagiarism ······ 23
2.4 Formulating a Thesis ··· 25
2.5 Outlining the Paper ·· 28
 2.5.1 Types of Outline ····································· 29
  2.5.1.1 Topic Outline ···································· 29
  2.5.1.2 Sentence Outline ································· 30
  2.5.1.3 Paragraph Outline ································ 31
 2.5.2 Outline Style ··· 32
2.6 Writing the First Draft ······································· 33
2.7 Revising, Editing and Proofreading ···························· 35
 2.7.1 Revising ··· 35
 2.7.2 Editing ·· 37
 2.7.3 Proofreading ··· 38
2.8 Finalizing the Paper ··· 38
Exercises ··· 39

Chapter 3 The Structure of a Research Paper ···················· 43

3.1 The Front Matter ·· 43
 3.1.1 Title Page ··· 44
 3.1.2 Outline Page ·· 46
 3.1.3 Abstract in English ·································· 46
 3.1.4 Abstract in Chinese ·································· 48
 3.1.5 Acknowledgments ··································· 48
 3.1.6 Table of Contents ··································· 49
 3.1.7 List of Illustrations/Figures ·························· 50
 3.1.8 List of Tables ······································· 51
 3.1.9 List of Abbreviations ································ 51

3.2 The Text ·· 51
  3.2.1 Introduction ·· 52
    3.2.1.1 Background Information ··· 52
    3.2.1.2 Thesis Statement ··· 53
  3.2.2 Body ··· 53
  3.2.3 Conclusion ·· 54
3.3 The Back Matter ··· 55
  3.3.1 References ··· 55
  3.3.2 Appendices ·· 56
  3.3.3 Notes ··· 56
Exercises ·· 57

Chapter 4 Language and Style ··· 61

4.1 Diction ··· 61
4.2 Tone ·· 62
4.3 Voice ··· 63
4.4 Economy ··· 64
4.5 Verb Tense ·· 64
4.6 Sentence Type and Length ··· 65
  4.6.1 Sentence Type ··· 65
  4.6.2 Sentence Length ·· 65
4.7 Verb Voice ··· 66
4.8 Parallelism ·· 66
4.9 Logical Consistency ·· 67
4.10 Coherence ·· 68
4.11 Transition ··· 69
4.12 Unbiased Language ·· 70
4.13 Constructing Paragraphs ·· 72
Exercises ·· 74

Chapter 5 Mechanics ··· 83

5.1 Capitalization ··· 83
5.2 Abbreviations ··· 86
  5.2.1 Use of Periods ·· 86
  5.2.2 Social and Professional Titles and Similar Terms ·········· 87

5.2.3 Organization ··· 88
  5.2.4 Units of Measurement ··· 89
  5.2.5 General Scholarly Abbreviations ·· 89
 5.3 Italicizing and Underlining ··· 91
 5.4 Spelling ·· 92
 5.5 Plural of Noun ·· 93
 5.6 Foreign Word ·· 93
 5.7 Hyphenation ·· 93
 5.8 Number ·· 94
  5.8.1 Use of Word or Numeral ··· 94
  5.8.2 Punctuation of Number ·· 95
  5.8.3 Fraction ·· 95
  5.8.4 Decimal and Percentage ··· 96
  5.8.5 Number from Mathematical and Statistical Calculation ·········· 96
  5.8.6 Number with Abbreviation or Symbol ······························ 97
  5.8.7 Date and Times of the Day ·· 97
  5.8.8 Inclusive Number ·· 98
  5.8.9 Plural of Number ·· 99
  5.8.10 Roman Numeral ·· 99
 5.9 Work Title ··· 99
  5.9.1 Capitalized Title ·· 100
  5.9.2 Underlined (Italicized) Title ·· 101
  5.9.3 Title in Quotation Marks ·· 101
  5.9.4 Title without Underlining or Quotation Marks ················ 102
  5.9.5 Title Containing Another Title ··· 102
 5.10 Enumeration ·· 103
 5.11 Table and Figure ·· 104
  5.11.1 Table ·· 104
  5.11.2 Relation of Table and the Text ······································· 105
  5.11.3 Figure ··· 106
  5.11.4 Relation of Figure and the Text ······································ 106
  5.11.5 Placement of Table and Figure ·· 106
 5.12 Numbering of Pages ··· 107
 5.13 Personal Name ·· 107
 5.14 Personal Title ·· 107

5.15 Use of Notes ··· 108
5.16 Spacing ··· 110
    5.16.1 Space around Punctuation Marks ······································· 110
    5.16.2 Margin ·· 110
    5.16.3 Indentation ··· 111
    5.16.4 Centered Material ·· 111
5.17 Division of Words and Division of Lines of Text ·························· 111
    5.17.1 Division of Words ·· 111
    5.17.2 Division of Initial, Number, and Lines of Text ···················· 112
5.18 Chapter Title and Heading ··· 113
    5.18.1 Part ·· 113
    5.18.2 Chapter ·· 113
    5.18.3 Section, Subsection and the Heading ································· 114
Exercises ··· 115

Chapter 6 Punctuation ··· 120

6.1 Comma ··· 120
6.2 Semicolon ·· 122
6.3 Colon ·· 123
6.4 Dash ··· 124
6.5 Parentheses ·· 126
6.6 Quotation Mark ·· 127
6.7 Square Bracket ··· 128
6.8 Slash ··· 128
6.9 Period ··· 128
6.10 Question Mark ·· 129
6.11 Exclamation Point ··· 130
6.12 Ellipsis ··· 131
Exercises ··· 134

Chapter 7 Documentation (1): Modern Language Association (MLA) Style ··· 138

7.1 MLA Parenthetical Citation ·· 139
    7.1.1 Placement and Punctuation of Citation ································ 139
    7.1.2 Basic Rules for Print and Electronic Sources ······················· 140
        7.1.2.1 Author Named in a Signal Phrase ···························· 140

- 7.1.2.2 Author Named in Parentheses ... 141
- 7.1.2.3 Author Unknown ... 141
- 7.1.2.4 Page Number Unknown ... 141
- 7.1.3 Variations on the Basic Rules ... 142
  - 7.1.3.1 Two or More Titles by the Same Author ... 142
  - 7.1.3.2 Two or Three Authors ... 142
  - 7.1.3.3 Four or More Authors ... 143
  - 7.1.3.4 Corporate Author ... 143
  - 7.1.3.5 Authors with the Same Last Name ... 143
  - 7.1.3.6 Indirect Sources (Sources Quoted in Other Sources) ... 144
  - 7.1.3.7 Encyclopedia or Dictionary ... 144
  - 7.1.3.8 Multivolume Work ... 144
  - 7.1.3.9 Two or More Works (Multiple Citations) ... 145
  - 7.1.3.10 An Entire Work ... 145
  - 7.1.3.11 Work in an Anthology ... 145
  - 7.1.3.12 Legal Source ... 145
- 7.1.4 Literary Work and Sacred Text ... 145
  - 7.1.4.1 Literary Work without Part or Line Number ... 146
  - 7.1.4.2 Verse Play and Poem ... 146
  - 7.1.4.3 Novel with Numbered Divisions ... 146
  - 7.1.4.4 Sacred Text ... 147
- 7.2 Information Note ... 147
  - 7.2.1 Use of *ibid.* and *op. cit.* ... 147
  - 7.2.2 Use of Superscript ... 148
- 7.3 List of Works Cited ... 149
  - 7.3.1 Author ... 150
    - 7.3.1.1 Single Author ... 151
    - 7.3.1.2 Multiple Authors ... 151
    - 7.3.1.3 Corporate Author ... 151
    - 7.3.1.4 Unknown Author ... 152
    - 7.3.1.5 Two or More Works by the Same Author ... 152
  - 7.3.2 Books ... 152
    - 7.3.2.1 Author with an Editor ... 152
    - 7.3.2.2 Author with a Translator ... 153
    - 7.3.2.3 Editor ... 153

7.3.2.4	Work in an Anthology	153
7.3.2.5	Edition Other Than the First	154
7.3.2.6	Multivolume Work	154
7.3.2.7	Encyclopedia or Dictionary Entry	154
7.3.2.8	Foreword, Introduction, Preface, or Afterword	155
7.3.2.9	Book with a Title within Its Title	155
7.3.2.10	Book in a Series	156
7.3.2.11	Republished Book	156
7.3.2.12	Publisher's Imprint	156
7.3.2.13	Book in a Foreign Language	156
7.3.3	Magazine and Journal	157
7.3.3.1	Magazine	157
7.3.3.2	Journal Paginated by Volume and by Issue	157
7.3.4	Daily Newspaper	158
7.3.5	Book or Film Review	158
7.3.6	Electronic Sources	159
7.3.6.1	An Entire Website	159
7.3.6.2	Short Work from a Website	160
7.3.6.3	Online Book	161
7.3.6.4	Online Periodical	161
7.3.6.5	CD-ROM	162
7.3.6.6	E-mail	162
7.3.7	Multimedia Source	162
7.3.7.1	Work of Art	162
7.3.7.2	Advertisement	163
7.3.7.3	Map or Chart	163
7.3.7.4	Musical Composition	163
7.3.7.5	Sound Recording	163
7.3.7.6	Film or Video	164
7.3.7.7	Radio or Television Program	164
7.3.7.8	Lecture or Public Address	164
7.3.7.9	Personal Interview	165
7.3.8	Other Sources	165
7.3.8.1	Government Publication	165
7.3.8.2	Pamphlet	165

   7.3.8.3 Dissertation ·············· 165
   7.3.8.4 Published Proceedings of a Conference ·············· 166
   7.3.8.5 Published Interview ·············· 166
   7.3.8.6 Personal Letter ·············· 166
 Exercises ·············· 166

Chapter 8 Documentation (2): The American Psychological Association (APA) Style ·············· 172

 8.1 Reference Citation in Text ·············· 172
  8.1.1 Work by a Single Author ·············· 172
  8.1.2 Work by Multiple Authors ·············· 173
  8.1.3 Work by Associations, Corporations, Government Agencies, Etc. ·············· 173
  8.1.4 Work by Unknown Author ·············· 173
  8.1.5 Work from Electronic Source ·············· 173
 8.2 References Cited ·············· 174
  8.2.1 Book ·············· 175
  8.2.2 Essay or Chapter in Edited Book ·············· 176
  8.2.3 Encyclopedia or Dictionary and Entry in an Encyclopedia ·············· 176
  8.2.4 Journal, Magazine, and Newspaper ·············· 177
  8.2.5 Thesis or Dissertation ·············· 178
  8.2.6 Technical and Research Report ·············· 178
  8.2.7 Audio-Visual Media ·············· 178
  8.2.8 Article from Electronic Source ·············· 179
 Exercises ·············· 180

Chapter 9 Documentation (3): The Chicago Manual Style ·············· 183

 9.1 Note-Bibliography System ·············· 183
  9.1.1 General Guidelines: Creating Chicago Notes ·············· 183
  9.1.2 General Guidelines: Creating Chicago Bibliography ·············· 184
  9.1.3 Examples: Creating Chicago Notes and Bibliography ·············· 185
   9.1.3.1 Book ·············· 185
   9.1.3.2 Book Chapter ·············· 191
   9.1.3.3 Journal Article ·············· 193
   9.1.3.4 Newspaper Article ·············· 196
   9.1.3.5 Conference Paper ·············· 197
   9.1.3.6 Statistics from Agency Database ·············· 198

	9.1.3.7 Encyclopedia and Dictionary	199
	9.1.3.8 Thesis/Dissertation	199
	9.1.3.9 Website Document	201
9.2	The Author-Date System	202
	9.2.1 Author-Date Text Citation	202
	9.2.1.1 Basic Form	202
	9.2.1.2 Page or Other Specific Reference	203
	9.2.1.3 Multiple References	204
	9.2.2 Reference List	204
	9.2.2.1 Book	205
	9.2.2.2 Periodical	210
	9.2.2.3 Newspaper	212
	9.2.2.4 Interview	212
	9.2.2.5 Secondary Source	212
	9.2.2.6 Thesis, Dissertation and Other Unpublished Work	213
	9.2.2.7 Paper Read at Meeting	213
	9.2.2.8 Sound Recording	213
	9.2.2.9 Slide, Film, and Videocassette	214
	9.2.2.10 Electronic Document	214
Exercises		214

Appendix A General Exercises for MLA, APA and Chicago Manual (Author-Date System) Styles 219
Appendix B Samples 225
Appendix C Revision Symbols 230
Bibliography 233
Index 236

9.1.3.7. Ibn-e-Jordon and Dictionary 199
9.1.3.8. Thesis/Dissertation 199
9.1.3.9. Website Document 201
9.2. The Author-Date System 201
9.2.1. Author-Date Text Citation 202
9.2.1.1. Basic Form 202
9.2.1.2. Page or Other Specific Reference Indicators 203
9.2.1.3. Multiple Reference 204
9.2.2. Reference List 204
9.2.2.1. Book 205
9.2.2.2. Periodical 210
9.2.2.3. Newspaper 212
9.2.2.4. Interview 212
9.2.2.5. Secondary Source 212
9.2.2.6. Thesis, Dissertation and other Unpublished Work .. 213
9.2.2.7. Paper Read at Meeting 213
9.2.2.8. Sound Recording 214
9.2.2.9. Slide, Film, and Videocassette 214
9.2.2.10. Electronic Document 214
Exercises 215

Appendix A. General Exercises for MLA, APA and Chicago Manual
(Author-Date System) Styles References 216
Appendix B. Sample Paper 225
Appendix C. Revision Symbols 230
Bibliography 233
Index 236

Chapter 1
Introduction: Research and Research Paper

1.1 Research

The English word *research* derives from the French *cerchier*, which means "search" and from the Late Latin *circare*, which means "circle around, explore". As the word suggests, research involves tracking down information from various sources.

The word *research* has been defined in a number of different ways. Martyn Shuttleworth defines it as "any gathering of data, information and facts for the advancement of knowledge." J. W. Creswell defines it as "a process of steps used to collect and analyze information to increase our understanding of a topic or issue." The Merriam-Webster Online Dictionary defines it in more detail as "a studious inquiry or examination; especially investigation or experimentation aimed at the discovery and interpretation of facts, revision of accepted theories or laws in the light of new facts, or practical application of such new or revised theories or laws". Research is in essence creative work undertaken on a systematic basis to increase the stock of knowledge. People use it to establish or confirm facts, reaffirm the results of previous work, solve new or existing problems, support certain theories, or develop new theories.

Research is absolutely vital to human beings. Without it, no authoritative words could have been written, no scientific discoveries or inventions made, no theories of any value propounded, and the world would have come to a standstill. Broadly speaking, research permeates people's life. Work in many professions — news reporting, medical treatment, police detection, prosecution, just name a few — relies heavily on research. When people investigate something — whether a college, a course, a TV program, or a portable computer — by reading up on it, discussing its features with their friends or seek advice from experts, they are acting as researcher. When a person, who wants to buy a pair of shoes, checks the shoes' size, color, price and the level of after-sales service, he or she is also acting as a researcher.

It is important and beneficial for people to acquire certain research skills. As an undergraduate, you should know how to combine experience, observation, and new information when you try to solve a problem, make a decision, or analyze a situation. You should know how to seek out pieces of information, evaluate their usefulness, fit them all together, and then use them to make an "educated guess". No matter what subject you study, learning to investigate, to review, and to use information, ideas, and opinions of other researchers productively will play a major role in your development as a student. Keep this in mind: Research increases our knowledge and understanding of a subject — Just do it!

1.2 Research Paper

A research paper is a sort of report describing some original research that a researcher has done or has been doing. It is a formal, substantial and well-documented paper that explores, discusses or analyzes some factual or theoretical questions. Normally, college research papers consist of two kinds: ① the argumentative paper, which evaluates research and takes a stand on it; ② the report paper, which simply lists the results of research. Whether argumentative or report, a research paper does not differ essentially from other essays whose purpose is to explain or persuade, interpret or criticize. But some of the procedures have special pertinence. For one thing, it is imperative to budget your time and work systematically at every stage of the project. However thorough your research and however lucid your report on your findings is, your paper will not be satisfactory if the footnoting is inconsistent and the proofreading careless. However elegant the footnoting is, sloppy basic research will undermine its effect. A good reference paper shows deliberate care in all its aspects — enough evidence of care that the reader feels he can take for granted the accuracy of text, documentation and mechanics and can concentrate on the thesis, the evidence and the qualities of style.

A research paper is an ambitious and complicated undertaking; every stage takes time, patience, and judgment. If you are to produce a good research paper, your intelligence and your intellectual curiosity must dominate your research. In a research paper, you should not merely review publications and extract a series of quotations from them. Rather, you should look for sources that provide new information, that helpfully survey the various positions already taken on a specific subject, that lend authority to your viewpoint, that expand or nuance your ideas, that offer methods or modes of thought you can apply to new data or subjects, or that furnish negative examples against which you wish to argue. As you use and scrupulously acknowledge

Chapter 1
Introduction: Research and Research Paper

sources, you should always remember that the main purpose of doing research is not to summarize the work of others but to assimilate and to build on it and to arrive at your own understanding of the subject.

Different paths can and do lead to successful research papers. Some researchers may pursue a more or less standard sequence of steps, but others may find themselves working less sequentially. In addition, certain projects lend themselves to a standard approach, whereas others may call for different strategies. Keeping in mind that researchers and projects differ, we will discuss activities that nearly all writers of research papers perform, such as selecting a topic, conducting research, compiling a working bibliography, taking notes, formulating thesis outlining, preparing and formatting the paper, and so forth.

If you are writing your first research paper, you may feel overwhelmed by the many tasks discussed here. As you follow the book's advice on how to locate and document sources, how to format your paper, and so forth, you may be tempted to see doing a paper as a mechanical exercise. But, in fact, writing a research paper is an adventure, an intellectual adventure rather like solving a mystery: It is a form of exploration that leads to discoveries that are new — at least to you if not to others. The mechanics of the research paper, important though they are, should never override the intellectual challenge of pursuing a question that interests you. This quest or search should guide your research and your writing.

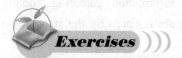

I. Answer the questions.

1. What is research? What is the importance of doing research?
2. What research skills should an undergraduate acquire?
3. How do you define the term *research paper*?
4. Why do we say some of the procedures of research paper have special relevance?
5. What is a good research paper? How can we produce a good one?

II. Fill in the blanks with proper words.

| research | assumptions | strategic | pursuit | view |
| objective | study | existing | application | important |

Research is the creation of new knowledge. It can be categorized into three distinct types: basic, strategic and applied. Basic research is the (1)_____ of new knowledge without any (2)_____ about what it might lead to — essentially knowledge for its own sake. (3)_____ research is the pursuit of new knowledge which might, in principle, have a practical (4)_____ but without a precise (5)_____ of the timescale or nature of the application. Applied research is knowledge which is developed with a specific (6)_____ in mind, particularly the conversion of (7)_____ knowledge into products, processes and technologies. Often people think of (8)_____ in terms of science and technology, but research takes place in every area of academic (9)_____. Research into our culture, our business practices or our economy can be as (10)_____ as medical and scientific research.

III. Read the passage and answer the questions.

The term research has been used in so many contexts and with such a variety of meanings that it is difficult for the student to sort it all out. Much of what we have been taught about research is based on misconceptions. Teachers give students an assignment called a "research paper" which mainly consists of gathering information from books and encyclopedias and reorganizing it and regurgitating it on a student-authored paper. These and other activities have been mislabeled research. They are more correctly, information gathering, note taking, library skills, or sales jobs. None of these are research by the standards of the KanCRN project.

What is research, then? The KanCRN project has specific requirements to teach regarding the research process. True research is a quest driven by a specific question which needs an answer. Paul Leedy, in his book *Practical Research: Planning and Design* lists eight characteristics of research which serve us well in defining research for the student.

Here are those eight characteristics.

(1) Research originates with a question or a problem.

(2) Research requires a clear articulation of a goal.

(3) Research follows a specific plan of procedure.

(4) Research usually divides the principal problem into more manageable sub-problems.

(5) Research is guided by the specific research problem, question, or

Chapter 1
Introduction: Research and Research Paper

hypothesis.

(6) Research accepts certain critical assumptions. These assumptions are underlying theories or ideas about how the world works.

(7) Research requires the collection and interpretation of data in attempting to resolve the problem that initiated the research.

(8) Research is, by its nature, cyclical; or more exactly, spiral or helical.

The KanCRN research process is represented by the Vee diagram, originally developed and refined by Bob Gowen and others at Cornell University. The modified KanCRN version of this Vee breaks the research process into component steps which are useful in organizing students work during the school year. These steps include, (1) establishing a research question, (2) finding background information, (3) planning and conducting a specific research method, (4) collecting and studying data, (5) analyzing the data, (6) formulating and establishing a conclusion, (7) looking for areas of further research, (8) stating the values associated with the research knowledge, and (9) publishing the research work for others to view. The KanCRN project has decided to use a modified form of the Vee diagram to conceptualize this research process. Actually, research is continual and expanding. As one question is answered, many more are generated. Researchers depend upon previous work to expand the knowledge base on any research frontier. A better representation of research might be a series of interconnected Vee's forming an upward spiral. Questions spurring research lead to conclusions which in turn lead to new questions or modifications of the original questions. These in turn lead to new conclusions and so on.

(— Gary Andersen, "What is research?" *KanCrn Collaborative Research Network*. 20 February, 2007 <http://kancrn.kckps.k12.ks.us/guide/research.html>)

(1) Why did the author say much of what has been taught at universities about research is based on misconceptions? Do you agree with him?

(2) What is research, according to Paul Leedy?

(3) What steps are included in the KanCRN research process?

(4) What is the suggestive meaning of the Vee diagram about research?

Chapter 2
The Process of Research and Research Writing

Writing is a task that no two people do the same way. However, there are some logical steps that every writer seems to follow in the creation of a research paper:

(1) Choosing a topic;
(2) Exploring data;
(3) Gathering data;
(4) Formulating a thesis;
(5) Organizing data and ideas;
(6) Drafting the paper;
(7) Reviewing and revising the paper;
(8) Finalizing the paper.

The process described here outlines those basic steps. These steps are not exclusive of each other. At times they are rather liquid. You will notice that, in the process of writing, work done in one area may necessitate returning to a step that you have already "completed."

2.1 Choosing a Topic

The first and most important step in writing a research paper is to choose a topic. Choosing a topic can be very difficult. It involves identifying a general subject area, defining the topic and narrowing it, and stating topic as a question or hypothesis. If your instructor assigns a specific topic, your job is considerably simplified. But usually you are given the freedom to choose a topic. Then choosing a topic will require discretion.

As you make decisions leading to a topic, you should consider the topic's importance and interest, its manageability, and its availability of sources.

Chapter 2
The Process of Research and Research Writing

2.1.1 Importance and Interest

The topic you choose should be intellectually significant and be interesting to you and, more important, to your readers. The topic "How dogs react to various brands of food" is not significant enough to warrant the effort of a research paper. The topic "What I've observed at rock concerts" is not appropriate because readers may not have any interest in your personal opinion. If you do not want to work on a subject that is neither meaningful nor interesting to you and your readers, you should give yourself plenty of time to read and think about what topic to choose. To choose a topic that is both significant and interesting, try to answer the following questions:

(1) What subject interests me? Will it interest my readers as well?

(2) What aspect of it interests you and your readers most?

(3) Is there anything you wonder about or you are puzzled about with regard to it? Is it intellectually important enough?

To a certain extent, importance and interest are subjective judgments. A topic that is trivial to people in one field of study may have special significance to people in another. Before you decide on a topic, it is always necessary for you to seek advice from your instructor, your classmates and friends. They will tell you if the topic you choose is worthwhile or not.

2.1.2 Manageability

Once you have a topic, you need to make it manageable for you. The topic you choose should neither be too broad nor too narrow. A topic that is too broad will yield inadequate information and limit your ability to reach a valid conclusion. A topic that is too narrow, too specialized or too technical may demand knowledge you cannot acquire in the time allotted for your project.

2.1.2.1 Avoid a Too Broad Topic

There are a few strategies to narrow a too broad topic. Periodical indexes can be especially helpful, because the sub-categories provide useful suggestions for narrowing the topic. Another method for narrowing a topic is to purposefully pick a broad subject, then to choose a second, narrower topic within this broad topic. You can repeat this process by choosing a third, still narrower topic within the second. For example:

(1) Broad topic： Americans
Narrow topic： Asian Americans
Narrower topic： Chinese Americans
(2) Broad topic： American poets
Narrow topic： Edgar Allan Poe
Narrower topic： the beauty-death theme in Edgar Allan Poe's poetry

You'd better narrow a broad topic down until the subject can be handled in ten or more typed pages.

2.1.2.2　Avoid a Too Narrow Topic

A too narrow or too technical topic is often trivial and uninteresting. You should avoid a topic upon which there is only a single or very few references derived from a single source. The subject may not be treated dispassionately in all its aspects or not analyzed sufficiently using different methods and ideas. You can see the following progression from the specific to the general, which demands you to include more data：

(1) Narrow topic： The Courtyard in Ximen Hutong
Broad topic： The Beijing-Style Courtyard
Broader topic： The Styles of the Courtyard in Northern China
(2) Narrow topic： Mark Twain's Animals
Broad topic： Mark Twain's Description of Animals
Broader topic： Symbolic Animals in Mark Twain's Fictions

2.1.3　Availability of Resources

Even if a topic is worthwhile and manageable, it may not be suitable if the necessary research materials are not available. The resources of the library in which you are working, as well as your access to electronic materials, should help guide your choice of topic. If your paper entails a survey or an experiment, you need to determine whether you can collect the required data within the time limits of the assignment.

2.1.4　Where to Find a Topic for Research

Possibilities for further research can be found even in fields that seem to have been well covered by scholars. Scholars sometimes suggest undiscussed areas of

Chapter 2
The Process of Research and Research Writing

inquiry or unresolved controversies in their own work; this kind of information often appears in notes. Commonly held but unsubstantiated conclusions or new ways of testing the basic assumptions in a field can provide subjects for your research. Contradictions or disjunctions among various books on the same subject also suggest possible research topics. Besides, recently published books or developments in current events often afford new insight into existing theories, they may give you opportunities to do research.

2.2 Exploring Data

All researches are based on data. According to the source of data, researches can be classified into primary research and secondary research. Primary research is often called empirical research or field research. It is the basic means of exploring and gathering information. By primary research, the data are collected directly from the researcher's experience or experiments. These data have not existed in any documents before. They are first-hand and original information. Secondary research is often called documentary or library research. It is a kind of study which makes use of data in documents, books and journals. These data have been collected by other people for their own purposes. Primary research and secondary research often walk hand in hand. In fact, neither of them can be conducted in isolation. Secondary research can only exist based on primary research, while primary research must start with secondary research.

Libraries are indispensable sources for information. They serve as the best place for you to start your research. In the library, thousands and perhaps millions of copies of newspapers, magazines, books, dictionaries, records, tapes, and other reference materials are collected and made available for researchers. A library's reference collection usually includes two broad types of reference materials: those that are general in scope and those that deal with specific disciplines. Guides to reference books can help you identify those that suit your purpose. Your research question can help you choose the best sources to use. Among the types most often consulted are encyclopedias, biographical dictionaries, sources for current events, and book indexes, periodical indexes, computer databases, internet sources and so forth.

2.2.1 Reference Works

Reference works are a good starting point because their articles almost always refer you to authoritative specialized works. Whatever your topic is, if you combine

orderly work habits with a certain alertness and ingenuity in following up clues, the sources of material in your topic will begin to spread out before you. So, a few minutes with them can be a shortcut to the books and/or articles that match your interest and purpose.

2.2.1.1 Encyclopedia and Dictionary

For general background on a subject, encyclopedias and dictionaries are a good place to start. Encyclopedias and dictionaries like *An Encyclopedia of World History*, *Encyclopedia of Psychology*, *Encyclopedia of the Social Sciences*, *the Oxford Companion to Classical Literature*, *Dictionary of World Literature* usually include bibliographies that could lead you to valuable sources. Though some of them do provide indepth information, more often they serve as a place to start your research.

Compared with general encyclopedias, specialized encyclopedias usually provide more detailed articles by authorities in the field as well as extensive bibliographies for locating sources. You should rely on these books for background material rather than as major sources of information.

2.2.1.2 Biographical Dictionary and Index

The lives and historical settings of famous people are the topics of biographical dictionaries and indexes. Before you use these sources, consider whether you need a volume covering people who are living or people who are dead. Before using such sources, consider if you need a volume covering living people or a volume covering deceased people. If the latter, consider whether you want a volume published currently or a volume published in the old days when these people who were still living.

2.2.1.3 Book Index

Book indexes can be helpful for quickly locating complete information on a book when you know only the author's last name, or the title. They can also be valuable for alerting you to other works by a particular author or on a particular subject.

2.2.1.4 Periodical Index

Periodicals — journals, magazines, and newspapers — are published frequently and more quickly, they can lend an immediacy to your research that books cannot. In addition, while an entire book may not be devoted to your specific topic, a number of articles may be.

Periodical indexes are guides to articles published in periodicals. Each index covers a specific group of periodicals, usually identified at the beginning of the index or volume. Many libraries also offer access to the online and CD-ROM computer database versions of many periodical indexes.

2.2.1.5 Computer Database

Your library may subscribe to online database networks and own CD-ROM machines that are accessed through the library's computer terminals. Most research databases are electronic indexes listing thousands of books and articles.

When you use a CD-ROM database, check the first screen, which lets you know what information you are accessing. Some large databases may require more than one disk, usually separated by date. Although you can search a database by author or title, most likely you will use descriptors (or keywords) describing subjects. Make your descriptors as precise as possible so that your database search results in a manageable list of sources relevant to your topic. Most databases include a thesaurus of descriptors and a set of guidelines for combining terms to narrow your search. In addition, most CD-ROMs include a browse function. When you enter a descriptor, the system automatically lists the terms that are close to it alphabetically. Once you have typed in your descriptors, the computer searches the database and lists every reference to them it finds.

2.2.1.6 Internet Sources

The internet is a global network made up of many smaller networks that enables computer users to share information and resources quickly and easily. With the internet, you can gather information about a research subject from sources all over the world. Common ways to conduct searches with search tools are by subject and by keyword. Some search tools, such as *Google*, *Yahoo*, *Baidu* and *Sina* offer hierarchically arranged subject directories through which you can navigate until you find specific topics you wish to explore. When you discover a seemingly useful document or site, add it to your bookmark list. In so doing, you can easily return to the source for further information or clarification. Always make note of the date or dates on which you consult a source. The date of access is important because the material could be revised between different visits to the site. The uniform resource

locator (URL) and the date of access are items of information you will need for your working bibliography and your list of works cited.

Most instructors permit and many encourage using Internet sources, but few consider a search of the World Wide Web alone adequate research for a paper. Other materials including print publications should be sought. Similarly, e-mail discussion lists and online "chat rooms" are helpful for sharing ideas but, except for rare occasions, they are not deemed acceptable resources for research papers.

2.2.2 Evaluating Sources

You will uncover many sources through your research, but not all of them will be equally useful. Do not waste time and energy on irrelevant and useless sources. Make sure to read the useful sources critically.

First, preview the source to get a general sense of it, to determine whether the source is related closely enough to your topic, and to decide whether it deserves reading further. If you determine that the source is useful, read it more carefully and take notes on it. Critical reading at this stage consists of responding — entering into a conversation with a text while you read — and reviewing — coming to a critical understanding of the text as a whole.

Reviewing to evaluate is particularly important when you are writing a research essay, since you are trying to determine the worth or validity of the text and the information it contains. If you determine that a source is irrelevant, unreliable, or out of date, you'll need to find another one. Because you want to know this as soon as possible, make the effort to evaluate each source continually: when reading, when taking notes, and when considering how to incorporate the source into your final paper.

The more you research, the more expert you become at determining whether a source is useful. When in doubt, confer with your instructor or a librarian. Here are some questions to ask yourself:

        Subject: Is the subject directly related to my research question?
                Does it provide information that supports my view?
                Does it provide helpful context or background information?
                Does it contain quotations or facts that I will want to quote in my paper?
        Author: What do I already know about the author's reputation?
                Does the book or periodical provide any biographical information?

Chapter 2
The Process of Research and Research Writing

                Is this author cited by other sources?

                Am I aware of any biases that might limit the author's credibility?

Date: When was this source published?

                Do my field and topic require current, up-to-date sources? or Would classic, well-established sources be more credible?

Publisher: Who published this source?

                Is it a major publisher, a university press, or a scholarly organization that would subject material to a rigorous review procedure?

Counter authority: Does the source address or present counter arguments on issues I intend to discuss or take?

To evaluate sources found on the Internet, apply the guidelines above whenever possible. That is, attend to author, publisher, date, and reputation if this information is available. Since anyone with a computer can put information on the Web, you need to take more precautions before you can trust the source to be as reliable and supportive as you wish.

2.3 Gathering Data

In this stage, you start collecting the information you need for your paper, be it from books, magazine or journal articles, pamphlets, handouts, interviews, or the Internet. Throughout the stage, you need to prepare a working bibliography, read the sources critically, access the author's arguments and evidence, and finally, take notes in correct forms.

2.3.1 Preparing a Working Bibliography

Once you have selected a broad subject, you need to begin research and determine how to narrow and shape the topic. This effort should result in a working bibliography, which is a list of sources that appear to be relevant at the initial stage of your research. During this first phase of your research, you should record information about every source you encounter, even if you are not certain if you will actually use it. If you ignore potential sources at this early stage, you may later wish that you had citations for works that seemed irrelevant early on but later proved significant. This bibliography includes as complete information as possible on everything you have

13

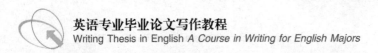

used as a source of information: encyclopedias, books, journal articles, interviews, recordings, films, etc. Such a bibliography is called a "working" one because it is not finalized — you change it continually as you work on your research. You should add to, but never delete references from it.

Complete information about a particular source should be placed on note card. For the convenience of later sorting, one reference should be placed on one card. Entries for bibliographies and lists of works cited require some or all of the following types of information for a book:

— Full name of the author (In case of coauthors, for the first author, give the surname followed by the given name)

— Title and any subtitle of the book

— Title of chapter or part of the book (If the whole book or several parts of a book are used, this is not necessary)

— Full name of the editor, translator, or compiler

— Edition (if it is other than the first)

— Series name (if the book is in a series)

— Number of volumes (if all volumes are referenced) and volume number (if one or a few volumes are referenced)

— City of publication, the publisher, and the year of publication

— Page number(s) the information was gathered from

The title page and copyright page of the book contain most of this information. The title page is one of the first, if not the first, pages in a book. Usually, the title is given at the top; the author's name in the middle; and information about the publisher at the bottom. Publishers often have several offices. If this is the case, use the first city named on the left. This is where the copy of the book you are using was published. On the copyright page, the word "copyright" appears, followed by the copyright symbol "©" (the letter c circled). Use the most recent date given here.

For an article, this information should include:

— Full name of the author (In case of coauthors, for the first author, give the surname followed by the given name)

— Title and any subtitle of the article

— Name of the periodical

— Volume number (if periodical uses it)

— Issue number (if periodical uses it)

— The date (if periodical uses it)
— Page number you took data or ideas from
— Page numbers of the first and last pages of the article

You may not find all of this information about a potential source in a reference work, but when you find the source itself, you will be able to complete the entry.

For electronic sources, particularly information networks and on-line databases, you need data sufficient to allow your readers to recover material identical to whatever you consulted. Consequently, you will need even more information for an electronic source than for a book. Because essential information, such as the electronic address or path you followed to locate the material, usually does not appear on the part of the screen that can be printed or downloaded, you will have to be certain that you write down all identifying data before you leave the document.

A working bibliography should include all necessary information that will allow you and your reader to access the work and to trace the citation back to the index or bibliography in which you found it. Whatever format you choose for it, it should be able to allow you to rearrange, alphabetize and delete its entries, and be portable for use wherever you conduct your research. It will save you time if all its entries correspond to the documentation system that you will use for your paper. As an English major, you may choose one of the following three documentation systems: Modern Language Association style (MLA), American Psychological Association style (APA), or The Chicago Manual of Style (Chicago Manual).

2.3.2 Reading Sources with a Critical Eye

Because all sources make an explicit or implicit argument, they often disagree with one another. Disagreements among sources arise sometimes from differences about facts, sometimes about interpretation of facts. A writer may well tell the truth, but he or she can never tell the whole truth, for people are not all-knowing. Thus you must examine sources critically, using them not as unquestioned authorities but as contributions to your own interpretation. You should continually evaluate the materials with regard to the objectivity of the source, the qualifications of the author, the date and form of publication, the level of the source, and its primary or secondary nature for your purpose.

2.3.2.1 Objectivity

The objectivity of a source refers to being free from bias or prejudice. Total

objectivity is not humanly possible, but the most valuable sources identify any biases that might be caused by the author's affiliations or allegiances — whether economic, political, philosophical, or academic — any limitations inherent in the author's approach or the materials used.

2.3.2.2 Qualifications of the Author

Before you choose to read a source, you may ask the question: Is the author an expert on the topic? The author's qualifications for writing a work, such as academic degrees, professional credentials, and experience and status in the field, may influence your choice. Information about an author's qualifications may be found in preliminary or appendix materials in the source itself. The information may provide clues to the quality, nature, and objectivity of a source.

2.3.2.3 Publication Background

The facts of publication can reveal a great deal about the potential usefulness of a source. The date of a work generally gives an indication of its perspective. Recent sources are often more useful than older ones, particularly in natural science. However, the most authoritative works are often older ones. Also, the identity of the publisher can suggest the nature of the source. Publication by a censorious publisher usually indicates that the book makes a substantial contribution to knowledge in its field and that it may be intended for specialists. Commercial publishers, however, release books for a wide range of readers, and their lists vary widely in level and quality.

2.3.2.4 Level

You should be aware of the level of specialization of the source and know for what audience the source was intended. Does the source provide a general or specialized view? General sources may be helpful as you begin your research, but you may then need the authority or up-to-dateness of more specialized works. If you find sources are too technical and too advanced, you will need either to seek guidance in understanding them or to omit them from your purview. You should also avoid too general or too simplistic sources.

2.3.2.5 Primary Source and Secondary Source

A primary source is an artifact, a document, a recording, or other source of information that serves as an original source. A secondary source builds upon the original source. It involves generalization, analysis, synthesis, interpretation, or evaluation of the original information. A given source may be either a primary source or a secondary source, depending on how you make use of it. Most textbooks and reference works are secondary sources. To write a research paper on a work of literature, you should come to grips with the original work in your subject before immersing yourself in making comment on it.

2.3.3 Assessing the Author's Argument and Evidence

Just as every author has a point of view, every piece of writing has what may be called an argument, a position it takes. As you read, try to identify the author's argument, the reasons given in support of his or her position. Then try to decide *why* the author takes this position.

The following questions can help you recognize — and assess — the author's argument:

— What is the author's main argument? How much and what kind of evidence supports his or her argument?
— How persuasive is the evidence? Can I offer any counterarguments or refutations to the evidence?
— Is there any questionable logic or fallacious thinking in it?

2.3.4 Taking Notes

After you have decided that a source is useful, you will need to take careful notes on it. Doing so most efficiently calls for approaching a source with some general questions in mind: What do I expect to learn about the topic? What can the source help me demonstrate? To what part of my research is the source most relevant?

2.3.4.1 Note-taking Methods

Note-taking methods vary greatly from one researcher to another. Whatever method you adopt, your goals will include ① getting down enough information to help you recall the major points of the source, ② getting down the information in the form in which you are most likely to want to incorporate it into your essay, and ③ getting down all the information you will need to cite the source accurately.

1. Index-card method

When you are researching, write down every idea, fact, quotation, or paraphrase on a separate index card (usually 12.5 cm by 7.5 cm). When you have collected all your cards, reshuffle them into the best possible order, and have an outline. It will be more helpful for you to use both white and colored cards. When you come up with a point that you think may be one of the main points in your outline, write it at the top of a colored card. Put each supporting note on a separate white card, using as much of the card as necessary. When you feel ready, arrange the colored cards into a workable plan. Some of the points may not fit in. If so, either modify the plan or leave these points out. You may need to fill gaps by creating new cards. You can shuffle your supporting material into the plan by placing each of the white cards behind the point it helps support.

2. Computer method

Recording notes by computer has the advantage of allowing you transfer quotations directly into your paper without having to recopy them. You can collect your points consecutively, then sort your ideas when you are ready to start planning. Take advantage of "outline view" in Word, which makes it easy for you to arrange your points hierarchically. This method is fine so long as you don't mind being tied to your computer from the first stage of the writing process to the last. Of course, the data in your computer file must be correct if you are to avoid perpetuating errors.

2.3.4.2 Note Form

Most of your notes will take the form of direct quotation, paraphrase, or summary.

1. Quoting sources directly

To quote a source directly, you reproduce the writer's or speaker's own words, exactly as they were in the original source. Direct quotation provides strong evidence and can add both life and authenticity to your paper. However, too much quotation can make it seem as though you have little to say for yourself. Long quotations also slow readers down. Unless the source quoted is itself the topic of the paper (as in a literary interpretation), limit brief quotations to no more than two per page and long quotations to no more than one every three or four pages.

Generally, when you quote someone, slight change in wording is permitted, but such changes must be clearly marked. Although you can't change what a source says, you do have control over how much of it you use. Use only as long a quotation as you need to make your point. You should remember that quotations should be used to support your points, not to say them for you.

Be sure that when you shorten a quotation you have not changed its meaning. If you omit words within quotations for the sake of brevity, you must indicate it by

Chapter 2
The Process of Research and Research Writing

using ellipsis points. Any changes or additions must be indicated with brackets.

1) Integrating quotation

Direct quotations will be most effective when you integrate them smoothly into the flow of your paper. You can do this by providing an explanatory "tag" or by giving one or more sentences of explanation. Readers should be able to follow your meaning easily and to see the relevance of the quotation immediately.

Brief quotations (according to MLA style guidelines, four or fewer typed lines) should be embedded in the main body of your paper and enclosed in quotation marks:

> Photo editor Tom Brennan took ten minutes to sort through my images and then told me, "Most photography editors wouldn't take more than two minutes to look at a portfolio."

Long quotations (five lines or more) should be set off in block format. Begin a new line, indent ten spaces, and do not use quotation marks:

> Kate Kelly focuses on Americans' peculiarly negative chauvinism, in this case, the chauvinism of New York residents:
>> New Yorkers are a provincial lot. They wear their city's accomplishments like blue ribbons. To anyone who will listen they boast of leading the world in everything from mafia murders to porno movie houses. They can also boast that their city produces more garbage than any other city in the world.

2) Introducing quotation

When you introduce quoted material into your essay, you usually need to use signal phrase. A signal phrase is a verb that introduces the quoted part, as *assert* in the sentence:

> Henry David Thoreau *asserts* in *Walden*, "The mass of men lead lives of quiet desperation."

To avoid monotony, you can vary the placement of signal phrase in the sentence. As different words have different meanings, you also need to choose right words to indicate your tone and intention. Watch out for the slight or significant differences in the following introductory signals:

acknowledge	add	admit	agree	argue	assert
believe	claim	comment	compare	confirm	contend
concede	conclude	declare	deny	dispute	emphasize
endorse	find	grant	illustrate	imply	insist
maintain	note	observe	point out	reason	refute
reject	report	respond	reveal	say	show
state	suggest	think	write		

3) Adjusting grammar when using quotations

A passage containing a quotation must follow all the rules of grammatical sentence structure: tenses should be consistent, verbs and subjects should agree, and so on. If the form of the quotation doesn't quite fit the grammar of your own sentences, you can quote less of the original source, change your sentences, or make a slight alteration in the quotation. Use this last option sparingly, and always indicate any changes with brackets.

Unclear: In Sand County Almanac, Aldo Leopold follows various animals, including a skunk and a rabbit, through fresh snow. He wonders, "What got him out of bed?"

Clear: In Sand County Almanac, Aldo Leopold follows various animals, including a skunk and a rabbit, through fresh snow. He wonders, "What got [the skunk] out of bed?"

Grammatically incompatible: If Thoreau believed, as he wrote in *Walden* in the 1850s, "The mass of men lead lives of quiet desperation," then what would he say of the masses today?

The verb *lead* in Thoreau's original quotation is present tense, but the sentence might call for the past tense form *led*.

Grammatically compatible: If Thoreau believed, as he wrote in *Walden* in the 1850s, that the mass of men led "lives of quiet desperation," then what would he say of the masses today?

Grammatically compatible: In the nineteenth century, Thoreau stated, "The mass of men lead lives of quiet desperation." What would he say of the masses today?

Grammatically compatible: If Thoreau thought that in his day, the "mass of men [led] lives of quiet desperation," what would he say of the masses today?

2. Paraphrasing sources

To paraphrase, you restate a source's ideas in your own words. The point of paraphrasing is to make the ideas clearer (both to your readers and to yourself) and to express the ideas in the way that best suits your purpose.

Chapter 2
The Process of Research and Research Writing

The best way to make an accurate paraphrase is to stay close to the order and structure of the original passage, to reproduce its emphasis and details, without using the same sentence patterns or vocabulary. But if the original source has used a wellestablished or technical term for a concept, you do not need to find a synonym for it. If you believe that the original source's exact words are the best possible expressions of some points, you may use brief direct quotations within your paraphrase, as long as you indicate these with quotation marks. Be careful not to introduce your own comments or reflections in the middle of a paraphrase, unless you make it clear that these are your thoughts, not the original author's or speaker's.

3. Summarizing sources

To summarize, you distill a source's words down to the main ideas and state such ideas in your own words. A summary includes only the essentials of the original source, not the supporting details, and is consequently shorter than the original. As you draft, summarize often so that your paper doesn't turn into a string of undigested quotations. The following guidelines may help:

(1) For main points. Use summary when your readers need to know the main points rather than the supporting details.

(2) For overviews. Use summary to provide an overview or an interesting aside without digressing far from your paper's focus.

(3) For condensation. Use summary to condense lengthy or rambling notes into a few effective sentences.

Keep in mind that summaries are generalizations and too many generalizations can make your writing vague and tedious. You should occasionally supplement summaries with brief direct quotations or evocative details collected through observation to keep readers in touch with the original source.

Summaries vary in length, and the length of the original source is not necessarily related to the length of the summary you write. Depending on the focus of your paper, you may need to summarize an entire novel in a sentence or two, or you may need to summarize a brief journal article in two or three paragraphs. Remember that the more material you attempt to summarize in a short space, the more you will necessarily generalize and abstract it. Reduce a text as far as you can while still providing all the information your readers need to know. Be careful — you should never distort the original meaning.

Original passage:

For a long time I never liked to look a chimpanzee straight in the eye — I assumed that, as is the case with most primates, this would be interpreted as a threat or at least a breach of good manners. Not so. As long as one looks with gentleness, without arrogance, a chimpanzee will understand and may even return the look.

Inaccurate summary:

Goodall learned from her experiences with chimpanzees that they react positively to direct looks from humans.

Accurate summary:

Goodall reports that when humans look directly but gently into chimpanzee's eye, the chimps are not threatened and may even return the look.

2.3.5 Avoiding Plagiarism

Plagiarism is the use of someone else's words or ideas as your own without crediting the original writer. You are aware of cases of deliberate plagiarism. Just avoid it. But you do need to know about unintended plagiarism — a direct quotation without quotation marks, a paraphrase that too closely resembles the original, background details gleaned from a source but used without acknowledgment. To avoid unintended plagiarism, you should understand what material you must document; take systematic, accurate notes; and give full credit to sources in both parenthetical citations and your list of sources cited.

2.3.5.1 Materials Not Requiring Acknowledgment

When the material you quote is from one of the following sources, the acknowledgment is generally unnecessary.

(1) Common knowledge. If most readers would be likely to know something, you need not credit it.

(2) Facts available in a wide variety of sources. If a number of encyclopedias, almanacs, or textbooks include the information, you need not cite a specific source.

(3) Your own findings from field research. If you conduct field research — observation, interviews, surveys — and produce results, simply announce those results as your own.

2.3.5.2 Materials Requiring Acknowledgment

You should credit the materials that do not come under one of the afore-said headings. Such materials include:

(1) Direct quotations. You need to cite the sources for all direct quotations. Do not forget to set off the author's original expressions in quotation marks in your paraphrase.

(2) Facts that are not widely known or are arguable. If your readers would be unlikely to know a fact, or if an author presents as fact an assertion that may or may not be true, cite the source.

(3) Judgments, opinions, and claims of others. Whenever you summarize or paraphrase anyone else's opinion, give the source for that summary or paraphrase. Even though the wording should be completely your own, you need to acknowledge the source.

(4) Statistics, charts, tables, and graphs from any source. Credit all statistical and graphical material derived from other people's research, even if you yourself create them from the source.

(5) Help provided by friends, instructors, or others. A conference with an instructor may give you the idea that you need to clinch an argument. Give credit. Friends may help you conduct surveys, refine questionnaires, or think through problems. Credit them, too.

2.3.5.3 Recognizing and Avoiding Unintended Plagiarism

When material is taken directly from a book, article, speech, statement, remarks, the Internet, or some other source, the writer must provide proper attribution. The following passage is from preface to the first edition of the book *The Origins of Totalitarianism* by Hannah Arendt (New York: Harcourt Brace Jovanovich, Inc., 1973 ed.), page vii.

Original passage:

> This book has been written against a background of both reckless optimism and reckless despair. It holds that Progress and Doom are two sides of the same medal; that both are articles of superstition, not of faith. It was written out of the conviction that it should be possible to discover the hidden mechanics by which all traditional elements of our political and spiritual world were dissolved into a conglomeration where everything seems to have lost specific

value, and has become unrecognizable for human comprehension, unusable for human purpose.

Word-for-word plagiarism:

　　This book has been written against a background of both reckless optimism and reckless despair. It holds that Progress and Doom are two sides of the same medal; that both are articles of superstition, not of faith. Interestingly enough, Arendt avoids much of the debates found in some of the less philosophical literature about totalitarianism.

Revised:

　　Arendt points out, "This book has been written against a background of both reckless optimism and reckless despair. It holds that Progress and Doom are two sides of the same medal; that both are articles of superstition, not of faith" (vii). Interestingly enough, Arendt avoids ...

When material is quoted word-for-word, a footnote or endnote (in Chicago Manual style) alone is insufficient. The material that represents a direct quotation must either be put within quotation marks or indented.

Footnote without quotation marks:

　　This book has been written against a background of both reckless optimism and reckless despair. It holds that Progress and Doom are two sides of the same medal; that both are articles of superstition, not of faith.[1] Interestingly enough, Arendt avoids much of the debates found in some of the less philosophical literature about totalitarianism.

Note:

　　[1] Hannah Arendt, The Origins of Totalitarianism (New York: Harcourt Brace Jovanovich, Inc., 1973 ed.), vii, Preface to the First Edition.

Revised:

　　As Hannah Arendt explains, her book was "written against a backdrop of both reckless optimism and reckless despair."[1] The book "holds that Progress and Doom are two sides of the same medal ..."[2]

Note:

　　[1,2] Hannah Arendt, The Origins of Totalitarianism (New York: Harcourt Brace Jovanovich, Inc., 1973 ed.), vii, Preface to the First Edition.

　　Or:

　　As Dr. Arendt has explained:

　　This book has been written against a background of both reckless optimism and reckless

Chapter 2
The Process of Research and Research Writing

despair. It holds that Progress and Doom are two sides of the same medal; that both are articles of superstition, not of faith.[1]

Interestingly enough, Arendt avoids much of the debate found in some of the less philosophical literature about totalitarianism.

Note:
[1] Hannah Arendt, The Origins of Totalitarianism (New York: Harcourt Brace Jovanovich, Inc., 1973 ed.), vii, Preface to the First Edition.

Even if the author's exact language is not used, a footnote or endnote is required for material that is paraphrased.

Hannah Arendt's book, *The Origins of Totalitarianism*, was written in the light of both excessive hope and excessive pessimism. Her thesis is that both Advancement and Ruin are merely different sides of the same coin. Her book was produced out of a belief that one can understand the method in which the more conventional aspects of politics and philosophy were mixed together so that they lose their distinctiveness and become worthless for human uses.[1]

Note:
[1] Hannah Arendt, The Origins of Totalitarianism (New York: Harcourt Brace Jovanovich, Inc., 1973 ed.), vii, Preface to the First Edition.

2.4 Formulating a Thesis

A thesis is a short passage — usually only a single sentence — summarizing the fundamental argument of the thesis (hence also called thesis statement). Typically, the thesis statement will appear near the end of the introductory paragraph, functioning as a promise to the readers, letting them know what will be discussed. Though you will probably not have a finished thesis when you begin to write, you should establish a tentative, working thesis early on in your writing process.

In spite of the fact that it will probably change, a working thesis is important for two reasons: ① it focuses your thinking, research, and investigation on a particular point about the topic and keeps you on track; and ② it provides concrete questions to ask about purpose, audience, and your stance and tone.

A working thesis statement has two parts: a topic part and a comment part. The topic part states the topic; the comment part makes an important point about the topic.

(1) Recent studies of depression (— *topic*) suggest that it is much more closely related to physiology than scientists had previously thought (— *comment*).

(2) The current health care crisis (— *topic*) can be traced to three major causes (— *comment*).

A successful working thesis has the following three characteristics.

(1) Be potentially interesting to your intended audience.
(2) Be as specific as possible.
(3) Limit the topic enough to be manageable.

You can evaluate a working thesis by checking it against the above criteria. Suppose a preliminary working thesis is.

Theories about "global warming" are being debated around the world.

INTEREST — The topic itself holds interest, but it seems to have no comment attached to it. The sentence merely states a bare fact, and it seems to go from facts to facts.

SPECIFICITY — The statement is clear, but not specific. Who is debating these theories? What is at issue in this debate?

MANAGEABILITY — The thesis is not manageable: it would require research in many countries and in many languages and would be beyond the capacities of most if not all undergraduates.

ASSESSMENT — The thesis is too general and needs to be narrowed by a workable comment before it can be useful. Also, the field for investigation is too large and vague.

This preliminary thesis can be narrowed into the following working thesis.

> Scientists from several different countries have challenged "global warming" theories and claimed that they are more propaganda than science.

There are seven errors to avoid when composing a thesis:

(1) A thesis cannot be a fragment; it should be expressed in a sentence.
(2) A thesis must not be in the form of a question.
(3) A thesis must not contain such phrases as *I think*.
(4) A thesis must not contain elements that are not clearly related.
(5) A thesis must not be expressed in vague language.
(6) A thesis must not be expressed in muddled or incoherent language.
(7) A thesis should not be written in figurative language.

The scope and precision of your thesis statement will vary depending on your field of study and the level at which you are writing. You will want to get some idea from your instructor about the scope of conclusions you are expected to draw for your research work. Remember: Your final thesis statement should cover all the points made in the paper. It need not enumerate each point, but you should not disconcert your reader by straying into an area of inquiry not suggested by the thesis statement.

Chapter 2
The Process of Research and Research Writing

The following is a useful method for writing thesis statements.

(1) Decide what you are writing about. A clear, concise thesis statement does more than outline the subject in question; it makes the reader aware of the writer's stand on the subject in question.

(2) Think about all the elements your paper will deal with. A thesis generally consists of a subject that contains a number of smaller facts; the topic sentence of each paragraph should refer back to the ideas contained within the thesis statement in order to keep the paper from digressing.

(3) Think about the purpose and tone of your paper. A thesis statement should contain the main point of the paper and suggest to the reader a direction that the paper will take in exploring, proving, or disproving that main point.

(4) State your main point in a sentence or two. A good writer asserts the main idea of an essay briefly. Instead of rambling, be as straightforward as possible.

(5) Revise your thesis as you develop your paper. A final version of a thesis statement will only be available after a draft of the paper has been completed. The focus of the paper may change and evolve in the course of writing; necessarily, the thesis statement should be revised to reflect the alterations in the paper.

So far, we have considered thesis statements that are one sentence long. You might keep your thesis statement one sentence long, if your paper is fairly short and direct. However, if your idea seems to be complex or your paper is long and involved, you might need to write a thesis longer than one sentence, as the underlined part in the following introduction.

> Mobility is an essential and enduring characteristic of American life. The freedom to go where we will, how we will, has had a strong impact on the style and structure of this country. Perhaps the single most important contribution to this American ethos has been the private automobile. For many people, the automobile is a symbol of freedom, providing both status and autonomy. Unfortunately, our national love affair with the private automobile threatens to become a national disaster — producing air, water, and land pollution, consuming valuable and irreplaceable resources, destroying both city and countryside, and, ironically, denying freedom of movement to those unable, or unwilling, to drive.
>
> <u>The purpose of this paper is to examine various aspects of transportation in the United States. The subject may be logically divided into several categories: the private automobile, alternatives to the private automobile, the feasibility of implementing those alternatives, and the economic and social implications of adopting them.</u>

In this case, the thesis takes two sentences: the first describes the writer's purpose; the second describes the points the writer will take up.

The following thesis is even longer.

> Most of the changes in Buddhism can be attributed to four factors: first, the lack of any documentation of Gautama Buddha's original teachings; second, the fact that Buddhism has spread throughout many countries all with a myriad of traditions; third, the inherent differences in man, every individual interpreting a certain teaching differently; and fourth, and perhaps most important, the changes that have come about through modernization. As many of the Buddhist countries become more Westernized, much of the old religion is being lost. These four factors have influenced the division of sects, especially the two major sects. An understanding of these four factors will clarify why it was inevitable that changes in Buddhism would take place.

2.5 Outlining the Paper

The outline should serve as a road map for your journey of writing. When writing an outline, keep your destination in mind. Put the thesis statement at the top of the page where it can be referred to often. Your instructor can help guide you through the outlining process. It is just common that the outline needs to be revised several times, for many materiats will be proved to be irrelevant and have to be deleted. One thing you have to remember is that even if the revised outline appears to be satisfactory and has been approved by your instructor, it will inevitably undergo changes along with the progress of your research and writing.

In an outline, entries of the same level of importance should be expressed in the same grammatical form, i.e., if capital roman numeral *I* is a noun, *II*, *III*, and so forth, should also be nouns; if capital *A* is an infinitive phrase, *B*, *C*, and so forth, should also be infinitive phrases.

Compare the following example of a partial outline in which entries at the same level are not in the same grammatical construction. Notice how easily the conversions to correct forms can be made.

Wrong:

    I. The ancient harp [noun]

        A. It is a musical instrument of great antiquity [sentence]

            1. Read about it in the Bible [sentence]

            2. References to it by writers all over the world [noun]

            3. Pictured in ancient art [incomplete sentence]

            4. Examples found by archaeologists [noun]

        B. Origin [noun]

Revised:

I. The ancient harp [noun]
   A. Antiquity [noun]
      1. References in the Bible [noun]
      2. References by writers from all over the world [noun]
      3. Delineations in ancient art [noun]
      4. Examples found by archaeologists [noun]
   B. Origin [noun]

2.5.1 Types of Outline

There are three types of outlines: topic outline, sentence outline, and paragraph outline. In the topic outline, every heading should be a noun or its equivalent (a gerund or an infinitive phrase). In the sentence outline, every heading should be a complete sentence, although an acceptable alternative is one in which the main heading is noun and every subheading a sentence, and vise versa. In the paragraph outline — except perhaps for the main heading being nouns — every heading is a paragraph.

2.5.1.1 Topic Outline

Topic outlines are undeniably easy to make, but they offer few other advantages. A topic outline is an organized list of the subjects with which a paper will deal. Here is a simple example of a topic outline.

Working Title: Modern Drama and the Tradition of Farce
Working Thesis: Farce, mere slapstick in the sixteenth century, developed a serious dramatic theory, absurdism, and finally became a permanent part of popular comedy.

  I. Ancient Models
     A. Greece
     B. Rome
  II. French Developments
     A. Extemporaneous Additions
     B. Establishment of Form
  III. English Farce
     A. Brief Comedies
     B. Low Humour
     C. Farce-Comedy

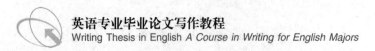

IV. **Modern and Contemporary Drama**
   A. Jarry
   B. Pirandello
   C. Ionesco
   D. Beckett
   E. Pinter
   F. Stoppard

V. **Beyond the Legitimate Theatre: Farce and Popular Culture**
   A. The Fringe
   B. Monty Python
   C. Saturday Night Live
   D. SCTV
   E. Kids in the Hall

2.5.1.2　Sentence Outline

Sentence outlines are formatted exactly as topic outlines are, but whole sentences replace the brief headings. The sentences state the crucial point of each stage of the paper. Consequently, a sentence outline provides a real test of your argument. The following is a sentence outline developed from the above topic outline.

Working Title: Modern Drama and the Tradition of Farce

Working Thesis: Farce, mere slapstick in the sixteenth-century, became the idiom of existential expression in the twentieth. Because farce combines theatrical and intellectual elements, it has become a permanent part of all serious comedy.

　I. The comedies of antiquity established the models for later playwrights.
　　A. The germs of both satire (Old Comedy) and farce (New Comedy) exist in Greek comedies.
　　B. Roman dramatists produced well-made farces, developing the traditions of Greek New Comedy.
　II. During the mid to late Renaissance, French dramatists developed an elaborate comic literature, while farces, lacking a literary tradition, grew spontaneously out of theatrical tradition.
　　A. Farces began as extemporaneous additions made by comic actors to the action of a more serious play.
　　B. Dramatists, attracted by the energy and theatrical success of these improvisations, began to write them into their plays.
　III. The English Farce, growing from brief interludes, came to dominate whole plays.
　　A. Farces began as very brief comedies marked by knockabout humour.

Chapter 2
The Process of Research and Research Writing

    B. The Farce became a full play, still characterized, however, by low humour.

    C. The growth of the Farce was completed when the Farce-Comedy, a hybrid mixture of plot and comic action, appeared in the eighteenth century.

IV. Modern dramatists, intent on demonstrating the rootlessness of human experience, made elements of the Farce the idiom of modernity.

    A. Absurdists and Pre-Absurdists such as Pirandello, Jarry, and Ionesco capitalized upon the manic, confusing qualities of farce to express human alienation.

    B. Beckett bridged the English and French theatrical cultures with *Waiting for Godot*, which brought farce to the attention of the North American and British intellectuals.

    C. Pinter, Stoppard, and Ayckbourn drew upon the work of the Absurdists and upon the tradition of farce, creating a popular theatrical idiom for serious, mainstream comedy.

V. The new farce quickly outgrew the legitimate theatre and found a new home in mass entertainment.

    A. The idiom of farce passed from the new playwrights to the new television comedians: The Fringe, Monty Python, and their many imitators.

    B. Troupes in the United States and in Canada (e.g., Saturday Night Live, SCTV, Kids in the Hall), working directly with the new tradition of farce, brought the technique to a growing audience.

Once you have reached the stage of a sentence outline, you will have an excellent idea of how valid your argument is, as well as a sense of its shape. A good sentence outline supplies all the basic information you need in order to write your essay. By merely adding a few transitional phrases to effect coherence, and by rounding out the bare ideas with some details, you can shape your essay into final form with content as well as direction. A sentence outline is more than an organizational device: it is a test of your ideas. When you make a sentence outline, you will find some ideas are weak and some assumptions are unsupported. Then you will make necessary adjustment. Note that the last two sections in the sentence outline are not quite unlike their counterparts in the topic outline. They group their components and establish connections between them.

2.5.1.3 Paragraph Outline

Paragraph outline is a variation on the sentence outline. The advantage of paragraph outline is clear: it forces you to begin your paragraphs with strong topic sentences rather than vague introductions and transitions. Against this real gain is poised the complexity of the task. You may well find that this exercise takes so much effort that it interferes with the actual writing of the paper. A sentence outline is a

very useful middle form, neither so easy as to be pointless nor so demanding as to steal time from the paper itself.

In organizing the facts and ideas gained in your early reading so as to construct a rough outline, you have come to understand the kinds of information that your further reading and your notetaking must supply. At the same time you should not feel too much bound by the preliminary outline, for, as wider reading increases your knowledge and develops your point of view, the relative values of the subtopics may change; you may even decide to drop some and add others. The outline, then, will almost certainly be adjusted as you go along and will not reach its final form until the reading and note-taking are finished.

2.5.2 Outline Style

The two basic styles for an outline are the number-letter sequence and decimal pattern. With either format, logic requires there be at least two items at each level or subdivision; that is, *A* must not appear without *B* and *1.1.1* must not appear without *1.1.2*. In the following example, the use of *1* under *A* is wrong for there is no use of *2*.

Wrong:

I. The ancient harp
  A. Origin
    1. The hunter's bow
  B. Styles

II. ...

When you find that you have only one subdivision for a section, either restate the major heading to include the subdivision or search for another logical division for the heading.

1. Number-letter sequence outline format

I. Wars of the nineteenth century
  A. United States
    1. Civil War, 1861–65
      a. Cause
        (1) Slavery
          (a) Compromise
            i) Missouri Compromise
            ii) 1850 Compromise

Chapter 2
The Process of Research and Research Writing

```
                    (b) ...
                (2) ...
            b. ...
        2. ...
    B. ...
II. Wars of the twentieth century
    A. United States
        1. First World War
        2. ...
...
```

2. Decimal outline format

```
1. Wars of the nineteenth century
    1.1 United States
        1.1.1 Civil War, 1861-1865
            1.1.1.1 Cause
                1.1.1.1.1 Slavery
                    1.1.1.1.1.1 Compromise
                        1.1.1.1.1.1.1 Missouri compromise
                        1.1.1.1.1.1.2 1850 compromise
                    1.1.1.1.1.2 ...
                1.1.1.1.2 ...
            1.1.1.2 ...
        1.1.2 ...
    1.2 ...
2. Wars of the twentieth century
    2.1 United States
        2.1.1 First World War
        2.1.2 ...
...
```

Note that the numerals are aligned on the periods that follow them, and are either set flush with the text or indented. Note that the numerals or letters denoting the top four levels are set off by periods (I., A., 1., a.) and those for the lower levels are set off by single or double parentheses [(1), (a), i)].

2.6 Writing the First Draft

Writing a research paper involves preparing a first draft, revising and editing the draft, preparing the documentation, attending to the elements of the format, and proofreading. Although to some extent you will approach these tasks in the order listed, you should not expect to complete any of them until you have a finished copy. Each activity proceeds both linearly and recursively. Even as you proceed with writing your first draft, you will constantly be thinking back to the sentences and paragraphs you have already written and thinking ahead to the projected design of your entire paper. You should remain flexible, allowing the organization and development of the body of the paper to emerge from your growing understanding of the topic.

The introduction will focus your reader's attention on your argument by making clear why the paper is written, what is being argued in the paper, and how the author situates the argument in the field's literature. If writing an introduction is difficult, start with the thesis statement. Here are some popular strategies to begin the paper:

— Relate the topic with something that is well known;
— Open with the thesis statement;
— Provide background information to the reader;
— Review the literature;
— Take exception to critical views;
— Challenge an assumption;
— Provide a brief summary;
— Supply data, statistics, and special evidence;
— Define key terms (avoiding "Webster says").

The directness of the introduction varies from field to field. Review exemplary papers or published articles from that field for models, but, most importantly, let the purpose of your paper and your argument drive the nature of the introduction.

The body develops the argument by presenting evidence to support the thesis statement. As you use your notes, keep track of the origin of your outside information by jotting down the source information that is on your note card.

The conclusion provides the reader with a summary of the argument as well as its implications. Possible concluding strategies include:

— restating the thesis and going beyond it;
— closing with an effective quotation;
— comparing past to present;
— offering a directive or solution;
— discussing test results.

You might start off by trying to set down all your ideas in the order in which you want them to appear. Do not be concerned if the writing in the first draft is hasty and

Chapter 2
The Process of Research and Research Writing

fairly rough. Stay focused by following your outline closely. Revise the outline, of course, whenever new ideas occur to you and whenever it no longer works.

You should resist the temptation to perfect opening sentences or paragraphs. Good introductions do not surface until you finish writing the entire paper. When doing the rough draft, get to the heart of the subject without regard for stylistic considerations. Save such considerations for your final draft. If your note taking was solid and your outline is good enough, follow your outline and keep the focus on your thesis. At this stage of composition, do not be concerned with the length of the paper; just go on writing until you have used all of your notes.

2.7 Revising, Editing and Proofreading

The terms *revising*, *editing*, and *proofreading* are sometimes used to mean the same thing, but there is good reason to understand each as a separate process, each in its own way contributing to good finished writing. Revising is reseeing, rereading, rethinking, and reconstructing your thoughts on paper until they match those in your mind. In contrast, editing is changing language more than ideas. You edit to make precise what you want to say, testing each word or phrase to see that is accurate, appropriate, or necessary. Editing is stylistic and mechanical work, generally taking place at the level of the sentence or word. Proof reading is checking a manuscript for accuracy and correctness. It is the last phase of the editing process, completed after conceptual and stylistic concerns have been addressed. When you proofread, you review spelling, punctuation, capitalization, and usage to make sure no careless mistakes have occurred that might confuse or distract readers.

2.7.1 Revising

There are two good reasons to revise before you edit. First, in revising you may cut out whole sections of a draft because they no longer suit your final purpose. If you have already edited those now-deleted sections, all that careful work goes for naught. Second, once you have invested time in carefully editing sentences, you become reluctant to cut them, even though these sections no longer suit your purpose. Of course, writers are always circling back through the stages, editing when it makes more sense to revise, inventing when they mean to edit. Nonetheless, you will save time if you revise before editing, and edit before proofreading.

In revising your paper, you should be concerned with the major matters of organization, the development of ideas, logic, and continuity. Read through your paper carefully to see whether it flows smoothly. You may even want to read it out loud, keeping in mind that if it does not sound good to you, it will not sound good to the reader. This may necessitate adding a transitional paragraph here or there to carry the reader from one point to another. This may also be the time to determine if you need to add or delete information that will help strengthen the support for your thesis. Try to set aside your draft for a day or two before revising. This makes it easier to view your work objectively and see any gaps or problems.

The computer makes revision immeasurably easier, most notably by eliminating the need for recopying multiple drafts. Not only can you add and delete words with the stroke of a key, but you can also block and move paragraphs and sections from one part to another. You can use the search feature to locate particular words or series of words, a good way to determine how you have previously used your terminology and how often you have repeated a particular word. A thesaurus, which permits you to see synonyms and antonyms, can help you find alternative words. Also, your printed copy will give you a view of your drafts that is different from the view that appears on the screen.

Although computers facilitate revision, they can inhibit certain kinds of improvements, most importantly the integration of parts into a whole. Working on a screen that allows you to see only twenty-four lines at a time makes it difficult to keep the structure of the entire paper in mind. It is quite common for writers to rework a sentence or paragraph on the computer screen, only to find that it no longer fits logically into the paper. Any change in the position of a paragraph nearly always requires other revisions, such as changes in transitions and the reordering of sentences elsewhere in the paper. You can compensate for these problems by printing your document occasionally and making revisions on paper.

It is wise to keep all versions of your draft because you may find that you want to restore something you had deleted. Some writers keep each draft in a separate file organized by date; others keep a file of deleted paragraphs, sentences, or even single words for possible use in another part of the paper.

The following questions can help you notice passages in your work that need revision. After you have answered all these questions affirmatively, you can begin editing.

— Does the writing have a clear sense of purpose?

— Does the thesis statement govern everything in the paper?

— Does the introduction prepare the reader for the paper?

Chapter 2
The Process of Research and Research Writing

— Could the major divisions and sub-points be presented in a better order?
— Are the paragraphs developed logically and arranged in a coherent sequence?
— Do any sections contradict other sections?
— Does the entire paper read smoothly, with transitions that carry the reader from one idea to the next?
— Does the paper address the appropriate audience?
— Is the style authentic and engaging?
— Is the language precise and appropriate to the writing context?

2.7.2 Editing

Readers expect a final copy that is clean and correct in every way. You need to make time for thorough and careful editing. All writers have personal trouble spots, problems that come up again and again in their writing. You may already be aware of some of your own trouble spots and will probably have others pointed out to you by advisers. Paying attention to the patterns of editing problems you find in your writing can help you overcome errors.

After identifying any typical trouble spots in your writing, organize the information you have gathered in a systematic way. To begin, list all the errors or corrections marked on the last piece of writing you did. Then note the context of the sentence in which error appeared. Finally, try to derive a guideline to spot future errors of the same kind. You can broaden these guidelines as you begin to find patterns of errors, and you can then add to your inventory every time you write and edit a draft. Here is an example of such a checklist.

MARKED ERRORS	IN CONTEXT	LOOK FOR
wrong preposition	*to* for *on*	*to*
spelling	*to* for *too*	*to* before adjectives, adverbs
fragment	starts with *when*	sentences beginning with *when*
missing comma	after *however*	sentences opening with *however*
missing apostrophe	*Michael's*	all names

Some errors, such as the use of wrong words or misspellings, may seem so unsystematic that you may not be able to identify patterns in them. But keeping an editing checklist will gradually allow you to identify most of the characteristic problems that trouble you. And because keeping up your checklist takes only a few minutes for each piece of writing, doing so is well worth the time.

Writing with a computer, you may use features of word-processing programs to help identify and correct errors. When you find an error, you can use the search command to retrieve other instances of this error and replace them with the correct form automatically. An adjunct to most word-processing programs is the spell checker, which identifies the misspelling of any word in its dictionary. Other programs can be used to identify problems with grammar, punctuation, usage, and wordiness. When you use any of these features or programs, remember that the computer does not think and you should not rely on them too much. Spell checkers and grammar checkers do not always catch errors. The only misspellings that a spell checker can identify are errors in words that are in its dictionary. They will not recognize, for example, the difference between *horse* and *house*. Grammar checkers point out problems, but they cannot help you find the most effective way to revise your sentence. Besides, errors are harder to spot on a computer screen than on paper. If you type your paper on a computer, it is better for you to print out a copy to proofread.

2.7.3 Proofreading

Proofreading can make the difference between a mediocre paper and an excellent one. When you have a thoroughly revised draft ready for final typing, read through it at least once more, paying attention to every detail. Check for faulty source citings and bibliographical entries. Look for careless errors such as misspelled words and incorrect punctuation and capitalization. Evaluate every sentence once again for clarity, check every paragraph for coherence, and think about every choice of diction and sentence structure.

Because writers are often too close to their work to view it objectively, an effective way to measure your audience's reaction is to read the paper to someone else, or read it aloud to yourself. The passages over which you hesitate or stumble probably need revision. Finishing the final draft a few days ahead of your deadline will give you an opportunity to improve your paper. You will be able to read and proofread and then set the paper aside so that you can return to it with a fresh perspective and a keen eye for detecting rough spots and errors.

2.8 Finalizing the Paper

Type the paper on one side of paper only. Use paper which is white and of a standard size $8\frac{1}{2}$ by 11 inches and double space throughout. Before you do this, make clear what format your instructor requires.

Chapter 2
The Process of Research and Research Writing

Exercises

I. Answer the questions.

1. Why are the writing steps reciprocal rather than exclusive of each other? Discuss the process of writing from your personal experience.
2. Why is it necessary for a writer to keep a working bibliography? What information should be included in the entry of a bibliography?
3. When we evaluate a source, what should we take into consideration? Why?
4. Talk about the advantages and disadvantages of the three note forms: direct quotation, paraphrase and summary. How can we use them properly?
5. What is plagiarism? How to avoid plagiarism?
6. What is the function of an outline in the writing of an essay? What are the advantages and disadvantages of the topic outline, sentence outline, and paragraph outline?
7. What is the most important principle that a writer must adhere to in the creation of an outline? Work out an outline of a journal article and see how the thesis statement is logically developed.
8. Why is revising essential for creating a research paper? What should be done in revising? If you have worked out a draft of an essay, revise it using the guidelines developed in the chapter.

II. Narrow down the general topics to a workable size.

Chinese Language
Translation
William Shakespeare
Intercultural Communication
The 19th-century American Literature
Language Teaching
Advertising
School Education

III. Choose a subject for a research paper, and prepare brief statements on the following.

A. Your reason for choosing the subject.

39

B. Your present knowledge about the subject and the gaps you will have to fill.

C. The reader you have in mind and the information you assume the reader could already have about the topic.

D. The bibliographies, indexes, and other reference works that you will consult.

E. The main points you will make and the methods you will use to develop them.

IV. **Which of the following theses is the best**? **Why**?

1. Forest fires are enormously destructive because they ravage the land, create problems for flood control, and destroy useful lumber.
2. Installment buying is of great benefit to the economy, having in mind the consumer to use a product while she pays for it and being like forced savings.
3. Television is a handicap.

V. **Consult encyclopedias and yearbooks in the library for information on one of the following topics.**

Chinese painting	Abraham Lincoln
Trade Union	Waterloo
French Revolution	English language

VI. **Compare the following thesis statements in pairs. In each pair, which one is immature? Which one is well-functioning and would best help the reader understand how the writer is going to develop the paper**?

1. a) The public behavior of some sports figures is poor.
   b) The public behavior of some sports figures is a poor example of illiteracy, arrogance, and violence for our youth.
2. a) Many college athletes graduate as functional illiterates because they have much ground training and little academic learning.
   b) Many college athletes graduate as functional illiterates.
3. a) Rocks are commonly divided according to their origin.
   b) Rocks are commonly divided according to their origin into three major

Chapter 2
The Process of Research and Research Writing

classes — igneous, sedimentary, and metamorphic.

4. a) Before any so-called Right to Die laws are enacted, many people should be consulted.

   b) Before any so-called Right to Die laws are enacted, representatives from the fields of law, medicine, and theology must be consulted.

5. a) Capital punishment should be abolished for both legal and moral reasons.

   b) One of the best things that can happen in the US is the abolishment of capital punishment.

6. a) All in all, I believe *The Godfather* is a highly dangerous film.

   b) *The Godfather* is a dangerous film because it romanticizes violence and encourages people to think all Italians are gangsters.

7. a) The members of some fraternities are incredible conformists: they wear the same clothes, take the same courses, and have the same political beliefs.

   b) The members of some fraternities are incredible conformists.

8. a) Theodore Roosevelt raised the consciousness of Americans.

   b) Although he had his detractors, Theodore Roosevelt raised the consciousness of Americans regarding such issues as conservation and physical fitness.

9. a) Writing is useful in clarifying your own thoughts and in communicating them to others.

   b) Writing is a useful thing for educated people to know how to do things.

10. a) School is a waste of time.

    b) For many children school is a waste of time because they get little attention, are made to feel inferior, and have few successes.

VII. Rewrite the following poorly worded theses. Make them clear and effective.

1. In my opinion, birth control is the most urgent need in today's world.

2. Just how far should the law go in its tolerance of pornography?

3. The problem with sound pollution is, How much longer can our ears bear the noise?

4. The noteworthy relaxation of language taboos both in conversation and in print today.

5. Education should train all young people for jobs, and many are impatient with

conditions today.

6. How missionaries are sent to other parts of the world in order to replace the local civilization with Western civilization.

VIII. Find some thesis statements and discuss with your partner whether they are good or not. If they are not good enough, work with your partner to improve them.

Chapter 3
The Structure of a Research Paper

A research paper consists of three main parts: the front matter, the text, and the back matter. In a long paper, each of these main parts may be made up of various sections.

The Front Matter:
  Title page
  Outline page
  Abstract
  Acknowledgements
  Table of contents
  List of tables
  List of figures

The Text:
  Composed of introduction, literature review, methodology, results, discussion, and conclusion as recommended by the American Psychological Association, or in other forms as required according to the discipline

The Back Matter:
  Reference list
  Appendix

The sequence presented above is not the actual writing sequence. A common practice is that the front matter is written last, the back matter second, and the text first. For the convenience of discussing, the sections are organized in the order of the sequence in a paper.

3.1 The Front Matter

The front matter includes the title page, the outline page, the abstract in English, the abstract in Chinese, acknowledgements, table of contents, list of tables and list of figures. But as undergraduates do not write long papers and do not use quite a few tables and figures in their paper, their beginning part usually does not include outline page and lists of tables and figures.

3.1.1 Title Page

Most universities and colleges have their own style of title page for theses and dissertations, and this style should be followed exactly in matters of content, capitalization, centering, and spacing. For graduation theses, the title page — the first page of the paper — should provide such information as the title of the manuscript, the label of the paper, the university at which the paper was written, author's name, instructor's name, and the date when the paper was finished. (See Sample 1 in Appendix B for one style that may be used for graduation theses.)

The title of your paper should be concise as well as descriptive and comprehensive. It should indicate the content of the paper so that readers will know whether it relates to their interest. A title like "The Tourist Industry in Hong Kong" does not sufficiently describe a paper devoted to the economic aspects of the industry there; a title such as "The Economic Dynamics of the Tourist Industry in Hong Kong" would more accurately describe the content.

The following are a few research paper titles:

The Rainbow under the Pen of Lawrence

The Role of Suppression in Understanding Metaphors

Form and Meaning in Text Cohesion

The Crises of the Character and Its Transformation in Modern British Fiction

L2 Proficiency and Comprehension Strategy Use of EFL Learners in Universities in China

How Do Postcolonial Theories Inspire Translation Studies in China?

Metaphor and Metonymy: Similarities and Differences

Although the title comes first in a research paper, it may sometimes be written last. Its final form may be long delayed and much thought about and argued over. As we can see from the above, good titles should meet the following requirements:

— The title should indicate the topic of the study.

— The title should indicate the scope of the study (i.e., neither overstating nor understating its significance).

— The title should be self-explanatory to readers in the chosen area.

Chapter 3
The Structure of a Research Paper

The expected length of research paper title is very much a disciplinary matter. In some areas, such as the life sciences, titles are usually longer and looking more and more like full sentences. In other areas, the preferred style is for short titles containing mostly nouns and prepositions, which can be seen in the above examples. Here are a few more examples:

(1) Chinese EFL Students' Learning Strategies for Oral Communication
(2) Children's Punctuation: An Analysis of Errors in Period Placement
(3) Is There a Female Style in Science?

Depending on your field, you may wish to consider using qualifications in your titles (as colon is used in 2.). In nearly all cases, the process of arriving at the final form of a title is one of narrowing it down and making it more specific. Colons are widely used in titles. One of the colon's typical functions is to separate ideas in such combinations as the following:

BEFORE	: (COLON)	AFTER
Problem	:	Solution
General	:	Specific
Topic	:	Method
Major	:	Minor

The following titles are from academic journals. Read them and pay attention to the relation between the ideas before and after colon.

— The Discourse Function of *Yes* and *No* in Narration: A Cognitive Functional Approach (Problem: Solution)
— The Conceptual Metaphors of "eye": A Comparative Study Based on Corpus Between English and Chinese (Problem: Solution)
— Scalar Implicature in Chinese Child Language: An Experimental Study (General: Specific)
— Translation: A Dialogue between a Text and Its Translators (General: Specific)
— Pound and Hu Shi: A Cultural Approach to Poetry Translation (Topic: Method)
— Discourse Pragmatics: Discourse Perspective on Syntactic Structure (Major: Minor)

We know that titles are important, as the research paper will be known by its title. A successful title will attract readers; an unsuccessful title will discourage readers. You can not give too much importance to the title of your paper.

3.1.2 Outline Page

The outline page of your paper presents a topic or sentence or paragraph outline, and sometimes includes the thesis statement. (See Sample 2-1, Sample 2-2 in Appendix B.) The numbers and headings on the outline page should not appear within the text of your paper.

3.1.3 Abstract in English

Abstracts usually consist of a single paragraph containing from about four to ten full sentences. Abstract is more important for the reader than for the writer. An unsatisfactory abstract is not likely affect whether the paper is finally accepted for publication but may affect how many people will read your paper. We know that readers of academic journals employ a vast amount of skimming and scanning. If they like your abstract, they may read your paper, or at least part of it. If they do not like it, they may not.

A well-written abstract provides the following information: the purpose of the study, the research questions to be addressed, the subjects involved, the instruments used to collect the data, the procedures for collecting and analyzing the data, the findings and the confusions. It should contain the most important words referring to method and content of the paper.

Use the following as a checklist for your abstract.

1. Motivation

Why do we care about the problem and the results? If the problem isn't obviously interesting, it might be better to put motivation first; but if your work is incremental progress on a problem that is widely recognized as important, it is probably better to put the problem statement first to indicate which piece of the larger problem you are breaking off to work on. This section should include the importance of your work, the difficulty of the area, and the impact it might have if successful.

2. Problem statement

What problem are you trying to solve? What is the scope of your work (a generalized approach, or for a specific situation)? In some cases it is appropriate to put the problem statement before the motivation, but usually this only works if most readers already understand why the problem is important.

3. Approach

How did you go about solving or making progress on the problem? Did you use simulation, analytic models, prototype construction, or analysis of field data for an actual product? What important variables did you control, ignore, or measure?

4. Results

What's the answer? Be concrete and specific with the results. Avoid vague results such as "very," "small," or "significant."

5. Conclusion

What are the implications of your answer? Is it going to change our conventional concept, be a significant "win," be a nice hack, or simply serve as a road sign indicating that this path is a waste of time. Are your results general, potentially generalizable, or specific to a particular case?

Abstracts can be descriptive, or informative. A descriptive abstract merely identifies the areas to be covered in the paper. It includes the purpose, methods, and scope of the research. It introduces the subject to readers, who must then read the paper to find out the author's results, conclusions, or recommendations. It is usually short, under 100 words. For example,

> With the development of computers and the internet, webchat has become more and more popular. This particular communicative form generates some unique linguistic features, which can hardly be found in other variants of English. Yet, to analyze its linguistic features from the point of view of stylistics is still a new realm. Adopting the theories of modern stylistics, this paper analyzes the English used in webchat from four levels — graphology, lexicon, syntax/grammar and context.

The abstract consists of 75 words. It introduces the purpose of the research (to analyze the linguistic feature of webchat), the method (adopting the theories of modern stylistics), the research scope (four levels — graphology, lexicon, syntax/grammar, and context), but does not tell the reader about the results, conclusions or recommendations.

An informative abstract summarizes the entire report and gives the reader an overview of the facts that will be laid out in detail in the paper itself. It is rarely longer than one page. It communicates specific information from the paper, includes the purpose, methods, and scope of the paper, provides the results, conclusions, and recommendations. For example,

Intercultural communication studies have scored great progress in China since they were introduced in the early eighties of the last century. Over 30 monographs and textbooks have been published and more than 2,000 articles have appeared in academic journals. An increasing number of colleges and universities now offer intercultural communication as a required or optional course. However, empirical research has been fairly weak. A comparison is made between articles published in Chinese journals and those published in the *International Journal of Intercultural Relations* for the period 1999–2002. It is found that while articles based on empirical research predominate in *IJIR*, only a very small percentage of articles in Chinese journals are data-driven. It is urged that more empirical research should be done in the future.

(— Hu Wenzhong, On Empirical Research in Intercultural Communication, *Foreign Language Teaching and Research*, Vol.37 No.5, 400)

The abstract is 125-word long. It not only includes the purpose of the research ("solving a problem in intercultural communication studies in China"), the method adopted ("comparison"), the scope of research ("articles published in Chinese journals and those published in the *International Journal of Intercultural Relations* for the period 1999–2002"), but also introduces the result ("only a very small percentage of articles in Chinese journals are data-driven"), the conclusion ("empirical research has been fairly weak"), and the recommendation ("more empirical research should be done in the future").

Keywords always come after the abstract. A keyword is a particular word or phrase that describes the contents of the paper. They are intended to act as shortcuts that sum up an entire paper and help search engines match a paper to an appropriate search query. Normally, keywords vary from three to five in number.

3.1.4 Abstract in Chinese

In general, the content of the abstract in Chinese should be the same as that in English. But a literal translation of the English version (except key words) is definitely unsatisfactory. Some English majors seem to be weak in writing in Chinese. Very often the draft of an abstract in Chinese contains some sentences that do not sound like Chinese and some are even difficult for readers to understand. To ensure the readability of the abstract, you may ask the students from other departments — the Chinese department, for instance — to read it and make comments on it before you submit it to your instructor.

3.1.5 Acknowledgments

In Acknowledgments, you thank those people who offered help in the process of your research and writing. You usually give thanks to: (1) your instructor; (2) the teachers and classmates who once gave you suggestions or advice on your research; (3) those who helped you correct data and/or do proof-reading; (4) those who gave you physical and/or mental support; (5) those who kindly permitted you to use their research instruments or materials.

Acknowledgments should be expressed simply and tactfully. The statements should be specific and coucrete. You should provide the information about the way you have been helped. Being general and abstract makes people think you are not sincere — you express your thanks just out of formality rather than from the bottom of your heart. You should say what the person had done in relation to your research and paper writing. For example,

> We wish to acknowledge the assistance and encouragement of many people who helped us to complete this project.
>
> We thank our mentors Mike Graves, John Hollowell, and Richard Shelton for the years of gentle guidance and friendship. Without them, we probably would not be teaching and writing.
>
> We thank our friend, colleague, and chief supporter Charles Davis, Director of Composition at the University of Arizona, for his never-ending support. We admire his unwavering commitment to quality education.
>
> (— Stuart C. Brown, Robert K. Mittan, & Duane H. Roen, *Becoming Expert*, xvii)

While you express your thanks to the people who helped you in your research and writing the paper, it is not necessary to be over-modest. Being over-modest could lead the reader to conclude that you are an incompetent researcher and, as a result, the reader will probably lose confidence in your argument.

3.1.6 Table of Contents

The table of contents, sometimes headed CONTENTS, list all the parts of the paper except the title page. If the chapters are grouped in parts, the generic headings (e.g., PART I) and titles (e.g., EARLY FINDINGS) of the parts also appear in the contents. Subheadings within the chapters are frequently included in one of various ways (see Sample 3 in Appendix B) or they may be omitted entirely from the table of contents.

If the subheading of any level is longer than one line, the second line of the subheading must be indented three spaces, and the page number should follow the period leaders after the last word of the subheading. Double-space between items, and

single-space runovers.

If more than one level of subheading is included in the table of contents, each level is indented three spaces below the preceding higher level. If only the first level is shown, each subheading may be indented three spaces below the chapter title or, if the subheadings are short, the first one in each chapter may be indented three spaces below the chapter title and the following ones of the same level run in.

Capitalization and wording of the titles of all parts, chapters and sections should all agree exactly with the way they appear in the body of the paper.

Numbers designating parts and chapters should be given as they are in the text. Part numbers may be uppercase roman numerals (PART I, PART II, etc.) or spelledout numbers (PART ONE, PART TWO, etc.). The generic heading may precede the part title and be separated from it by a period, or it may be centered above the title and thus need no punctuation. Chapter numbers may be Arabic or uppercase roman numerals, or spelled-out numbers. The word "Chapter" may precede or be placed over the chapter number. Do not use the word "Chapter" in the contents if the sections of the paper are not so designated.

Page numbers in table of contents are always justified right following a line of periods. Note that only the beginning page number of each chapter or other section is given. Page numbers for parts may be omitted if they are all identical with the beginning page number of the first chapter under each part. Note that if the page number is given for one part, it must be given for all of them.

3.1.7 List of Illustrations/Figures

In a list of illustrations, sometimes headed ILLUSTRATIONS, the figure numbers are given in Arabic numerals followed by a period; the captions start two spaces after the period; and the page numbers (in Arabic) are separated from the caption by period leaders. Double-space between captions, single-space within.

The figure numbers in the list are aligned by their periods under the word "Figure," and page numbers are listed flush right under the word "Page," as in Appendix B Sample 4.

The captions in the list of illustrations should agree with those given beneath illustrations, unless the latter are long, in which case it is best to give them in shortened form in the list.

3.1.8 List of Tables

In a list of tables, the table numbers (in Arabic, followed by a period) are placed in a column flush left under the heading "Table", and the page numbers are listed flush right under the heading "Page". Table titles should begin two spaces after the period following the table number and should agree exactly with the wording of the titles as they appear above the tables in the text. The titles are capitalized in either sentence or headline style, as in Appendix B Sample 4, and runover lines are indented three spaces. Double-space between items, single-space within.

3.1.9 List of Abbreviations

A list of abbreviations is desirable only if the writer has devised abbreviations instead of using those that are commonly accepted. A list of abbreviations should be arranged alphabetically by the abbreviation itself, not the spelled-out term. Under the centered generic heading in uppercase, list abbreviations on the left in alphabetical order and leave two to four spaces between the longest abbreviation and its spelled-out term. Align the first letter of all other spelled-out terms with the first letter of the spelled-out term following the longest abbreviation, and use the longest line in the column to center the list on the page(s). Double-space between items, single-space within. A list of abbreviations should help the reader who wishes to read only a portion of the whole paper instead of reading it from beginning to end. Even when a paper includes a list of abbreviations, the spelled-out version of a term should be given the first time the term appears in the paper, and it should be followed by the abbreviation in parentheses.

3.2 The Text

Generally speaking, every essay or paper is made up of three parts: introduction, body, and conclusion. The following format outlines the major sections of an academic paper, but it does not specify how the body of the paper — the longest and most difficult section — should be organized.

    I. Introduction
        A. Background
        B. Thesis
    II. Body

    Literature Review, Methodology, Results and Discussion

III. Conclusion

    A. Summarize the issue

    B. Show importance or relevance

3.2.1 Introduction

The introduction is the first part of the paper. The introduction to an academic paper should serve two purposes:

(1) Provide background — general information of the subject and your particular perspective;

(2) State the thesis — the most important ideas that you will deal with in your paper.

3.2.1.1 Background Information

A good way to begin an academic paper is to provide general background information on the subject. By including background material you make the reader aware of the context surrounding your topic. For example, if you were writing a paper on Lincoln's Gettysburg Address, you might want to begin the paper by mentioning the background to that historic address. You could provide some information about the battle that took place at Gettysburg, and thereby help readers become more familiar with the context of the speech. Similarly, reports of psychological experiments usually begin with a discussion of past research related to the particular investigation reported. By mentioning these other studies, the writer presents a brief history of scientific activity in the field; in this way, the writer familiarizes the reader with the reason for the experiment and shows how the experiment is related to preceding work.

    William Wordsworth's "A Slumber Did My Spirit Seal" is the culmination of a series of lyric poems, written in early 1799, known collectively as the "Lucy" poems. Critics have argued for nearly two centuries over different interpretations of the last poem of this group. Some interpret it as the poet's personal reminiscence of a secret lover; others regard it as a symbolic "killing off" of Wordsworth's sister, Dorothy, whom (some suppose) Wordsworth subconsciously desired incestuously. Many claim that the subject of this poem is the physical horror of death, with the recognition that Lucy (whomever she may represent) is dead. However, Wordsworth has insisted that the poet's business is to give pleasure. For Wordsworth, pleasure has an absolute or mystical value, as a sign that our individual lives are rooted in a whole whose life is joy, are living branches of the tree of life, with its sap tingling in our veins. A proper understanding of Wordsworth's "A Slumber Did My Spirit Seal" enhances our chances of sharing in this pleasure, of feeling the "tingle" of life in our veins.

As background, the writer introduces Wordsworth's poem "A Slumber Did My Spirit Seal" and the history of controversy concerning its interpretation. Moreover, because she is going to build her argument around a particular view of "pleasure," she must define this term. Her definition provides the background necessary to understand the main point of her argument — a "proper understanding" of the poem "enhances our chances of sharing in this pleasure, of feeling the 'tingle' of life in our veins."

3.2.1.2 Thesis Statement

Practically speaking, you have two choices to put thesis statement: 1) in your introduction, specifically as its last sentence, so that your readers know where you are taking them; 2) in your conclusion, so that you reveal your destination to your readers after your evidence seems inevitably to have taken them there. Usually, it is unwise to blurt out your thesis in the first sentence. Most readers prefer to see the main point in the introduction, specifically at the end of the introduction. For example, in the above example, the thesis statement "A proper understanding of Wordsworth's 'A Slumber Did My Spirit Seal' enhances our chances of sharing in this pleasure, of feeling the 'tingle' of life in our veins" is the last sentence of the introduction. The same principle applies to major sections and subsections. Readers tend to look for the main point of a section at the end of its introduction. If that introduction is a single sentence, that point will be the first sentence of the section. If the introduction is longer, readers look for the main point in the last sentence of the introduction. You may have reason to put the point of a whole section at its end, but at the beginning of every section, readers still need an introductory sentence or two to lead them into its body. So, even if you put your point last in a section, you'd better draft a sentence or two for the beginning that will lead your readers to the point at the end.

3.2.2 Body

The body of the paper usually consists of a number of chapters. If your research involves certain experiment, the body will consist of Literature Review, Methodology, Results and Discussion chapters.

Literature review may be a free-standing part. It commonly serves to pave the way for your own research. It is a critical look at the existing research which is significant to your research. Some people think it is just a summary, this is not true. Although you need to make summary of the research work in the past, you need to compare the research results that have been achieved up to the time, and, more important, you need to evaluate them and make comment on them.

The Methodology chapter describes the design of the proposed study. It includes general as well as specific research questions or hypotheses, information about subjects, instruments, the procedures for data-collection and data-analysis. The information presented in this chapter should be explicit and transparent so that any other researcher can easily replicate your study if she/he wants to.

The Results chapter is a report of the findings, usually including scores and statistics, which are the answers to research questions. The Discussion is an interpretation of the results. In the Discussion chapter, you explain ① the possible reasons for a specific finding, ② the significance of the findings, and ③ the link between the present findings and the previous ones. Discussion may go along with each finding presented or it may be an independent chapter from the Results.

In the body of the paper your ideas should be developed in detail. You should prove your points continually by using specific examples and quotations from your note cards; and use transition words to ensure a smooth flow of ideas from paragraph to paragraph.

3.2.3 Conclusion

Conclusion is the ending part of the paper proper. Essays that move through several stages need recognizable endings if they are not to give the impression of having been cut off too abruptly. The ending is author's last chance to drive home the thesis. A good conclusion manages to bring out the significance of the whole discussion. A restatement of the course of the discussion, drawing out implications, is appropriate in long papers and may be necessary when the material is difficult. When evidence has been built up throughout the paper, the ending can repeat as an authoritative statement what was presented at the start as a tentative hypothesis. Or the ending may summarize only the strongest of the arguments made in the essay.

> It is true, from the teacher's point of view, that letter grades have a certain amount of utility: they make it easier to keep concise records. But when we weigh this small advantage against the great disadvantages of grades, the argument for the utility of letter grades seems weak. Grades are, as we have seen, the greatest cause of anxiety among students. This anxiety

disrupts both personal and academic development during the college years. Moreover, grades discourage a love of learning. By working for a grade rather than for knowledge, students learn to value the immediate rewards of a higher grade rather than to value the long-range goal of a love of learning. Thus, by using the antiquated system of letter grades, schools actually subvert the scholastic ideals which they proclaim.

Here, the writer is justified in restating the main points in the concluding part of the paper. By doing so he helps the reader put all the arguments together at one time. The good ending makes it clear that the essay has arrived at its destination; it strikes a note of finality and completeness. Whatever works against that sense of completeness weakens the paper. The ending is not the place for afterthoughts, for bringing in ideas that should have been treated in the body of the paper. Nor is it the place for apologies or confessions of inadequacy. It is the place for as much affirmation as is justified by the discussion that precedes it. It may also be the place for pointing to broader implications, for indicating the significance of the findings, or for throwing a challenge to the reader. An ending that brings an essay to a totally satisfying conclusion may at the same time open a door into another essay as yet unwritten.

3.3 The Back Matter

The Back Matter mainly contains a reference list and/or appendices. This is the place where you put the materials which are important for you to convince your reader but are unsuitable to be put intact in the context.

3.3.1 References

A bibliography is a list of the sources you use to get information for your paper. It is at the end of your paper, on the last page or last few pages.

You will find it easier to prepare your final bibliography if you keep track of each book, encyclopedia, or article you use as you are reading and taking notes. Start a preliminary, or draft, bibliography by listing all your sources on a separate sheet of paper. Note down the full title, author, place of publication, publisher, and date of publication for each source. (See 2.3.1.)

Also, every time a fact gets recorded on a note card, its source should be noted in the top right corner. When you are finished writing your paper, you can use the information on your note cards to double-check your bibliography.

When assembling a final bibliography, list your sources (texts, articles, interviews, and so on) in alphabetical order by authors' last names. Sources without

author's name (encyclopedias, movies) should be alphabetized by title. There are different formats for bibliographies. Use the one your instructor demands.

In a strict sense, there is difference between a bibliography and a reference list: A reference list contains only those works that you have cited in your paper, while a bibliography may include works that you have consulted during your research but you have not cited in your paper. Research paper usually requires a reference list rather than a bibliography.

A common problem in students' papers is that the reference list includes the works that are not cited in the text while the cited works are excluded. This is due to the lack of timely revision of the reference list along with repeated revisions of the text. A solution to it is to go through the whole paper by page and tick the references in the working bibliography that appear in the text. Delete those that have not been marked. Enter all those remaining ones into the section of references. Meanwhile you should add cited works to the reference list if they are not included in your working bibliography.

3.3.2 Appendices

An appendix, although by no means an essential part of every paper, is a useful device to make available to the reader the material related to the text but not suitable for inclusion in it. Appendices may contain tables which are too detailed for text presentation, a large group of illustrations, technical notes on method, schedules and forms used in collecting materials, copies of documents not generally available to the reader, case studies too long to be put into the text, and sometimes figures and graphs or other illustrative materials.

Materials of different categories should be placed in separate appendices. Where there is more than one appendix, each should be given a number or a letter (APPENDIX 1, APPENDIX 2, etc.; or APPENDIX ONE, APPENDIX TWO, etc.; or APPENDIX A, APPENDIX B, etc.).

Whether an appendix should be single- or double-spaced depends upon the nature of the material; spacing need not be the same for each of the appendices. Documents and case studies may well be single-spaced, whereas explanations of methods and procedures may be double-spaced, as is the text.

3.3.3 Notes

When you write a research paper, you can give credit for your sources by adding

Chapter 3
The Structure of a Research Paper

a note at the bottom of the page called footnote or at the end of the document called endnote (see 5.15). You can also use footnotes and endnotes to enter additional explanatory material or even just an aside comment that would not fit with the main flow of text. Compared with footnotes, endnotes are more commonly used in term papers than in theses or dissertations, where footnotes have been traditionally preferred and where parenthetical references are now commonly recommended. Both footnotes and endnotes are numbered consecutively in the text, with superscript Arabic numerals referring to corresponding notes (see 5.15, 7.2).

Exercises

I. Answer the following questions.

1. Discuss the overall structure of a research paper. What elements does each component part contain?
2. What information should the title page of a graduation thesis provide?
3. Why is "Abstract" an essential part of the research paper? What is a good "Abstract"? Find two or three "Abstracts" and comment on them using the guidelines developed in the chapter. Write an "Abstract" for your own paper in hand.
4. What is the point of writing the "Acknowledgements"? What is a good "Acknowledgements"? Find two or three "Acknowledgements" and make comment on them using the guidelines developed in the chapter. Write your own "Acknowledgements" for the paper in hand.
5. How to make a table of contents? a list of illustrations/figures? and a list of tables?
6. What are the component parts of the text? What function does an introductory part play in paper writing? What function does a conclusion part play?
7. Find a research paper and read it carefully. Does it include a review of the relevant literature? If any, where is it located — in the introduction? Or in a separate chapter? Why is the review of literature necessary for the paper?
8. Find some journal articles that include notes. Read the notes and its relevant text. Make an analysis of their form and purpose.
9. Is there any difference between a "bibliography" and a "reference list"? How to make an appropriate reference list for a research paper?
10. What materials should be put in "Appendices"? Why?

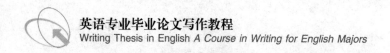

II. Read the two drafts of abstracts. Answer the questions that follow.

Version A

A count of sentence connectors in 12 academic papers produced 70 different connectors. These varied in frequency from 62 tokens (however) to single occurrences. Seventy-five percent of the 467 examples appeared in sentenceinitial position. However, individual connectors varied considerably in position preference. Some (e.g., in addition) always occurred initially; in other cases (e.g., for example, therefore), they were placed after the subject more than 50% of the time. These findings suggest that a search for general rules for connector position may not be fruitful.

Version B

Although sentence connectors are a well-recognized feature of academic writing, little research has been undertaken on their positioning. In this study, we analyze the position of 467 connectors found in a sample of 12 research papers. Seventy-five percent of the connectors occurred at the beginning of sentences. However, individual connectors varied greatly in positional preference. Some, such as *in addition*, only occurred initially; others, such *therefore*, occurred initially in only 40% of the cases. These preliminary findings suggest that general rules for connector position will prove elusive.

1. The journal requirements state that the abstracts accompanying papers should not exceed 100 words. Do versions A and B qualify?
2. Which version is a results-driven abstract? Which one is a summary abstract?
3. Compare the tense usage in versions A and B.
4. Which version do you prefer? And why?
5. Some journals also ask for a list of key words. Choose three or four suitable key words from them.

III. Read the following paragraph and answer the questions.

Several researchers addressed the problem of the optimal handling unit (pallet or container) size, to be used in material handling and warehousing systems. Steudell (13), Tanchoco and Agee (14), Tanchoco et al. (15) and

Grasso and Tanchoco (5) studied various aspects of this subject. The last two references incorporate the size of the pallet, or unit load, in evaluation of the optimal lot sizes for multi-inventory systems with limited storage space. In a report on a specific case, Normandin (10) has demonstrated that using the "best-size" container can result in considerable savings. A simulation model combining container size and warehouse capacity considerations, in an AS/RS environment, was developed by Kadosh (8). The general results, reflecting the stochastic nature of the flow of goods, are similar to those reported by Rosenblatt and Roll (12). Nevertheless, container size was found to affect strongly overall warehousing costs. In this paper, we present an analytical framework for approximating the optimal size of a warehouse container. The approximation is based on series of generalizations and specific assumptions. However, these are valid for a wide range of real life situations. The underlying assumptions of the model are presented in the following section.

(1) In which sentence does the writer group the similar information?
(2) In which sentence does the writer show the relationship between the work of different researchers?
(3) In which sentence does the writer indicate the position of the work in the research area history?
(4) What is the relationship between the previous work and the writer's own?

IV. Read the following concluding parts. Are they good ending parts? Why? or Why not?

1. The conclusion to a paper entitled "Rights of the Mentally Committed":

People are becoming more aware of the absurdities of the mental health system. Organizations, such as the National Association for Mental Health, have worked hard to enlighten people about mental illness. But as a whole, the public still distrusts and fears ex-patients. The most efficient way to make sure the mentally ill receive the rights they deserve is through legislation. Mental health reform continues to confront us with the problem of balancing the parental and police functions of the government against the rights of the individuals. Criminals lose their freedom because of what they do, but the non-criminal mentally ill lose their rights and liberty because of what others think they are. In any case, the procedures for commitment must be picked apart and redeveloped. Potential patients should be represented by counsel and an in-depth, fair hearing ought to be provided for them. The mental health system also masks a number of other problems which imply the need for more and better facilities for the mentally ill. Greater public awareness as well as concrete steps taken by Congress, state legislatures, and state and federal courts can make changes that will give back rights taken away from the large group of the mentally ill.

2. The conclusion to a paper on two styles of doing the high jump:

In conclusion, both the straddle and the flop require a great amount of technique. The high jump is an event which is successfully achieved by only a selected few. But of the two styles, the flop seems to be the more successful. This may be because the flop style of jumping allows the jumper a greater amount of velocity when approaching the bar, which in turn allows a greater jumping ability. The flop requires less body action than the straddle. The flop seems to allow more consistency in performance. If a jumper is running into a stiff head wind, the flop allows the athlete to perform closer to his ability under these conditions. Therefore, in training a young high jumper, it is best to start him out using the flop technique for better and more consistent performance.

V. Identify the background and thesis statement in each of the following introductions.

1. "I'm bald because my mother's father was" is a typical statement about how the baldness trait is acquired. People have perpetuated this homespun conclusion without much consideration for available information on the subject. An understanding of simple genetic property — sex trait determination — yields a different answer to the question of baldness determination.

2. Centuries separated the lives of the Hawaiians and visitors to the islands. The missionaries of the 1800s stepped into the past, a Stone Age compared to their modern Western civilization. The Hawaiians had been stranded in time, lost in a vast Pacific ocean, an isolated population since A.D. 400 or 500. Though totally oblivious to Western civilization, the Hawaiians had developed a unique and complex civilization of their own. Today, no written record exists of their ancient history, but the ancient chants and hulas link Hawaii's past to its present. They should be preserved in their original forms, not only for their historical value, but for their linguistic, musical, and artistic values as well.

Chapter 4
Language and Style

Effective writing depends as much on clarity and readability as on content. The organization and development of your ideas, the unity and coherence of your presentation, and your command of sentence structure, grammar, and diction are all important considerations. The key to successful communication is to use the right language for the audience you are addressing. In research writing, like in all other types of writing, the challenge is to find the words, phrases, clauses, sentences, and paragraphs that express your thoughts and ideas precisely and make them interesting to your readers.

4.1 Diction

Words that are often used can be divided into three types: formal, common, and colloquial. Formal words mainly appear in formal writing, such as scholarly or theoretical writing, political and legal documents, and formal lectures. Research paper writing is formal and words used in a research paper should be formal rather than colloquial. Colloquialisms, dialect, slang, and jargon are usually out of place in research papers. In general, technical words that are not a part of the vocabulary of the subject matter should also be avoided. And trite expressions should be everywhere excluded. Be alert to the proper meanings of the many pairs of words that are often mistakenly used for each other (allusion — illusion, practicable — practical). Avoid, too, the pretentious, the flowery, the poetic expressions that will seem forced and artificial, such as "beauteous" for "beautiful," "domicile" for "house," "knight of the road" for "tramp," "liquidate" for "kill."

Strive for exactly the right word to convey your meaning at a given place. Use the dictionary in selecting synonyms and antonyms and pay attention to the *precise* meanings of the words you choose. The synonyms listed for a word cannot always be used interchangeably with it; so notice particularly what the dictionary says of the different implications of the synonyms. Aim at a style that is simple and direct. Do not

use quotation marks to indicate that you do not really mean what the word means. When you need specialized vocabulary or jargon to accomplish your purpose, define your terms clearly.

4.2 Tone

In academic writing, the ideal writer is seen as someone who, after careful and impartial examination of all available evidence, comes to a careful and impartial judgment. The "impartial judge" is the idealized model of how an academic writer goes about his or her intellectual pursuits. In academic writing, arguments conventionally imply impartial judgment through the use of rational, impersonal and unemotional language, eventhough the author is passionate about the position he or she is arguing.

To achieve an impersonal, objective tone in your writing, it is essential to avoid judgmental language and emotive language.

(1) Judgmental language (I think, it seems, it is right, it is wrong). This is language that reveals the writer is making a personal judgment. Of course, the academic writer is *always* making a judgment, but using judgmental language makes it sound as if the writer is coming to his or her conclusions on his or her own, based on his or her previously-held beliefs and values, rather than letting the evidence guide the inquiry. Whether a word, a phrase, or a statement is judgmental sometimes depends on context. For example, a claim that would not be considered judgmental if accompanied by a justification based on evidence might be considered judgmental if the evidentiary justification is not provided or mentioned.

(2) Emotive language (great, marvelous, fantastic, extremely). This is language that appeals to emotions or values to make an argument. This emotive language loads the argument with emotion in an attempt to incite an emotional reaction in the reader. Emotive language reveals the writer's feelings just as judgmental language does, but more subtly — the writer is not revealing his or her feelings in an direct statement, such as "I believe X" or "X is good." Rather, the writer's feelings are revealed in the connotation of the phrases used, as in "History has provided us with *great* heroes." Whether a particular word or phrase is too emotive usually depends on its context. Basically, if the writer is using words or phrases with high emotional content that seem to be trying to persuade the reader, he or she is probably using emotive language.

4.3 Voice

Voice here refers to the quality of prose that indicates the presence of a human speaker. Voice conveys your relationship or connection to the ideas you present. You do not need to use first-person pronouns to give your paper a voice. Using a first-person pronoun (*I, me, my,* or *mine*) to call attention to the fact that a statement is your opinion often weakens the assertion by implying uncertainty. The reader assumes that statements in your paper, unless otherwise attributed, are your opinion and represent your point of view. So, most writers like to use the third person instead — with nouns or third-person pronouns (*he, she, they,* or *it*) as subjects of the sentences. At the same time, you should not use impersonal labels such as "the researcher" or "the writer," because they tend to remove you entirely from your paper.

Though not recommended in academic writing, the first-person pronoun is appropriate when you relate a personal experience, such as your own process of research, or when you wish to call particular attention to your opinion as distinguished from the views of others. In papers that call for a subjective response to texts, ideas, or situations you will want to use first-person pronouns. The plural first person, the editorial *we*, should not substitute for *I*, but it may be used to refer to a group of researchers that includes you. Whatever choice of pronouns you make for the text, you may freely use the first person in the preface and acknowledgments.

Because your reader will assume that you are addressing him or her, second-person pronouns (*you, your*) usually do not belong in a research paper. The edited sentences below demonstrate ways of eliminating unnecessary first- and second-person constructions:

Original: In my opinion, presidential candidates should debate in an uncontrolled forum.
Revised: Presidential candidates should debate in an uncontrolled forum.
Original: I firmly believe that previous researchers have misinterpreted the evidence.
Revised: Previous researchers have misinterpreted the evidence.
Original: I think that these statistics substantiate the previous study.
Revised: These statistics substantiate the previous study.

4.4 Economy

In research writing, you can not repeat or multiply words just for the sound of them — the way you do in creative writing. This is because the research paper is judged on a different standard — economy of expression. You should not use more words than you need to accomplish your goal. Many students, however, do not know how to write concisely. They use phrases when a single word will do. Or they offer pairs of adjectives and verbs where one is enough. Or they over-write, saying the same thing two or three times with the hope that, one of these times, they will get it the way they want it. To write concisely. You can delete unnecessary words and phrases by asking yourself the following questions: Do I really need words like "actually," "basically," "generally," and so on? If I do not need them, why are they there? Do I use two words where one will do? For example, Isn't "first and foremost" redundant? What is the point of "future" in "future plans?" And why do I keep saying, "In my opinion?" Doesn't the reader understand that this is *my* paper, based on *my* point of view? Of cause, during the drafting stage, as a means of keeping their momentum, you can use as many words as you want to, but during revision, you should eliminate all excessive verbiage.

4.5 Verb Tense

Tense choice in reviewing previous research is subtle and somewhat flexible. But studies have shown that at least two-thirds of all citing statements fall into one of the three major tenses: Past, Present Perfect, and Present.

Past — researcher activity as agent

Jones (1987) *investigated* the causes of illiteracy.

The causes of illiteracy *were investigated* by Jones (1987).

Present Perfect — researcher activity not as agent

The causes of illiteracy *have been* widely *investigated* (Jones 1987, Ferrara 1990, Hyon 1994).

There *have been* several investigations into the causes of illiteracy (Jones 1987, Ferrara 1990, Hyon 1994).

Several researchers *have studied* the causes of illiteracy. [1-3]

Present — no reference to researcher activity

The causes of illiteracy *are* complex (Jones 1987, Ferrara 1990, Hyon 1994).

Illiteracy *appears to have* a complex set of causes. [1-3]

In general, an event, be it a survey, an experiment or a study of some kind done by any researcher, should be reported or described in the past tense, while interpretations, evaluations, assessments, discussions or ideas arising from it, should be in the present tense. Note that present tense is sometimes also used with famous or important sources (hence called *citational present*), as in *Plato argues that...; Confucius says...; The Bible says...*, etc.

4.6 Sentence Type and Length

4.6.1 Sentence Type

Grammatical correctness is not the sole attribute of a good sentence. A good sentence reinforces your meaning through its structure and pace. Different types of sentences have different functions in conveying ideas. The simple sentence is good for clarity and directness. When you want to make an assertion clear and emphatic, use the simple sentence. The compound sentence emphasizes the equality of coordinated ideas, reduces wordiness and relieves monotony. The complex sentence contains a main clause (with the main idea in it) and one or more dependent clauses (with the minor ideas in them), with a connective word denoting the relationship between them. And the compound-complex sentence is good for a show of eloquence. It can be used to move the reader on account of its long sweeping movement and cadence. Careful attention to your sentences can help you refine your ideas and make your argument more persuading.

4.6.2 Sentence Length

You frequently need to take the length of sentence into account when you are trying to make a difficult sentence easier to read, a dull one more arresting, an ambiguous one precise. At best, short sentences (say under eighteen words) have a simplicity and directness that makes them easy to understand, and a briskness and drive that carries the reader along. But they can become choppy and jerky, breaking ideas into units that are too small to be followed easily; and several in succession can become unemphatic and monotonous. Long sentences offer comparable risks and opportunities. They can be so convoluted or so rambling that the reader, if not the writer, loses track of the main idea. But handled well, a long sentence — even a very long one — can gather up and convey the full measure of a complex thought, with all its distinctions and refinements and qualifications. Alternation is often necessary: A long sentence coming after a series of short ones can pull particulars together into an inclusive statement that summarizes or interprets or evaluates; a short sentence following a long one can have a powerful effect. Just make the length of your sentences appropriate to what they are saying.

4.7 Verb Voice

The active voice is the dominant voice used in English. The active voice is more vigorous than the passive voice because it allows a subject to stand in its familiar position in front of its verb. *I took a walk* is better than *A walk was taken by me. I will always remember my last trip to Paris* is better than *My last trip to Paris will always be remembered.* Sentences in active voice are generally — though not always — clearer and more direct than those in passive voice. However, the passive voice has important uses. The passive voice is useful for emphasis, or when the receiver of the action is more important than the actor. *There, before our eyes, two human beings were burned alive by gasoline flames.* In this case, human beings are more important than gasoline flames.

4.8 Parallelism

Parallelism is the repetition of syntactically similar constructions of coordinate sentences or phrases. To help your reader move quickly from one idea to the next, you should pair and sequence the ideas you want to stress equally in the same grammatical form. For example, in the sentence "Oregon's bottle law *has saved* taxpayer's money, *conserved* energy, and *created* jobs.", all verbs in the present perfect tense are grammatically alike. But in the sentence "Oregon's bottle law *has saved* taxpayer's money, *conserves* energy, and *creates* jobs.", the logic of the sentence is upset, because the writer sets up an expectation in the reader's mind but it is not fulfilled. The first verb in the present perfect tense *has served* sets the framework for the action in the sentence. The sentence starts this way, then readers expect to be enlightened on what Oregon's bottle law has *already* achieved, but they are thrown off balance when they stumble onto the simple present tense — *conserves* and *creates*. The sentence suffers, therefore, from a lack of parallel structure.

Parallelism is among the most useful tools of all writers. Through well-balanced construction, parallelism gives emphasis, clarity and coherence of ideas as well as the rhythm of the language. Because of its unique characteristics, parallelism is often used in research paper writing. For example, elements in an outline or list, as well as chapter titles, subtitles, and headings — all should be parallel and in the same grammatical form. If you use a noun or noun phrase for one heading, the next heading should also be a noun or noun phrase. Similarly, in a sentence outline all entries at the same level should be complete sentences (see also 2.5.1).

The entries in the following outline are not parallel: *I.* is a sentence, whereas *II.* is an infinitive phrase; in *I.*, *A.* is a noun phrase, whereas *C.* is a complete sentence.

Unparallel:

I. Nuclear Opponents Cite Dangers
   A. Leakage
   B. Disposing of Nuclear Waste
   C. Groups Threaten Sabotage
II. To protect against Nuclear Accidents
   A. Sound Design and Construction
   B. Monitoring Systems
   C. Correcting Problems with Automatic Devices

The entries in the following outline are parallel because they are in the same grammatical form.

Parallel:

I. Dangers of Nuclear Power Plants
   A. Leakage of Radiation
   B. Disposal of Nuclear Waste
   C. Sabotage by Terrorist Groups
II. Safety Features of Nuclear Power Plants
   A. Sound Design and Construction
   B. Monitoring Systems
   C. Automatic Correction Devices

You may use any constructions in an outline as long as each entry at the same level takes the same form. You may combine sentences in all first-level headings with noun phrases for all subordinate categories.

4.9 Logical Consistency

The requirement for parallelism is not exclusively a grammatical one, but a logical one as well. Grammatical inconsistencies often signal problems in logic. Logical consistency requires that headings at the same level of an outline have

approximately equivalent importance and refer to similar categories of ideas. For example, the first three headings designating historical periods and the fourth one designating procedural difficulties would not be logically consistent. Moreover, each heading at a given level should represent the same degree of generalization and refer to approximately the same kind of information. The following set of headings is logically unbalanced:

I. China's primary schools during the first half of the twentieth century

II. Changes in primary school programs in Jiangsu province from 1930 to 1949

III. Nature of primary school curricular changes from 2003 to 2005

IV. Percentages of teenagers enrolled in high schools

The fourth heading is considerably narrower in focus than the others and calls for purely statistical information rather than interpretation. In addition, the scope of the inquiry changes from national in the first heading to local in the second heading.

4.10 Coherence

Coherence is product of many different factors, which combine to make every paragraph, every sentence, and every phrase contribute to the meaning of the whole piece. Coherence in writing is much more difficult to sustain than coherent speech because writers have no nonverbal clues to inform them if their message is clear or not. Therefore, writers must make their patterns of coherence much more explicit and much more carefully planned. Generally speaking, coherence is the product of two main factors — paragraph unity and sentence cohesion.

To achieve paragraph unity, a writer must ensure two things only. First, the paragraph must have a single generalization that serves as the focus of attention, that is, a topic sentence. Secondly, a writer must control the content of every other sentence in the paragraph's body such that ① it contains more specific information than the topic sentence and ② it maintains the same focus of attention as the topic sentence.

To achieve sentence cohesion — the link of one sentence to the next, use the following techniques.

(1) Repetition. In sentence B (the second of any two sentences), repeat a word from sentence A.

(2) Synonymy. If direct repetition is too obvious, use a synonym of the word you wish to repeat. This strategy is called "elegant variation."

(3) Antonymy. Use the "opposite" word. In language, antonyms actually share more elements of meaning than you might imagine.

(4) Pro-forms. Use a pronoun, pro-verb, or another pro-form to make explicit reference back to a form mentioned earlier.

(5) Collocation. Use a commonly paired or expected or highly probable word to connect one sentence to another.

(6) Enumeration. Use overt markers of sequence to highlight the connection between ideas. This system has many advantages: ① it can link ideas that are otherwise completely unconnected, ② it looks formal and distinctive, and ③ it promotes a second method of sentence cohesion.

(7) Parallelism. Repeat a sentence structure. This technique is the oldest, most overlooked, but probably the most elegant method of creating cohesion.

(8) Transitions. Use a conjunction or conjunctive adverb to link sentences with particular logical relationships.

4.11 Transition

Strong organization demands the parts of the paper be in the right and apparent order. Explicit transitions signal relationships and establish connections. Transitional paragraphs are the most overt signals you can use in the body of an essay. They are usually brief — often only a sentence long. Because they normally have a strong imperative force, they should be reserved to mark major turns in the discussion. Transitional sentence normally comes either at the beginning or at the end of a paragraph. It signals a shift from one idea to another, indicates that the discussion is to take a new turn, or marks a digression from the main thread. The following are some of the explicit transitions.

(1) To show addition: again, and, also, besides, equally important, first (second, etc.), further, furthermore, in addition, in the first place, moreover, next, too, etc.

(2) To give examples: for example, for instance, in fact, specifically, that is, to illustrate, etc.

(3) To compare: also, in the same manner, likewise, similarly, etc.

(4) To contrast: although, and yet, at the same time, but, despite, even though, however, in contrast, in spite of, nevertheless, on the contrary, on the other hand, still, though, yet, etc.

(5) To summarize or conclude: all in all, in conclusion, in other words, in

short, in summary, on the whole, that is, therefore, to sum up, etc.

(6) To show time: after, afterward, as, as long as, as soon as, at last, before, during, earlier, finally, formerly, immediately, later, meanwhile, next, since, shortly, subsequently, then, thereafter, until, when, while, etc.

(7) To show place or direction: above, below, beyond, close, elsewhere, farther on, here, nearby, opposite, to the left (north, etc.), etc.

(8) To indicate logical relationship: accordingly, as a result, because, consequently, for this reason, hence, if, otherwise, since, so, then, therefore, thus, etc.

Transitional markers seem to be the simplest of the devices for achieving coherence, but to use them well requires care and discrimination. If you use too few overt connectors, the sentences may seem to be mutually repellent particles, and the sequence of thought will be hard to follow. If you use too many, the style will be heavy-handed.

Note, too, that transitions can be implied as well as expressed. A colon often does the work of *for example*. The simple juxtaposition of two statements may signal a relation of addition, contrast, causality or inclusiveness.

4.12 Unbiased Language

You need to be careful about words that designate gender, sexual orientation, race, ethnicity, disability, and age, especially when such identification is unjustified, or unnecessary for your purpose.

Avoiding biased language usually demands only minor editing. Here are a few of the strategies for revising to avoid gender bias.

(1) Change a sentence using the generic masculine pronoun from singular to plural.

Example:

>Give each student his paper as soon as he is finished.

Alternative:

>Give students their papers as soon as they are finished.

(2) Substitute the pronouns *he or she* or, as some writers prefer, *she or he* for *he* used generically.

Chapter 4
Language and Style

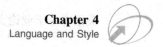

Example:

If he is to succeed, a new teacher requires intelligent supervision.

Alternative:

If he or she is to succeed, a new teacher requires intelligent supervision.

(3) Use gender-neutral designations for professions and positions.

BIASED	NEUTRAL
chairman	presiding officer, head, chair, chairperson, coordinator (of a committee or department), moderator (of a meeting)
mankind	humanity, humankind, human beings, people
man-made	synthetic, manufactured, machine-made
manpower	workers, work force, personnel
male nurse	nurse
the common man	the average person, ordinary people
businessman	business executive
fireman	firefighter
policeman and policewoman	police officer
steward and stewardess	flight attendant
mailman	mail carrier

(4) Reword to eliminate gender problems.

Example:

The average student is worried about his grade.

Alternative:

The average student is worried about grades.

(5) Replace the masculine pronoun with *one, you,* or (sparingly) *he or she,* as appropriate.

Example:

If the student was satisfied with his performance on the pretest, he took the post-test.

Alternative:

A student who was satisfied with her or his performance on the pretest took the post-test.

(6) Alternate male and female examples and expressions. (Be careful not to confuse the reader.)

71

Example:

Let each student participate. Has he had a chance to talk? Could he feel left out?

Alternative:

Let each student participate. Has she had a chance to talk? Could he feel left out?

Using the masculine pronouns to refer to an indefinite pronoun (everybody, everyone, anybody, anyone) also has the effect of excluding women. In all but strictly formal uses, plural pronouns have become acceptable substitutes for the masculine singular.

Example:

Anyone who wants to go to the game should bring his money tomorrow.

Alternative:

Anyone who wants to go to the game should bring their money tomorrow.

4.13 Constructing Paragraphs

A paragraph is generally understood as a single "unit" of a paper. What your reader expects when he enters a new paragraph is that he is going to hear you declare a point and then offer support for that point. If you violate this expectation — if your paragraphs wander aimlessly among a half dozen points, or if they declare points without offering any evidence to support them — the reader becomes confused or irritated by your argument. He won't want to read any further. Therefore, writers, especially inexperienced writers, should bear the reader's expectations in mind and write their paragraphs analytically.

However, experienced writers paragraph intuitively rather than analytically. Sometimes their paragraphs fulfill conventional expectations, presenting a single well-organized and well-developed idea; sometimes their paragraphs serve other purposes. For example, they break the text into a new paragraph to help readers pause and take a break while reading, allowing them to imagine or remember something sparked by the text, or to recapture the reader's flagging attention when detail may overwhelm them. But remember the use of one-sentence paragraphs (especially in succession) is usually out of place in academic writing.

In a research paper, every content paragraph should have one focus or one single idea which should be included in a topic sentence. A topic sentence has several functions: ① It substantiates or supports an essay's thesis statement; ② it unifies the

Chapter 4
Language and Style

content of a paragraph and directs the order of the sentences; ③ it advises the reader of the subject to be discussed and how the paragraph will discuss it. Topic sentences often act like tiny thesis statements. As the thesis statement is the unifying force in the paper, so is the topic sentence in the paragraph. Further, as is the case with the thesis statement, when the topic sentence makes a claim, the sentences that follow must expand, describe, or prove it in some way.

Topic sentence usually appears at the beginning of a paragraph. In the following example the writer backs up his claim with examples of characters from literature, religion and mythology whose tragic stature is a function of their ability to mediate between their fellow human beings and a power that transcends the merely human:

> The tragic hero is typically on top of the wheel of fortune, half-way between human society on the ground and the something greater in the sky. Prometheus, Adam, and Christ hang between heaven and earth, between a world of paradisal freedom and a world of bondage. Tragic heroes are so much the highest points in their human landscape that they seem the inevitable conductors of the power about them, great trees more likely to be struck by lightning than a clump of grass. Conductors may of course be instruments as well as victims of the divine lightning: Milton's Samson destroys the Philistine temple with himself, and Hamlet nearly exterminates the Danish court in his own fall.

The structure of the paragraph is simple but powerful: the topic sentence makes an abstract point, and the rest of the paragraph elaborates on that point using concrete examples as evidence.

Sometimes a transitional sentence or two will come before a topic sentence:

> We found in comedy that the term *bomolochos* or buffoon need not be restricted to farce, but could be extended to cover comic characters who are primarily entertainers, with the function of increasing or focusing the comic mood. The corresponding contrasting type is the suppliant, the character, often female, who presents a picture of unmitigated helplessness and destitution. Such a figure is pathetic, and pathos, though it seems a gentler and more relaxed mood than tragedy, is even more terrifying. Its basis is the exclusion of an individual from the group; hence it attacks the deepest fear in ourselves that we possess — a fear much deeper than the relatively cosy and sociable bogey of hell. In the suppliant pity and terror are brought to the highest possible pitch of intensity, and the awful consequences of rejecting the suppliant for all concerned is a central theme of Greek tragedy.

In this paragraph, the writer begins by drawing a parallel between the figure of the buffoon in comedy and that of the suppliant in tragedy. His discussion of the buffoon occurred in an earlier section, a section devoted to comedy. The first

sentence of the paragraph is transitional: it prepares the way for the topic sentence. The delayed topic sentence contributes to the coherence of the writer's discussion by drawing an explicit connection between key ideas in the book. In essays, the connection is usually between the last paragraph and the current one.

If you do not want to give away your point at the beginning of a paragraph and want to build your argument toward an effective climax, you may save the topic sentence for the end of the paragraph:

> In Ghana or Nigeria, pupils in school are exposed to much greater quantity of English in other subjects than they are in their English lessons alone. If they have different teachers for other subjects from those who teach them English, then it is likely that the general standard of English of these teachers will have more influence on the pupils than the standard of their English specialist teachers. It has been suggested that if the classes called English were removed from the time-tables of schools in Nigeria, when the children now starting at school eventually come to leave, no difference in their ability in English, compared with the present standard, would be detected. <u>Although I do not accept this as true, I insist that no discussion of language-teaching problems in Africa can avoid this crucial question of the part-played in teaching a language by teaching all subjects in that language.</u>

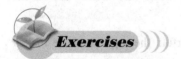

I. Compare the following paragraphs. Which one presents the ideas in a much more formal, academic way?

1. Capital is a complex notion. There are many definitions of the word itself, and capital as applied in accounting can be viewed conceptually from a number of standpoints; that is, there is legal capital, financial capital and physical capital. The application of financial and physical concepts of capital is not straightforward as there are various permutations of these concepts applied in the business environment ...

2. Capital is a difficult thing to understand. We can explain it in different ways, and in accounting we can look at it from different angles. Accountants talk about legal capital, financial capital and physical capital. How we apply financial and physical concepts of capital isn't easy because people in business use it differently ...

Chapter 4
Language and Style

II. **Combine the sentences into either a compound or complex, or simple sentence with modifiers.**

1. Gasoline is becoming expensive. Automobile manufacturers are producing smaller cars. Smaller cars use less gasoline.
2. The computer has undoubtedly benefited humanity. The computer has also created problems for humanity.
3. Government and private agencies have spent billions of dollars advertising the dangers of smoking. The number of smokers is still increasing.
4. Some students go to college to get a degree. Some students go to college to get an education.
5. The grading system at our college should be abolished. The students don't like getting grades. The instructors don't enjoy giving grades.
6. Radio offers short programs, interrupted between and within by commercial. They are also often unrelated. TV does this too.
7. The pilgrims were on the road for many days and stopped at places for the night. Chaucer does not tell us how many or where.
8. The further restrictions are placed on one-party rational arguments. Such arguments require us to pay special attention to certain aspects of argument. These aspects are not so important in everyday argument.

III. **Rewrite the following choppy sentences and make them effective.**

    The purpose of speech is most often to persuade. It is seldom to generate understanding or to stimulate thoughtful response. Speeches on television take advantage of this fact. A televised speech gives viewers the time only to receive information, to respond emotionally to it, to "feel" it. Viewers can simply enjoy or deplore its impact. Unlike a televised speech, a written speech can be read, reread, and analyzed. The reader can thoroughly process and analyze it. For this reason, I prefer to read and study a speech, not watch and instantly swallow it. This preference is limited to speeches that may be of great importance to me.

IV. **Eliminate unnecessary word in the sentence. Make change accordingly, if necessary.**

1. He was not only a famous scholar but also a great patriot as well.
2. As a rule, my father usually worked late into the night.

3. I was merely sitting in class, letting my mind wander, when the professor asked me to explain the principle.
4. As for her family we know nothing about them.
5. My father is a veteran worker who has retired.
6. She took good care of her brother though she was in poor health.
7. I decided that I should take the exam.
8. There is an increase in membership in sororities and fraternities this year.
9. At the time of registration, students are required to make payments of their fees.
10. Due to the fact that she inquired with reference to the dormitory hours, specifically in regard to when the girls in most cases had to return at night, we sent her a copy of the new regulations.

V. Fill in the blank with one word in the parentheses that you think will best fit what the author intends the sentence to mean.

1. She was a _____ blonde. (curvaceous, plump, fleshy)
2. She knew that black raven circling the sky was a bad _____ (sign/omen/symbol).
3. The congressman gave a(n) _____ answer. (judicious, ambiguous, cautious)
4. It was an _____ insult. (intentional, unmistakable, implied)
5. He was in a _____ mood. (fault-finding, quarrelsome, irritable)
6. He said that he would write an English course book if he could find a(n) _____ to deal with the less interesting parts. (collaborator, accomplice, helper)
7. The whole audience was _____ by her sad story and many shed tears. (affected, infected, influenced)
8. If you put any more potatoes into that bag, it will _____. (crack, burst, break)
9. Sometimes husbands live under the _____ that they can do anything even when they have been repeatedly proved wrong. (delusion, illusion, imagination)
10. Careful planing should _____ the success of the party. (assure, insure, secure)

Chapter 4
Language and Style

VI. Choose the suitable word to complete the sentence.

1. In my memory I have never _____ your invitation. (refused, declined)
2. The enemy troops were driven back when they _____ to cross the border. (attempted, tried)
3. Empress Dowager Cixi was _____ for her cruelty. (noted, notorious)
4. I am quite _____ of your opportunity to study at such a famous university. (jealous, envious)
5. This servile man is especially _____ before his superiors. (modest, humble)
6. Soon, the audience were _____ and some began to doze off. (disinterested, uninterested)
7. The young lady's behavior is rather _____. (childlike, childish)
8. Her clothes, though made of _____ material, are quite elegant. (cheap, inexpensive)

VII. Arrange words in a line according to their stylistic meaning.

1. drunk, inebriated, loaded
2. impoverished, poor, broke
3. shrewd, perspicacious, sharp
4. kisser, countenance, face
5. kids, children, descendants
6. guy, individual, man
7. thrills, kicks, gratification
8. investigate, pry, sneak
9. pooped, exhausted, tired
10. pedagogue, prof, teacher

VIII. Rewrite the sentences by putting the verbs in the other voice. Compare the different versions. Which version do you find preferable? Why?

1. In Gower's research, it was found that pythons often dwell in trees and live near rivers.
2. They started shooting pool, and, before Cathy knew it, she owed the kid ten dollars.

77

3. When I was eight, my father's crazy dreams uprooted our family from Florida to California.
4. For me, living in a dorm was more easily adjusted to than living in an apartment.
5. The image of native Americans has been totally distorted by Hollywood in most of its films about the West.

IX. Read the paragraph and delete the irrelevant information.

Since 1960, the number of married post-graduate students at Leeds University has grown considerable and the problem of finding places for them and their families to live has become a serious one. The University does have a few flats for married post-graduates, but there are not enough for all of them. These students do not usually have much money, and the houses and flats in the city and near the University are too expensive for them. Indeed, they are too expensive even for many of the professors and staff. Therefore, many of them have to live a long way from the University in district where the houses and flats are cheaper. This explains why the buses to the University are so crowded in the mornings.

X. Identify the gap in logical consistency.

1. a) John went to the store. Elephants are supposed to have good memories.
   b) John went to the store. He bought an apple and returned home.
2. a) Oil is one source of energy. Other sources are coal, the sun, and the wind.
   b) I could not do the sixth problem. The painting of fire hydrants in different colors is a part of an attempt to beautify the environment.
3. a) Baths are not needed so frequently by the older patient because of the decreased sweat secretion. The hospital does not have sufficient health care facilities for the older patients.
   b) Baths are not needed so frequently by the older patient because of the decreased sweat secretion. Less frequent bathing will help to preserve the major skin areas; however, special attention must be given to the perineum to prevent skin excoriation.

Chapter 4
Language and Style

XI. Put an appropriate transition in the blank.

1. | in this way   finally   and   furthermore   for example |

   Through the class activities, the teacher can develop creativity in the preschool child by giving importance and value to what the child has made and by encouraging him to develop his own ideas and thoughts. (1) _____, when the child paints a boat on the sea, the teacher could ask him what he had painted, what colors he had used, (2) _____ why he had painted. (3) _____, not only the teacher but also the child is evaluating and describing the product, (4) _____, if the teacher ascertains that a child is not happy with the task he has accomplished, the teacher should show him the value of the task. This will give the child security in his work and will allow him to further develop his creativity. (5) _____, the dual evaluation of the task by teacher and child will be constructive; the teacher can suggest new ideas by asking the child if there is another way he can accomplish the task and by making the child aware of various alternatives available to him.

2. | as   however   because   first   so   and   therefore   since |

   (1) _____, today, as we see in the societies where the women go to work, there are many problems which may in the end destroy society (2) _____ we know it. (3) _____, many people, especially men, do not find jobs (4) _____ women have taken those jobs. (5) _____, the men, with decreased job chances, (6) _____ unemployment, are pushed to commit crimes. Children also take the wrong way because they have the feeling that their fathers and mothers ignore them; their parents push them off on the baby-sitters, and these parents have no time to direct and look after their children. The fathers do not even know what their children do during the day (7) _____ their mothers are also absent from the home, and (8) _____ the fathers cannot discipline the children. This breaking apart of the family is the cause of the high race of divorce; as the women become financially independent, they flee the responsibilities of being wives and mothers.

XII. Make the passage coherent by using the correct linking words.

| another   first   also   finally   for instance |

Despite these problems, there are a number of advantages that favor the development of photovoltaics. (1) _____, photovoltaics attain the highest efficiency conversion of solar to electrical energy devices. Here, the efficiency is the percent of the incident light energy that is converted into electrical energy. Cells are now being produced that are about 30 percent efficient. (2) _____ advantage is the long life expectancy of solar cells. They can provide their rated output for perhaps a dozen years with virtually no maintenance required. (3) _____ advantageous is their high power to weight ratio. This has made solar cells essential in the development of our space program and, in view of the probable need for large arrays as a means of reducing cost, will allow practical construction of such arrays. (4) _____, photovoltaics have the advantage of being easy to apply. The proper combination of cells can provide any DC voltage and current which can power any intended load. Once activated, the installation can run unattended for a number of years.

XIII. Revise the passage, substituting nonsexist language as necessary.

Feeling his oats. One year old is an exciting age. Your baby is changing in lots of ways — in his eating, in how he gets around, in what he wants to do and in how he feels about himself and other people. When he was little and helpless, you could put him where you wanted hem, give him the playthings you thought suitable, feed him the foods you knew were best. Most of the time he was willing to let you be the boss, and took it all in good spirit. It's more complicated now that he is around a year old. He seems to realize that he's not meant to be a baby doll the rest of his life, that he's a human being with ideas and a will of his own.

XIV. Identify the thesis statement. Arrange the topic statements in proper order.

1. ____ a) Adjusting to life at college is difficult because suddenly I find myself plagued with more freedom, more uncertainty, and more money problems than ever before.

Chapter 4
Language and Style

        ____ b) Finally, there are the money problems, the frustrating, never ending, money problems.

        ____ c) With more freedom, comes uncertainty.

        ____ d) The freedom one feels in college can be a benefit but also a burden.

2. ____ a) Decreased oxygen means that the stove fails to take in enough oxygen to burn efficiently.

       ____ b) Decreased air pressure means less efficient cooking.

       ____ c) High altitude affects a camping stove's performance because of two phenomena: a decrease in oxygen and a decrease in air pressure.

3. ____ a) After forsaking his suicidal intentions, Hamlet begins to reflect more deeply on the meaning and purpose of death.

       ____ b) Hamlet progresses in his attitude toward death from an early contemplation of suicide to his final philosophical acceptance of death.

       ____ c) After he has recognized and accepted death, Hamlet proceeds to avenge his father's death with determination, and with stoic acceptance of the consequences.

       ____ d) In the beginning of the play, Hamlet shows that he takes death seriously, both because he grieves intensely for his father and because he seriously contemplates suicide.

XV. Read the following suggested topic sentences in pairs. Which one provides a clear guide for both the writer and the reader?

1. a) Dayton is a city in the state of Ohio.
   b) Dayton is a great industrial city.
2. a) London is the capital of England.
   b) London is one of the world centers for banking and insurance.
3. a) The war of 892 had three definite causes.
   b) A war broke out in the year of 892.
4. a) The United States has a space travel program.
   b) A program of space travel involves great expense of time, money, and manpower.
5. a) Whenever he stayed on his grandfather's farm during his holidays,

George always had plenty to do.

b) When he was a little boy, George used to spend his summer holidays on his grandfather's farm.

6. a) Abraham Lincoln was the sixteenth President of the United States of America.

b) Abraham Lincoln, the sixteenth President of the United States of America, came from a family which was humble and undistinguished.

Chapter 5

Mechanics

One of the biggest challenges in writing is to feel confident about appropriately applying the mechanics of writing. The term *mechanics* generally refers to matters of manuscript form rather than to conventions which express meaning. That is, mechanics determine what the text looks like rather than what it says. The writer's use of margins, indentation, italics, numerals, symbols (@ , $, %, & and ∗), capital letters, abbreviations, even the convention of writing from left to right — all belong to mechanics. This chapter deals with those areas of mechanics that relate most directly to a research paper. You'll explore the rules of capitalization and abbreviations. You'll learn some of the special situations that influence how numbers are used, and you'll get tips and techniques to make spelling troublesome words easier. Your creativity will be enhanced when you're confident about writing mechanics. Unless otherwise specified, all guidelines here apply to papers written according to the Chicago Manual, MLA, and APA style sheets.

5.1 Capitalization

At one time, all letters were written as capitals. By the time the movable type was invented, a new system had evolved, and printers used a capital letter only for the first letter of any word they felt was particularly important. Today, the conventions of capitalization are fairly well standardized, although they vary from language to language.

1. Capitalize the first word of a sentence or a line of poetry

Capitalize the first word of a sentence:

> Posing relatives for photographs is a challenge.

If you are quoting a full sentence, capitalize its first word:

> Everyone was saying, "What will I do after I graduate?"

Capitalization of a sentence following a colon is optional:

Gould cites the work of Darwin: The (or the) theory of natural selection incorporates the principle of evolutionary ties between all animals.

A sentence that is set off within another sentence by dashes or parentheses should not be capitalized.

Those assigned to transports were not humiliated like washouts — *somebody* had to fly those planes — nevertheless, they, too, had been *left behind* for lack of the right stuff.

The disagreement between the two men (its origins have been discussed by Westover in considerable detail) ultimately destroyed the organization.

But a sentence within parentheses that stands by itself is capitalized:

The expression such as *that is, namely, i.e., e.g.,* and the element it introduces, may be enclosed in parentheses if the break in continuity is greater than that signaled by a comma. (For comparative examples see 5.62.)

The first word of each line in a poem is traditionally capitalized.

Loveliest of trees, the cherry now
Is hung with bloom along the bough,
And stands about the woodland ride
Wearing white for Eastertide.

— A. E. Housman, *Loveliest of Trees*

Some poets do not capitalize each line, however. When citing poetry, therefore, be careful to follow the original capitalization.

2. Capitalize proper nouns and proper adjectives

In all languages written in the Latin alphabet, proper nouns (those naming specific persons, places, and things) and proper adjectives (those formed from proper nouns) are capitalized:

John and Jane Doe	Niagara Falls
European	Shakespearean
Brazil	Brazilian

However, proper nouns and proper adjectives that have lost their original meanings and have become part of everyday language are not capitalized:

french doors	india ink	roman numerals

3. Capitalize titles of individuals

Capitalize titles used before a proper name. When used alone or following a proper name, most titles are not capitalized. The only exceptions are titles of some very powerful officials — for example, many writers capitalize the word *president* when it refers to the President of the United States.

> Professor Lisa Ede   Lisa Ede, an English professor
> Governor Ann Richards   Ann Richards, governor of Texas

4. Capitalize academic institutions and courses

Capitalize the names of specific schools, departments, or courses, but not the common nouns for institutions or subject areas.

> University of California (*but* a California university)
> History Department (*but* a history major)

5. Capitalize titles of works

In giving titles of published works in text, note, reference list, or bibliography, the spelling of the original should be retained, but capitalization and punctuation may be altered to conform to the style used in the paper (see 5.9). In most scientific fields, sentence-style capitalization is used. In the humanities and most of the social sciences, however, it is customary to capitalize titles headline style.

1) Sentence-style capitalization

In parenthetical references and reference-list entries in APA style, titles of books and articles in English are capitalized sentence style, that is, the first word of a title or subtitle is capitalized and only proper nouns and proper adjectives thereafter:

> *The triumph of Achilles*
> "Natural crisis: Symbol and imagination in the American farm crisis"

2) Headline-style capitalization

Capitalize the first and last words in titles and all other words with the exception of articles (*a, an, the*), coordinate conjunctions (*and, but, or, for, nor, yet, so*), prepositions (*to, at, before, between,* etc.), and the word *to* in an infinitive.

> *Metaphors We Live By*
> *Across the River and into the Trees*

Note that the subtitle, following a colon, is capitalized the same way as the main title:

> *Emily Dickinson: The Mind of the Poet*
> "Thesis to Book: What to Get Rid Of"

Rules for capitalizing compound words vary widely. A rule of thumb that usually proves satisfactory is ① always capitalize the first element and ② capitalize the

second element if it is a noun or proper adjective or if it has equal force with the first element:

Twentieth-Century Literature in the Making
Computer-aided Graphics: A Manual for Video-Game Lovers

6. Notes to parts of works

References to such parts of a work as contents, preface, foreword, introduction, bibliography, and appendix should not be capitalized:

The variables within the experiment are listed in table 2.
Copies of supporting documents are in appendix 3.

References to divisions of your paper may be capitalized when they substitute for a title and are followed by a number or letter.

Chapter 7　　　Section 3　　　Appendix C

References to divisions of sources are not capitalized:

chapter 7 in Morrison　　　volume 3 of Pelikan's History

References to tables and figures are capitalized, but not references to elements of them:

column 3 in Smith's Table 7　　　note 5 in Figure 3

5.2 Abbreviations

In tabular matter, notes, bibliographies, illustrations, and lists of all kinds, abbreviations are normally preferred and are formed according to a standard list accepted within any given field. Such forms of address as Mr., Mrs., and Dr. are almost never spelled out. The writer who must form new abbreviation for the purposes of a paper should place them in a list of abbreviations within the front matter.

5.2.1 Use of Periods

The trend now is strongly away from the use of periods, especially in uppercase abbreviations. In the examples that follow, the periods have been left wherever they have traditionally appeared. Periods may be omitted from many of these examples, but it is still common practice to use periods after lowercase abbreviations (e.g., in, act, no.) and to use a period and a space after the initials for personal names (e.g., E. F. Bowman). In an abbreviation with an internal period (e.g., N.Y., Ph.D, N.Dak,

Chapter 5
Mechanics

U.S.), there should be no space after the internal period.

5.2.2 Social and Professional Titles and Similar Terms

Social titles are always abbreviated, whether with full name or last name only (note that after *Mlle* and *Mme* there traditionally is no period):

    Mr.   Mrs.   Ms.   M.   Messrs.
    Mlle   MM.   Mme   Dr.

The abbreviations Sr., Jr., III, and IV (for Senior, Junior, Third, and Fourth) follow a full name and are not used with the family name alone, although in informal writing it is permissible to use these terms with given names (e.g., John, Jr.). The terms are never spelled out when part of a name. A comma precedes Jr. and Sr. (and one also follows, if these forms appear within a sentence), but a comma should not be used before III and IV:

    Mrs. Joseph P. Turner, Sr., sent her regrets.
    Adlai E. Stevenson III announced his candidacy.
    Rev. Oliver C. Jones, Jr., spoke to the group.
    Do you know Ralph Smith, Jr.'s address?

Abbreviations for scholarly degrees and titles of respect, which follow full names, are preceded by a comma and followed by another comma when they are given in text.

    Leroy S. Wells, Ph.D., belonged to the committee.
    The Reverend Jesse E Thorson, S.T.B., was nominated by the board of trustees.

The following list includes many frequently used abbreviations for scholarly degrees and professional and honorary designations:

A.B.	Artium Baccalaureus (Bachelor of Arts)
A.I.A.	American Institute of Architects
A.M.	Artium Magister (Master of Arts)
B.A.	Bachelor of Arts
B.S.	Bachelor of Science
D.D.S.	Doctor of Dental Surgery
LL.B.	Legum Baccalaureus (Bachelor of Laws)
LL.D.	Legum Doctor (Doctor of Laws)
M.A.	Master of Arts
M.B.A.	Master of Business Administration

M.D.	Medicinae Doctor (Doctor of Medicine)
M.P.	Member of Parliament
M.S.	Master of Science
Ph.D.	Philosophiae Doctor (Doctor of Philosophy)
S.M.	Master of Science
S.T.B.	Sacrae Theologiae Baccalaureus (Bachelor of Sacred Theology)

Spell out a civil, military, professional, or religious title when it precedes the family name alone:

    Senator Proxmire   General Patton

But use the appropriate abbreviation before a full name:

    Sen. William F. Proxmire   Gen. George S. Patton

Spell out Reverend, Honorable, and Colonel if preceded by "the"; otherwise abbreviate to *Rev*, *Hon*, or *Col*. Never use these titles, either spelled out or abbreviated, with family names alone (never use: Rev. Bentley, Reverend Bentley, the Rev. Bentley, the Reverend Bentley). Use them only when the title is followed by the person's full name or by Mr., Mrs., Miss, Ms., or Dr. with the family name alone:

    The ceremony was in honor of the Reverend Martin Luther King, Jr.'s birthday observance.

    Rev. Dr. Wilson gave the address.

    The Honorable Mr. Collins closed the final session of the conference.

5.2.3 Organization

The names of government agencies, network broadcasting companies, associations, and other groups are often abbreviated, even in text, preferably after one spelled-out use. Such abbreviations are set in uppercase with no periods:

    AT&T   NAACP   NATO   OPEC   UN   UNESCO

Within the text, company names should be given in their full form, without including the terms *Inc.* or *Ltd.* and without capitalizing the word *the*, even when it is part of a company's full name.

    A.G. Becker and Company was incorporated in 1894.

    The book was published by the University of Chicago Press.

In notes, bibliographies, parenthetical references, and reference lists, etc., the

Chapter 5
Mechanics

following abbreviations may be freely (but consistently) used:

    Co.   Corp.   Inc.   Ltd.

5.2.4 Units of Measurement

Except for scientific and technical writing, most units of measurement should not be abbreviated in the body of a paper.

    five miles   150 pounds   14.5 meters

In scientific and technical writing, standard abbreviations (km., ft., lb., gal.) for units of measurement are used if the amount is given in numerals.

5.2.5 General Scholarly Abbreviations

app.	appendix
art.	article (plural, arts.)
b.	born
bk.	book (plural, bks.)
c.	copyright
ca., *circa*	about, approximately
cf., *confer*	compare (Note that *confer* is the Latin word for "compare"; *cf.* must be used as the abbreviation for the English "confer," nor should *cf.* be used to mean "see.")
ch.	chapter (in legal references only)
chap.	chapter (plural, chaps.)
col.	column (plural, cols.)
comp.	compiler (plural, comps.); compiled by
dept.	department (plural, depts.)
d.	died
div.	division (divs.)
e.g., *exempli gratia*	for example
ed.	edition; edited by; editor (plural, eds.)
et al., *et alii*	and others
et seq., *et sequens*	and the following
etc., *et cetera*	and so forth
fig.	figure (plural, figs.)

89

英语专业毕业论文写作教程
Writing Thesis in English *A Course in Writing for English Majors*

fl., *floruit*	flourished (for use when birth and death dates are not known)
ibid, *ibidem*	in the same place
i.e., *id est*	that is
id., *idem*	the same (used to refer to persons, except in law citations; not to be confused with ibid.)
infra	below
l. (el)	line (plural, ll.) (Not recommended because the abbreviation in the singular might be mistaken for "one" and the plural for "eleven.")
n.	note, footnote (plural, nn.)
n.d.	no date
n.p.	no place; no publisher
no.	number (plural, nos.)
n.s.	new series
o.s.	old series
p.	page (plural, pp; these abbreviations always precede the numbers; when "p." follows a number, it can stand for "pence.")
par.	paragraph
passim	here and there
pt.	part (plural, pts.)
q.v., *quod vide*	which see (for use with cross-references)
sc.	scene
sec.	section (plural, secs.)
[*sic*]	so, thus
supp.	supplement (plural, supps.)
supra	above
s.v.	under the word
trans.	translator, translated by
v.	verse (plural, vv.)
viz., *videlicet*	namely
vol.	volume (plural, vols.)
vs, *versus*	against ("v." is used in law references.)

5.3 Italicizing and Underlining

In all fields except some of the sciences, titles of published books and some other kinds of works are underlined. Other titles are enclosed in double quotation marks, and still others are capitalized but neither underlined nor enclosed in quotation marks. The general rule is to underline the titles of *whole* published works and to put the titles of *parts* of these works in quotation marks. Titles of unpublished material are also in quotation marks. Titles of series and manuscript collections, and various kinds of descriptive titles, are neither underlined nor in quotation marks.

Underline the titles of books, pamphlets, bulletins, periodicals (magazines, journals, newspapers), and long poems (such as *Paradise Lost*). It should be noted that although a published work is thought of as set in type and printed in conventional form, it may be a typewritten script reproduced by one of the photoduplicating processes, or it may be published in microform. If the work bears a publisher's imprint, it should be treated as published rather than unpublished material; that is, the title should be underlined wherever it appears.

Titles of chapters or other divisions of a book, and titles of short stories, short poems, essays, and articles in periodicals are set in quotation marks:

> "The New Feminism", <u>Saturday Review</u>
> <u>The First Circle</u>, chapter 2, "A Puzzled Robot"

Titles of dissertations and other unpublished works are also put in quotation marks:

> "Androgen Action and Receptor Specificity" (Ph.D. dissertation. University of Chicago, 1995)

Italic is a typeface in which the letters slant to the right (in MLA format, words that would be italicized in print are usually underlined). When italics are used, adjacent punctuation — except parentheses or brackets — must also be italicized. Italics may be used to provide emphasis in your text or in direct quotations.

> Gil's homer pulled the cork, and now there arose from all over the park a full, furious, happy shout of "Let's go, *Mets!* Let's go, *Mets!*" There were wild cries of encouragement before every pitch, boos for every called strike ... The fans' hopes, of course, *were* insane.
> — Roger Angell, *The Summer Game*

When you use italics to add emphasis within direct quotations, indicate your alteration of the original with a note enclosed in brackets: [my emphasis] or [emphasis mine]. Similarly, if you want to point out that the original contains italics, you may do so within brackets: [original emphasis] or [italics in original].

Also, italics can serve to indicate the correct reading of a word when it might be misunderstood. These uses of italics should be kept to a minimum because an overabundance of emphasized words reduces the impact of them all.

Italic type is sometimes not distinctive enough for this purpose, and you can avoid ambiguity by using underlining when you intend italics. Underline words and letters that are referred to as words and letters.

> Shaw spelled <u>Shakespeare</u> without the final <u>e</u>.
> The word <u>albatross</u> probably derives from the Spanish and Portuguese word <u>alcatraz</u>.

In general, foreign words and phrases used in an English text should be underlined except when they have become anglicized, or accepted as English words if the word is familiar in ordinary language (see also 5.6).

Several exceptions are worth noting. Sacred books such as the Bible or the Koran, and public documents, such as the Constitution, are not italicized. Notice also with magazines and newspapers that an initial *the* is neither italicized nor capitalized, even if it is part of the official name.

5.4 Spelling

When you are in doubt about the spelling of a word or when variant spellings exist, consult a standard dictionary. Spelling, including hyphenation, should be consistent throughout the research paper. You can best ensure consistency by always adopting the spelling that your dictionary gives first in any entry with variant spellings. To save time and avoid possible errors, do not divide words at the ends of lines. The "word-wrap" feature of your computer performs this operation automatically. If you choose to divide a word, consult your dictionary about where the break should occur.

For the correct spelling of proper names not found in a dictionary, refer to an authority such as a biographical dictionary or an encyclopedia. If you decide to use an uncommon spelling, specify the reason for your decision in a note. When you find a misspelled word in a passage that you wish to quote directly, underline the word exactly as you find it and indicate that the error is not yours by adding [*sic*] immediately after the word.

Chapter 5
Mechanics

5.5 Plural of Noun

The plurals of English words are generally formed by adding the suffix *-s* or *-es* (*laws, taxes*), with several exceptions (e.g., *children, halves, mice, sons-in-law*).

5.6 Foreign Word

If you quote material in a foreign language, you must reproduce all accents and other marks exactly as they appear in the original. If you need marks that are not available on your computer, write them in by hand.

> He was *un católico* before he was a Catholic.

In general, underline foreign words used in an English text. The numerous exceptions to this rule include quotations entirely in another language ("Julius Caesar said, 'Veni, vidi, vici'"); non-English titles of short works (poems, short stories, essays, articles), which are placed in quotation marks and not underlined; proper names; and foreign words anglicized through frequent use. Since English language rapidly naturalizes words, use a dictionary to decide whether a foreign expression requires italics or underlining. Following are some adopted foreign words, abbreviations, and phrases commonly not underlined:

| et al. | etc. | e.g. | i.e. | versus |
| cliché | genre | bourgeois | pasta | kowtow |

5.7 Hyphenation

Hyphens are used to create compound words. Compounds that function as nouns may be open (school year), hyphenated (self-concept), or closed (schoolroom). The current trend discourages use of the hyphen; generally, it is dropped when a compound becomes common. Words designating new areas of endeavor offer good examples of rapid change in policy on hyphenation. The compound word *on-line* will probably close to *online*, just as the compound *psycho-analysis*, standard usage in the first half of this century, changed to *psychoanalysis*.

Some hyphenated compounds are permanent, or hyphenated regardless of increased usage or placement in the sentence (post-World War II, self-serving, two-thirds, great-grandfather), whereas others are temporary, or hyphenated when they precede a noun but not when they follow it (nineteenth-century poet but poet of the nineteenth century, a spelled-out number, but a number spelled out). Keep in mind

that there are occasional exceptions to the rules for permanent and temporary compounds and that you may find an instance where you need to add a hyphen to ensure readability.

5.8 Number

5.8.1 Use of Word or Numeral

In scientific and statistical material, all numbers are expressed in numerals. In nonscientific material, numbers are sometimes spelled out and sometimes expressed in numerals, according to prescribed rules. The general rule followed by many writers is to spell out all numbers through one hundred (e.g., sixty-five, ninety-eight) and all round numbers that can be expressed in two words (e.g., one hundred, two hundred, five thousand, forty-five thousand).

> At that time the population of the district was less than three million.

All other numbers are written as figures.

> There are 514 seniors in the graduating class.

The general rule applies to ordinal as well as cardinal numbers:

> On the 122d and 123d day of his recovery, he received his eighteenth and nineteenth letters from home.

A sentence should never begin with a figure, even when there are figures in the rest of the sentence. Either spell out the first number or, better, recast the sentence.

Original: Five hundred and seventeen people visited the gallery last week.
Revision: Last week 517 people visited the gallery.
Original: Nineteen ninety-two began with several good omens.
Revision: The year of nineteen ninety-two began with several good omens.
Original: Two hundred and fifty passengers escaped injury; 175 sustained minor injuries; 110 were so seriously hurt that they required hospitalization.
Revision: Of the passengers, 250 escaped injury, 175 sustained minor injuries, and 110 required hospitalization.

To avoid confusion, you may spell out one set of figures in an expression that involves two or more series of figures:

> In a test given six months later, 14 children made no error; 64 made one to two errors; 97 made three to four errors.

Although a round number occurring in isolation is spelled out, several round numbers occurring close together are expressed in figures:

> They shipped 1,500 books in the first order, 8,000 in the second, and 100,000 in the third; altogether there were now about 1,000,000 volumes in the warehouse.

Very large round numbers are frequently expressed in figures and units of millions or billions:

> This means that welfare programs will require about $7.8 million more per day compared with $3.2 million spent each day at the current rate of inflation.

Use figures for the following: dates, page, street, serial, telephone numbers, fractions accompanied by a whole number, decimals, percentages, and quantities combined with abbreviations and symbols. In writing that presents numbers for calculation, express all numbers in figures.

5.8.2 Punctuation of Number

Numbers consisting of four or more digits have commas at the thousand's and million's points: 1,000; 7,654,321. The exceptions are page numbers, street numbers, serial numbers, highway numbers, telephone numbers, numbers to the right of the decimal point, and four-digit dates.

(1) Page and line numbers: on page 1014.
(2) Addresses: at 4132 Broadway.
(3) Decimals: 0.5332.
(4) Four-digit year number: in 1999.

But commas are added in year numbers of five or more figures, for example, in 10,000 BC.

5.8.3 Fraction

A fraction standing alone should be spelled out, but a numerical unit composed of a whole number and a fraction should be expressed in figures:

> Trade and commodity services accounted for nine-tenths of all international receipts and payments.
> Cabinets with $10\frac{1}{2}$-by $32\frac{1}{4}$-inch shelves were installed.

APA does not hyphenate fractions used as nouns: two thirds of the population. Numerals in a fraction are separated by a slanted line without spacing: $1\frac{2}{3}$, $27\frac{5}{8}$.

5.8.4 Decimal and Percentage

Figures should be used to express decimals and percentages. The word *percent* should be written out, except in scientific and statistical writing, where the symbol "%" may be used:

> Grades of 3.8 and 95% are equivalent.
>
> With interest at 8 percent, the monthly payment would amount to $12.88, which he noted was exactly 2.425 times the amount he was accustomed to put in his savings monthly.

Use the symbol for *percent* (%) only when it is preceded by a figure. Note that *percentage*, not *percent* or %, is the correct expression to use when no figure is given:

> The September scores for students enrolled in summer school showed an improvement of 70.1% [or "70.1 percent"] over text scores recorded in June. Thus the percentage of achievers in the second text indicated that summer school had resulted in higher scores in a majority of cases.

The figure preceding either *percent* or % is never spelled out:

> 15 percent   55%

In formal nonscientific writing, the percent symbol (%) should be used only in tables and figures; in scientific or technical papers, the percent symbol follows a numeral. In the absence of a number, the word *percentage* is used.

> Sales have increased 37 percent this year, but the percentage increase was greater than last year's.

APA recommends using the percent symbol with all numbers, except at the beginning of a sentence.

> The current rate of inflation is 2.3%.

5.8.5 Number from Mathematical and Statistical Calculation

Textual reference to numbers derived from mathematical and statistical calculations, including those taken from figures and tables, should be in the form of numerals, even if the numbers might otherwise be written out.

> 2 of the 33 tests
>
> a ratio of 12:1
>
> a winning margin of 5,000 votes

Chapter 5
Mechanics

5.8.6 Number with Abbreviation or Symbol

Numbers accompanied by abbreviations or symbols are expressed in numerals: 6 ft, 25 km, 27 mm, $ 9.99.

The abbreviation B.C. (meaning "before Christ") and the designations B.C.E. ("before the Christian [or common] era") and C.E. (Christian [or common] era) follow the year, while the abbreviation A.D. (*anno Domini* in Latin, or "in the year of our Lord") precedes the year.

> Agriculture changed little between 1900 B.C.E. and 1400 C.E.
> Agriculture changed little between 1900 B.C. and A.D. 1400.
> Solomon's Temple was destroyed by the Babylonians in 587 B.C. Rebuilt in 515 B.C, it was destroyed by the Romans in A.D. 70.

MLA omits the periods in these abbreviations: AD, BC, BCE, CE.

Numerals are used to indicate most times of the day (2:00 p.m., the 6:20 flight). Exceptions include time expressed in quarter and half hours and in hours followed by o'clock.

> a quarter to twelve
> half past ten
> five o'clock

5.8.7 Date and Times of the Day

Dates in the text may be written in one of two ways. Chicago Manual and MLA prefer day-month-year order without commas.

> On 22 July 1989 the group met for the first time.

APA prefers month-day-year order, with the year set off by commas.

> On July 22, 1989, the group met for the first time.

When you refer to a month or season and a year, do not set off the year in commas.

> In January 1994 the mayor declared several snow days.
> Summer 1995 had record heat waves.

Be consistent in writing dates. Use either the day-month-year style or the month-day-year style but not both. If you begin with the month, be sure to add a comma after the day and also after the year, unless another punctuation mark goes there, such

97

as a period or a question mark. Do not use a comma between month and year (August 2004). Decades are usually written out without capitalization (the nineties), but it is acceptable to express them in figures (the 1990s, the '90s). Whichever form you use, be consistent.

5.8.8 Inclusive Number

The term *inclusive numbers* (sometimes also called *continued numbers*) refers to the first and last number of a sequence of numerical designations, such as pages or years. Continued numbers are separated by a hyphen in a paper and expressed according to the following scheme, which is based on the way one normally speaks these numbers. The table is taken from the Chicago Manual of Style, thirteenth edition, page 244.

FIRST NUMBER	SECOND NUMBER	EXAMPLES
Less than 100	Use all digits	3-10; 71-72
100 or multiple of 100	Use all digits	100-105; 600-630; 1100-1134
101 through 109 (in multiples of 100)	Use changed part only, omitting unneeded zeros	107-8; 505-17; 1002-6
110 through 199 (in multiples of 100)	Use two digits, or more as needed	321-25; 425-532; 1536-38; 11564-68; 13792-803
	But if numbers are four digits long and three digits change, use all digits	1496-1504; 2787-2816

The principal use of the foregoing scheme is for page numbers and other numbered parts of written works, and for inclusive year dates:

    These cities were discussed on pages 2-14, 45-46, 125-26, 200-210, 308-9.
    He lost everything he owned in the years 1933-36 of the Great Depression.
    This chapter covers the Napoleonic victories of 1800-1801. (Turabian 34-35)

But MLA recommends entering only the final two digits if all other numbers remain the same: 121-48, 300-07, 2176-78. Enter any numbers that have changed: 1989-3016, 23976-4801. Never use fewer than two digits, except for numbers below ten: 1-2, 5-8, but not 501-2.

In parenthetical notes and bibliographical entries, APA recommends entering complete page numbers both before and after the hyphen: 121-148, 1813-1816.

In references to inclusive years, both MLA and APA give only the final two digits when the century remains the same: 1975–78, 1901–09, 711–17. But when the century changes, the entire set of digits should be included: 1890–1950, 400–1000, 1994–2004.

5.8.9 Plural of Number

Plurals of numbers expressed in figures are formed by the addition of s alone: 1920s, the '60s, in his 30s.

> Pilots of 747s undergo special training.
> There was a heavy demand to trade 6½s for the new 8¼s.

Plurals of spelled-out numbers are formed like the plurals of other nouns: the nineteen twenties, thousands, trillions.

> There were many more twelves and fourteens than thirty-twos, thirty-fours, and thirty-sixes on sale.
> Most of the women were in their thirties or forties.

5.8.10 Roman Numeral

Current usage discourages roman numerals in all types of writing. They are acceptable for designating individuals in a series, such as Elizabeth II, Henry VIII, Philip II, and John D. Rockefeller IV; numbering outlines, and numbering preliminary matter in a dissertation or book. Otherwise, use Arabic numerals.

Use lowercase roman numerals for citing pages of a book that are so numbered (e.g., the pages in a preface). Treat inclusive roman numerals like inclusive Arabic numerals: xxv–vii (25–27), xlvi–li (46–51). Your instructor may prefer that you use roman numerals to designate acts and scenes of plays.

5.9 Work Title

Whenever you cite the title of a published work in your research paper, take title from the title page, not from the cover or from a running head at the top of a page. Since display headings, both on title pages and at the heads of articles, frequently set a title in two or more lines, and since punctuation is normally omitted at the ends of lines of display headings, it is often necessary to add marks of punctuation to a title as it will appear when written out in text, note, reference list, or bibliography. This need occurs most often in titles composed of a main title and a subtitle. Consider the following example of a title and its subtitle:

The Early Growth of Logic in the Child
Classification and Seriation

Here, as the title is shown on the title page, no punctuation follows *Child*. When the title and subtitle are referred to in text, they should appear as follows:

The Early Growth of Logic in the Child: Classification and Seriation

Do not reproduce any unusual typographic characteristics, such as special capitalization or lowercasing of all letters. For example, the display headings on the title pages are:

MODERNISM & NEGRITUDE

BERNARD BERENSON
The Making of a Connoisseur

Turner's early sketchbooks

In research papers, however, they should appear as follows:

Modernism and Negritude

Bernard Berenson: The Making of a Connoisseur

Turner's Early Sketchbooks

5.9.1 Capitalized Title

The rules for capitalizing titles are strict. In both titles and subtitles, capitalize the first words, the last words, and all principal words, including those that follow hyphens in compound terms. Capitalize the following parts of speech: nouns, pronouns, verbs, adjectives, adverbs, subordinating conjunctions (e. g, after, although, as if, as soon as, because, before, if, that, until, when, where, while). (See also 5.1.) Do not capitalize the following parts of speech when they fall in the middle of a title: articles, prepositions, coordinating conjunctions, and the word *to* in infinitives (as in *How to Play Chess*).

Death of a Salesman

The Teaching of Spanish in English-Speaking Countries

Storytelling and Mythmaking: Images from Film and Literature

Life As I Find It

The Artist as Critic

<u>What Are You Doing in My Universe?</u>
<u>Whose Music? A Sociology of Musical Language</u>
<u>Where Did You Go? Out. What Did You Do? Nothing.</u>
"Ode to a Nightingale"
"Italian Literature before Dante"
"What Americans Stand For"

5.9.2 Underlined (Italicized) Title

In general, underline the titles of works published independently (APA prefers italicizing the titles of works). Titles to be underlined include the names of books, plays, long poems that are published as books, pamphlets, periodicals (newspapers, magazines, and journals), films, radio and television programs, compact discs, audiocassettes, operas and other long musical compositions, paintings, works of sculpture, ships, aircraft (see also 5.3). When you underline a title, you should not break the underlining between words.

<u>The Awakening</u> (book)
<u>The Importance of Being Earnest</u> (play)
<u>The Waste Land</u> (long poem published as a book)
<u>New Jersey Driver Manual</u> (pamphlet)
<u>Wall Street Journal</u> (newspaper)
<u>Time</u> (magazine)
<u>It's a Wonderful Life</u> (film)
<u>Star Trek</u> (television program)
<u>Sgt. Pepper's Lonely Hearts Club Band</u> (compact disc, audio-cassette)

5.9.3 Title in Quotation Marks

Use quotation marks for the titles of works published within larger works, such titles include the names of articles, essays, short stories, short poems, chapters of books, individual episodes of television and radio programs, and short musical compositions (e.g., songs). Also use quotation marks for unpublished works, such as lectures and speeches. (See also 5.3.)

"Rise in Aid to Education Is Proposed" (newspaper article)
"Sources of Energy in the Next Century" (magazine article)
"Etruscan" (encyclopedia article)

"The Fiction of Langston Hughes" (essay in a book)
"The Lottery" (short story)
"Kubla Khan" (poem)
"The American Economy before the Civil War" (chapter in a book)
"Mood Indigo" (song)
"Preparing for a Successful Interview" (lecture)

5.9.4 Title without Underlining or Quotation Marks

The titles of sacred works, series, editions, and societies and words referring to the divisions of a book are neither underlined nor put in quotation marks. (See also 5.3.)

(1) Sacred writings: Holy Bible, New Testament, Koran.
(2) Series: New Accents, The Brain.
(3) Societies: American Psychological Association, Association of American Petroleum Geologists.
(4) Divisions of a book: foreword, preface, introduction, appendix, chapter, act, volume, scene.

5.9.5 Title Containing Another Title

Some titles may include another title. Underline the title that is normally indicated by underlining when it appears within a title enclosed in quotation marks.

"<u>Romeo and Juliet</u> and Renaissance Politics" (an article about a play)
"Language and Childbirth in <u>The Awakening</u>" (an article about a novel)

Enclose in single quotation marks a title which is normally indicated by double quotation marks.

"Lines after Reading 'Sailing to Byzantium'" (a poem about a poem)
"The Uncanny Theology of 'A Good Man Is Hard to Find'" (an article about a short story)

Also place single quotation marks around a quotation that appears within a title requiring quotation marks.

"Emerson's Strategies against 'Foolish Consistency'" (an article with a quotation in its title)

Use quotation marks around a title normally indicated by quotation marks when it appears within an underlined title.

> "The Lottery" and Other Stories (a book of short stories)
>
> New Perspectives on "The Eve of St. Agnes" (a book about a poem)

On the matter of titles including another title, *Chicago Manual* and MLA differ. (See Chapter 7 and Chapter 9.)

5.10 Enumeration

You may wish to give some items special emphasis by designating them in a series with numerals or lowercase letters. When the list of items is short enough to be run smoothly into the text, identifying numerals are enclosed in parentheses. Note that numbers (or letters) used to enumerate items in text stand out better when they are set in double parentheses than when they are followed by periods.

> The steps in writing a research paper include (1) choosing a topic, (2) preparing a working bibliography, (3) outlining the paper, (4) collecting information, and (5) writing the paper.

Enumeration may also be introduced with a colon following complete sentence.

> Writing a research paper includes the following steps: (a) choosing a topic, (b) preparing a working bibliography ...

To avoid confusion, when enumerated items appear in text that includes Arabic numerals in double parentheses referring to numbered items in a reference list, use underlined letters in double parentheses, rather than Arabic numerals, for the enumeration:

> Haskin's latest theory (2) has several drawbacks: (a) it is not based on current evidence, (b) it has no clinical basis, and (c) it has a weak theoretical grounding.

When the length or number of items listed would create a cumbersome or confusing sentence, set off the list. The items to be listed are most often indicated by Arabic numerals followed by a period and treated like the paragraphs of the text, that is, given paragraph indention and the runover lines begun at the margin. When the items to be listed are complete sentences, use the following format:

> The authors made three recommendations for keeping European markets open:
>
>   1. Companies must step up their strategic planning in Europe. (The paragraph may continue.)
>   2. Business leaders outside Europe must realize that there is strength in numbers.

3\. Non-European companies must enlist their governments' help at the highest levels.

Or they may be set flush with the margin, and the runover lines aligned with the first line of substantive matter:

> The authors made three recommendations for keeping European markets open:
> 1. Companies must step up their strategic planning in Europe. (The paragraph may continue.)
> 2. Business leaders outside Europe must realize that there is strength in numbers.
> 3. Non-European companies must enlist their governments' help at the highest levels.

In both styles, the periods immediately following the numerals must be aligned. Periods should be omitted at the ends of items, unless the items are composed of complete sentences or whole paragraphs:

> 1. Selective initial dissemination of published material — a direct responsibility of the library
> 2. Arrangement and organization of the collection

But, if the listed items are words or phrases that are a grammatical part of the lead-in statement, they should be punctuated as a series and a period should be put at the end of the last item.

> The syllabus for the seminar included sessions on
> a. new systems of discourse,
> b. the rhetorical inheritance,
> c. literacy, and
> d. do measurement of writing ability.

5.11　Table and Figure

Graphic representations of data can help make the results of your research comprehensible to your reader. Tables and figures (the general name for any illustrative material, including graphs, maps, diagrams, and photographs) can support your argument by revealing complex relationships in a way that prose alone often cannot. Computers can now be used to generate many types of tables and figures; the principles for presenting them are the same regardless of the medium you use to produce them.

5.11.1　Table

The data that you collect constitute the evidence on which your inferences and conclusions are based. Large quantities of statistics or numerical data should be tabulated in the interest of both brevity and clarity. Not all statistical matter, however, need be presented in tabular form. You would not tabulate the following numbers if you had no additional data: "The 607 delegates, representing seventeen nations, voted 402 to 205 in favor of the resolution." A simple array of data may be presented informally in the text.

And the class members were about evenly divided on the candidates, as is shown in these results:

	Boys	Girls	Total
For Smith	17	16	33
For Brown	13	15	28
Total	30	31	61

A table should have a unified and clearly stated purpose. It should not try to present too many kinds of data or show too many types of relationships. Of course, a table can be very useful for presenting a large quantity of data, but these data should be organized so that they can be easily assimilated.

Tables within the body of the text should be as brief as clarity permits. Very long and complex tables usually belong in an appendix.

5.11.2 Relation of Table and the Text

To help your reader understand the data in a table, you should provide a clear introduction. The introduction might explain the principles governing the table or state the significance of the data. It should explain how the data support your thesis.

Two general rules apply to the relationship between tables and text. First, a table should be so constructed that it may be read and understood without reference to the text. For those readers who wish to study only the statistical data, tables should be organized logically and explained fully in a caption, or title. Second, the text should be so complete that readers can follow the argument without referring to the tables. You should incorporate into the body of the paper enough analytical and summary statements that are derived from each table to provide a coherent and valid report of actual findings.

Tables should be placed as close as possible to the discussion of the facts or data in the text. If a table appears within the two or three pages following the first reference to it, only the number of the table need be given in the text ("Table 3 shows …"). Tables that are farther away from their initial mention in the text should be referred to by the table number and page number ("Table 4 on page 13 shows …"). Avoid using imprecise phrases such as "in the following table" and "in the table above"; these may be confusing when the table is not immediately visible.

5.11.3 Figure

The term *figure* usually refers to any kind of graphic representation or illustration, whether in the text or in an appendix. Figures include graphs, charts, drawings, diagrams, maps, photographs, blueprints, and some kinds of computer printouts. If you plan to use illustrations, be sure that you possess or have access to the skills and materials required for a satisfactory finished product.

5.11.4 Relation of Figure and the Text

Like tables, figures should be designed so that they can be read and understood without reference to the text. Captions should be fully descriptive. Moreover, the text should be so complete that the reader can follow the argument without examining the figures. The text, however, should refer to each figure and explain or analyze its content.

If a figure appears within the two or three pages following the first reference to it, only the number of the figure need be given in the text ("Figure 4 shows …"). When you refer to a figure that is farther away from its initial mention, you should provide both figure number and page number ("Figure 5 on page 19 shows …").

5.11.5 Placement of Table and Figure

The following guidelines apply to the placement of tables and figures in the text:

(1) Confine each table or figure to one page if possible. Leave the usual margins.

(2) Include textual material on the page with a table or figure that occupies no more than half the page. The page should begin with text. Leave a quadruple space both above and below a table or figure.

(3) Place a table or figure between complete paragraphs. Avoid inserting a table or figure into the middle of a paragraph, even if you have to leave some extra space on the page.

5.12 Numbering of Pages

All pages of the text of a research paper should be numbered, including the first page. Position numerals in the upper right-hand corner one inch from the top of the page. Flush with the right margin. Double-space to the first line of text.

MLA recommends placing the name of the writer before the numeral without intervening punctuation (Jones 2 or Smith 21) one-half inch from the top of the page. Double-space to the first line of the text, which sits approximately one inch from the top of the page.

For the running head, APA recommends using the first two or three words of the title, as in "EQUALITY OF ACCESS 5" for the fifth page of a paper entitled "Equality of Access in Public Higher Education." The running head appears in full capital letters. Leave five spaces between the running head and the page number. Place the head one inch below the top margin and double-space to the first line of text.

In a research paper, the front matter (such as the Abstract and the Acknowledgements sheet) should not be numbered or counted as part of the paper or dissertation. The title page should be counted but not numbered. Use lowercase roman numerals for the front matter and Arabic numerals running consecutively for the text and the back matter.

APA numbers the title page and all succeeding pages with continuous Arabic numerals.

5.13 Personal Name

In general, the first time you use a person's name in the text of your paper, spell it exactly as it appears in your source. Do not change Martin Luther King, Jr. to Martin Luther King. In subsequent references to the person, you may give the last name only (King) — unless you refer to two or more persons with the same last name. In casual references to the very famous — say, Shakespeare, Whitman, or Lincoln — it is not necessary to give the full name initially.

5.14 Personal Title

In general, do not use formal titles (Mr, Mrs, Miss, Ms, Dr, Professor) in referring to men or women, living or dead. A few women in history are traditionally known by their titles as married women (Mrs. Humphry Ward). Treat other women's names the same as men's.

First Use	Subsequent Use
Emily Dickinson	Dickinson (not Miss Dickinson)
Harriet Beecher Stowe	Stowe (not Mrs. Stowe)

5.15 Use of Notes

Notes have four main uses: (a) to cite the authority for statements in text — specific facts or opinions as well as exact quotations; (b) to make cross-references; (c) to make incidental comments upon, to amplify, or to qualify textual discussion — in short, to provide a place for material which the writer deems worthwhile to include but which would in the writer's judgment interrupt the flow of thought if introduced into the text; and (d) to make acknowledgments. Notes, then, are of two kinds: reference notes (*a* and *b* above) and content notes (*c* and *d* above). A content note may also include one or more references.

Tables, outlines, lists, letters, and the like, that are not immediately relevant to the text are best placed in an appendix and referred to in the text by a simple content footnote:

[5] The member banks and their contributors are listed in appendix 3.

In a paper using endnotes or parenthetical references, references to the above materials should be placed in parentheses in the text, so that the reader does not have to consult two parts of the back matter to find a source:

Auditors traced this error to the member banks and their contributors (see appendix 3).

The place in the text at which a note is introduced should be marked with an Arabic numeral typed slightly above the line (superscript). Note numbers preceding notes themselves are also typed slightly above the line (as in the above).

Leave no space between the note number in the text and the word or mark of punctuation that it follows. Put no period after a note number nor should you embellish it with parentheses, brackets, or slash marks. Place the note number before a dash, but after all other marks of punctuation. The note number should always follow the passage to which it refers. If the passage is an exact quotation, the note number comes at the end of the quotation, not after the author's name or at the end of the textual matter introducing the quotation.

Incorrect: Robert Heilbroner explains that "the profit motive as we know it is only as old as 'modern man.[1]'"

Correct: Robert Heilbroner explains that "the profit motive as we know it is only as old as 'modern man.'"[1]

Incorrect: Robert Heilbroner[1] explains that "the profit motive as we know it is only as old as 'modern man.'"

Correct: "The profit motive as we know it is only as old as 'modern man,'" according to Robert Heilbroner.[1]

Incorrect: "The profit motive as we know it is only as old as 'modern man'" —[1] ancient civilizations did not have that concept.

Correct: "The profit motive as we know it is only as old as 'modern man'"[1]— ancient civilizations did not have that concept.

Correct: "The profit motive as we know it is only as old as 'modern man'":[1] ancient civilizations did not have that concept.

Notes should be arranged in numerical order either at the foot of the page (footnotes) or at the end of the paper (endnotes). Because footnotes appear at the bottom of the page, readers can see them in context, when the source material or an additional explanation might be most useful. On the other hand, if sources or supplementary information can be looked at afterward, endnotes might be best. Use the one your instructor prefers.

If you are using footnotes, place every footnote at the bottom of the page on which the citation appears. Type a one-and-one-half-inch line with the underline key, starting from the left margin, one double space below the last line of the text. Place the first footnote one double space below the line. Indent the first line of each note five spaces. Subsequent lines start at the left margin. Place the number designating the note on the line; leave one space between the number and the first word of the note. Single-space within footnotes, and double-space between them. When a footnote cannot be included without running into the bottom margin (one inch) and cannot be omitted without making the page noticeably short, the footnote may be split and carried over to the next page. Conclude the footnote without indention, ahead of the next footnote in the series.

A research paper usually uses endnotes. If you are using endnotes, notes should be placed in a separate section entitled "Notes" (not "Endnotes"), either at the entire paper immediately preceding the bibliography or at the end of each chapter, as local regulations specify. Indent the first line of each note five spaces. Subsequent lines start at the left margin. Place the number designating the note on the line; leave one space between the number and the first word of the note. Double-space throughout, both within and between entries.

When you number the notes, you must take care to ensure that the final sequence is correct. If you find, on checking the manuscripts, that a note has been omitted or that one should be deleted, you must renumber the notes from the point of the desired change to the end of the chapter or paper.

5.16 Spacing

5.16.1 Space around Punctuation Marks

Periods, colons, commas, question marks, and semicolons follow the previous letter without spacing. One space follows a colon, a semicolon, and a comma. Dashes are indicated by two consecutive hyphens (—). Neither hyphens nor dashes have space on either side of them.

> She needs these materials: one saw, one hammer, and one nail.
> (One space after colon and comma in text)
> To err is human; to forgive, divine.
> New York: Holt, 1983.
> (One space after colon, semicolon and comma, whether in text or in notes)
> The stock — American Can — sold above par.
> (No space on either side of a dash)
> He won by a two-thirds majority.
> (No space on either side of a hyphen)

In typed copy, two spaces traditionally follow the periods at the end of sentences. APA now specifies that periods be followed by one space only. *Chicago Manual* and MLA also recommend following publishers' requirements for one space, but they continue to allow for two spaces in typescripts.

Within the text, a superscript should be placed without any intervening space after the end punctuation.

5.16.2 Margin

Margins should measure a minimum of one inch on all sides. Page numbers and running heads should sit one or one-half inch (as desired) from either the top or the bottom of the paper. For a graduation thesis, larger left-hand margins may be required

Chapter 5
Mechanics

to allow for a binding.

5.16.3 Indentation

Indent the first line of a paragraph five spaces. Bring all subsequent lines back to the left margin.

5.16.4 Centered Material

Any material to be centered on a page, such as title and first-level headings, should be centered between margins, not between the edges of the page.

5.17 Division of Words and Division of Lines of Text

5.17.1 Division of Words

1. The general rule

(1) When the division of words is necessary at the ends of lines, divide them according to their syllabication as shown in reliable dictionary.

(2) Avoid placing two or more hyphens in a row at the right margin.

(3) Divide according to pronunciation, rather than derivation. When a word is divided after an accented syllable, the consonant stays with the vowel when the vowel is short:

| signif-icant | param-eter | hypoth-esis |
| philos-ophy | democ-racy | pres-ent (a.) |

But the consonant goes with the following syllable when the preceding vowel is long:

| stu-dent | Mongo-lian | deci-sive |

The consonant goes with the accented syllable, however, in such cases as the following:

| philo-sophical | pre-sent (v.) | demo-cratic |

When *ing* or *ed* is added to a word whose final syllable contains the liquid *l* (e.g., *circle, handle*), the final syllable of the parent word becomes a part of the added syllable:

| cir-cling | bris-tling | chuck-ling | han-dling |
| cir-cled | bris-tled | chuck-led | han-dled |

111

In words where an end consonant is doubled before *ing* and *ed*, the division comes between the double consonants:

    set-ting   con-trol-ling

    per-mit-ting   per-mit-ted

Note that this rule does not apply to words originally ending in a double consonant:

    add-ing   in-stall-ing

2. Exceptions and special rules

(1) Never make one-letter or two-letter divisions, especially when the division would give a misleading appearance.

Wrong:	a-mong	u-nite	e-nough	man-y	pray-er
	mon-ey	loss-es	wo-man	of-ten	

(2) Never divide the syllable *able* and *ible*.

Wrong:	inevita-ble	permissi-ble	allowa-ble
Right:	inevi-table	permis-sible	allow-able

(3) Avoid division of hyphenated words except at the hyphen.

Wrong:	self-evi-dent	gov-er-nor-elect	well-in-ten-tioned
Right:	self-evident	governor-elect	well-intentioned

(4) Avoid division of a proper name unless it is one in which the correct division is obvious.

Right:	Wash-ing-ton	Went-worth	Bond-field
	John-son		

5.17.2 Division of Initial, Number, and Lines of Text

(1) Never divide initials for names of countries or states (U.S, N.Y.), names of organizations (UNESCO, NATO), or names of publications or radio or television stations (PMLA, CCTV). Never divide the name of the month (May, August) and the day (Monday, Friday), years (1997, 2006), hours of the day (05∶00, 19∶30), and monetary expressions ($10.50, ￥200).

In the case of proper names, the given name and surname or initials and surname should be on the same line when possible; very long names are an exception.

Chapter 5
Mechanics

Wrong: T./S. Eliot   J./B.S. Haldane   P./R. of China

But the following are allowable:

Allowable: T.S./Eliot   J.B.S./Haldane   P.R./of China (or P.R. of/China)

(2) When a word cannot be included in its entirety or properly divided and hyphenated within the established margin, the entire word should be placed on the next line. No more than two successive lines should end with hyphenated words.

(3) Words should not be broken between pages. Avoid carrying over just one line of a paragraph to the following page.

5.18   Chapter Title and Heading

Chapter titles and headings serve the purpose of guiding the reader through long or complex material. Short papers usually do not require divisions, but longer research papers (especially of literary type) often benefit from the insertion of headings, organization into chapters, and grouping of chapters into parts. Titles and headings should be used to clarify the organization, not to conceal incoherent development or insufficient transitions.

5.18.1   Part

If the chapters are grouped under "parts," part-title pages are required, placed immediately before the first chapter of the group composing the part. Since the Introduction is to the entire paper, whether the Introduction is titled CHAPTER 1 or not, it is not included in PART I. The first part-title page therefore follows rather than precedes the Introduction.

5.18.2   Chapter

The main body of the paper is divided into chapters. Each chapter begins on a new page and has a generic heading and a title. In a short paper, some writers prefer to omit the word CHAPTER and to use merely numerals — roman (I, II) or Arabic (1, 2) — in sequence before the headings of the several main divisions. The generic heading of a chapter consisting of the word CHAPTER is followed by a number. The number may either be spelled out, in capital letters, or given in the form of a numeral (Arabic or uppercase Roman). The form in which the chapter number is expressed

113

should be different from the form in which the part number is expressed (e.g., PART TWO, CHAPTER I). The title, which describes the content of the chapter, is centered in uppercase below the generic heading.

5.18.3 Section, Subsection and the Heading

In research papers the chapters or their equivalents are often divided into sections, which may in turn be divided into subsections, and subsections into sub-subsections, and so on. Such divisions are customarily given titles, called *subheadings*, which are differentiated and designated respectively first-, second-, and third-level subheadings. The first-level subdivision should have greater attention value than the lower levels. Centered headings have greater attention value than side headings. And underlined or boldfaced headings, centered or side, have greater attention value than those not underlined or in boldface. Each subhead should have two blank lines above if it follows text or three blank lines above if it follows a table or a figure. A blank line should go beneath each subhead that is not run in. A plan for the display of five levels of subheadings in a typed paper follows:

(1) First-level (centered heading, underlined or in boldface, capitalized headline style):

Traditional Controversy between Medieval and Renaissance Times

(2) Second-level (centered heading, not underlined or in boldface, capitalized headline style):

Reappearance of Religious Legalism

(3) Third-level (side heading, underlined or in boldface, capitalized headline style, beginning at the left margin):

Shakespeare's Early Sonnets

(4) Fourth-level (side heading, not underlined or in boldface, capitalized sentence style, beginning at the left margin):

The Gospel as it is related to Jesus

(5) Fifth-level (heading run into — at the beginning of — a paragraph, underlined or in boldface, capitalized sentence style):

The gospel legalized in the Church. The gospel that the early Christians preached within the pagan sects was also a product of their experiences ...

Chapter 5
Mechanics

If fewer than five levels are required, the style may be selected in any suitable descending order indicated above.

All headings at the same level should be parallel grammatically and logically. Double-space above and below centered headings (also see 5.16). Capitalize the first letter of each word except articles, conjunctions, and prepositions, unless they are the first or last word in the heading. Do not number unless required. If a heading is more than four inches long (forty pica spaces), use a double-spaced inverted-pyramid format. For example,

Orientations to Pedagogy: Interactive/
Experiential Versus Transmission

Do not use punctuation, unless it ends with a question mark or an exclamation point.

Leave a double space above and below freestanding side headings. Align with the left margin, and underscore with a solid line. Capitalize and punctuate as you would centered headings. If a side heading is more than about two and one-half inches long (twenty-five pica spaces), divide the heading, placing the second line a double space below, with a two-space hanging indention.

<u>Language Is Best Learned</u>
  <u>When Kept Whole</u>

<u>Language in the Classroom</u>
  <u>Should Be Meaningful and Functional</u>

Leave a double space above paragraph headings, indent five spaces, and underscore the run-in heading with a solid line. Capitalize the first word and proper nouns and adjectives only. End the heading with a period, and begin the text on the same line.

<u>Continued footnotes.</u> When a footnote cannot be included without running into the bottom margin (one inch) and cannot be omitted without making the page noticeably short, footnote may be split and carried over to the next page ...

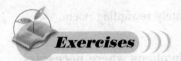

Exercises

I. Capitalize words as needed in the following sentences.

1. the town in the south where I was raised had a stature of a civil war soldier in

    the center of main street.

2. we had a choice of fast-food, Chinese, or Italian restaurants.

3. in *home before dark*, cheever tells how her father once panicked when driving east on the tappan zee bridge over the Hudson river.

4. the council of trent was convened to draw up the catholic response to the protestant reformation.

5. my favorite song by cole porter is "you'd be so nice to come home to."

II. Give a precise explanation for each of the following abbreviated forms.

bk.	ch.	et al.	Gen.	Matt.	ibid.	Dir.
Cond.	Perf.	Tran.	eds.	Rev.	Ed.	Diss.
cf.	Comp.	qtd.	rpt.	ser.		

III. Revise each of the following sentences to eliminate any abbreviations that would be inappropriate in academic writing.

1. An MX missile, which is 71 ft. long and 92 in. around, weighs 190,000 lbs.

2. The A.M. shift is easier because customers usually just order coffee, tea, doughnuts, etc.

3. A large corp. like AT&T may help to finance an M.B.A. for an employee.

4. The local NPR station has a broadcast range of 75 mi.

5. After less than a yr. at U.Va., Poe left and joined the U.S. army.

IV. Underline (or italicize) and capitalize the words where necessary.

1. Critics debated whether thelma & louise was a feminist film.

2. Hawthorne's story "my kinsman, major molineux" bears a striking resemblance to Shakespeare's play a midsummer night's dream.

3. An excerpt from his book waiting for the weekend was published in the Atlantic.

4. The word veterinary comes from the Latin veterinarius.

5. The washington post provides extensive coverage of Congress.

6. The waste land is a long and difficult but ultimately rewarding poem.

V. Using the dictionary as a reference, insert hyphens where necessary.

1. deescalate

2. pre World War II

3. happily married couple
4. self important
5. president elect
6. seven hundred thirty three
7. a hard working farmer
8. a politician who is quick witted

VI. Revise the numbers in the following sentences as necessary for correctness and consistency. If a sentence is correct, circle its number.

1. 307 miles long and 82 miles wide, the island offered little of interest.
2. Some call it the handbook for the 90s.
3. You can travel around the city for only 65 cents.
4. Cable TV is now available to 72 percent of the population.
5. The department received 1,653 calls and forty-three letters.
6. The parents considered 25 cents enough for a five-year-old.

VII. Correct the errors according to MLA style.

26-9   104-108   1550-562   George Gordon Byron(1788-824)
in 18000 BC 1 338 North Park Avenue   AD 1864-949

VIII. Correct the errors, if there are any, in the following notes.

1. The commentary of the sixteenth-century literary scholars Bernardo Segni and Lionardo Salviati shows them to be less-than-faithful followers of Aristotle[1].
2. 1For strong points of view on different aspects of the issue, see Public Agenda Foundation 1-10 and Sakala 151-88.
3. "Prosaic strength" (Donald Davie's phrase[4]) is a fitting term to apply to writing which explores the expressive resources of the language to the full, without noticeably exceeding them.
4. As a considerable part of the present book is concerned with what are traditionally known as "rhetorical figure" or "figures of speech"[4], it is well to bear in mind from the start the technical names for these figures are not sacrosanct, nor have their definitions been laid down once and for all time.

5. But it is because *eikôn* "always involves two relations" —[4] like metaphor by analogy — that relation can be inverted so easily.

6. Any particular situation in which language is used may be roughly described by answering the following questions: [3]

   (1) Who are the participants?

   (2) What objects are relevant to the communication?

   ...

IX. Put the work title in correct form.

1. Errors and Expectations: a Guide for the Teacher of Basic Writing (a book)
2. the Need for Theory in Composition Research   (a magazine article)
3. A Discourse-centered Rhetoric of the Paragraph   (an essay in a book)
4. Evaluation of teaching college English   (a book)
5. A Review of "Gone with the Wind"   (an article)
6. The Red Cap   (a short story)
7. "The Waste Land"   (a long poem)
8. Romeo And Juliet   (a play)

X. Identify error in enumeration.

1. Quotation marks are used to enclose the title of a) articles from periodical journals, magazines, and newspapers; b) chapters of books; c) short stories; d) short poems; and e) songs.

2. There have been several major theories advanced concerning alternative authors of the plays traditionally attributed to Shakespeare. Four areas which are usually discussed in the development of these theories are: 1. arguments for the refection of William Shakespeare as author; 2. arguments for the rejection of some other candidate as author; 3. reasons for the long concealment of the identity of the proposed author; and 4. reasons the authorship was formerly attributed to William Shakespeare. The theories differ most drastically in the second area, while the arguments for the other points are often nearly identical.

3. Of the signals that writers use to make the ideas in their papers cohere, linking words or phrases are probably the best known. These words can be grouped into four types according to the function they play in linking one

idea to the next.
- *a.* Making an additional (parallel) point: *moreover, furthermore, also, in addition, another.*
- *b.* Giving an example: *to illustrate, for example, similarly, for instance, in other words.*
- *c.* Making a contrasting point: *however, on the other hand, but, in spite of, on the contrary, yet, although.*
- *d.* Providing results, summary, or a concluding point: *therefore, consequently, hence, thus, finally, in summary, in conclusion, as a result.*

Chapter 6

Punctuation

The primary purpose of punctuation is to ensure the clarity and readability of writing. Punctuation clarifies sentence structure, separating some words and grouping others. It adds meaning to written words and guides the understanding of readers as they move through sentences. The rules set forth here cover many of the situations you will encounter in writing research papers.

6.1 Comma

Comma (,) is used to separate parts of a sentence from one another, and to mark a pause in reading. It is the most frequently used punctuation mark in English. A study of student writing reveals that a lot of students' common errors in writing involve the use of comma. But reducing comma use to hard and fast rules is very difficult for several reasons. First, comma can play a number of different roles in sentence, making general rules hard to come by. More important, many decisions about comma relate to matters of purpose, rhythm, and style rather than grammar alone. As a result, conventions for using comma differ from one English-speaking country to another, even from one professional writer to another. Getting full control of comma usage in your own writing thus involves not only learning some rules but also practicing the use of comma in writing and concentrating on the stylistic decisions you must learn to make as a writer.

(1) Use a comma before a coordinating conjunction (*and*, *but*, *for*, *nor*, *or*, *yet*, or *so*) joining independent clauses in a sentence.

> Most young Europeans spend their holidays in other European countries, and many students take vacation jobs abroad.
>
> The poem is ironic, for the poet's meaning contrasts with her words.

But if the sentence is short and clarity is not an issue, no comma is needed:

> John arrived early and Mary came an hour later.

(2) Use comma to separate words, phrases, and clauses in a series.

WORDS:

They found employment in truck driving, farming, and mining.

PHRASES:

He has plundered our seas, ravaged our coasts, burnt our towns, and destroyed the lives of our people. (Thomas Jefferson, Declaration of Independence)

CLAUSES:

In the Great Depression, millions lost their jobs, businesses failed, and charitable institutions closed their doors.

You may often see a series with no comma after the next-to-last item, particularly in newspaper writing, as in "The day was cold, dark and dreary." Occasionally, however, omitting the comma can cause confusion, and you will never be wrong to include it.

When the items in a series contain commas of their own or other punctuation, separate them with semicolons rather than commas.

Pollsters focused their efforts on Columbus, Ohio; Des Moines, Iowa; and Saint Louis, Missouri.

(3) Use comma between coordinate adjectives — that is, adjectives that separately modify the same noun.

They are sincere, talented, inquisitive researchers.

But in a sentence "The cracked bathroom mirror reflected his face.", "cracked" and "bathroom" are not coordinate because "bathroom mirror" is the equivalent of a single word, which is modified by "cracked". Hence they are not separated by commas.

(4) Use comma to set off a parenthetical comment, or an aside, if it is brief and closely related to the rest of the sentence.

The bill, you will be pleased to hear, passed at the last session.

Many people feel resentful because they think they have suffered an unjust fate; that is, they look upon illness, bereavement, or disrupted domestic or working conditions as being undeserved.

(5) Use comma to set off a nonrestrictive modifier — that is, a modifier that is not essential to the meaning of the sentence.

The theme song of the campaign, "Happy Days Are Here Again", is indelibly associated

with the Great Depression.

Scientists, who must observe standards of objectivity in their work, can contribute usefully to public-policy debates.

(6) Use comma after a long introductory phrase or clause.

If the appositive limits the meaning of the noun and is therefore restrictive, no commas should be used.

After years of anxiety over the family's finances, Linda Longman looks forward to the day the mortgage will be paid off.

(7) Use comma to set off alternative or contrasting phrases.

The king remains a tragic figure, however appalling his actions.

But in the sentence "Several cooperative but autonomous republics were formed.", the conjunction "but" links cooperative and autonomous, making a comma inappropriate.

(8) Use comma in date whose order is month, day, and year. If such a date comes in the middle of a sentence, include a comma after the year. (See also 5.8.7.)

Martin Luther King, Jr., was born on January 15, 1929, and died on April 4, 1968.

But no comma is used with dates whose order is day, month, and year.

Martin Luther King, Jr., was born on 15 January 1929 and died on 4 April 1968.

A comma is sometimes necessary to prevent misreading:

After eating, the lions yawned and then dozed off.

6.2 Semicolon

Semicolon (;) has the effect of creating a pause stronger than that of a comma but not as strong as the full pause of a period. They are used to link coordinate independent clauses and to separate items in a series.

(1) Use semicolon between independent clauses not linked by a conjunction.

My high school was excessively competitive; virtually everyone went on to college, many to the top schools in the nation.

Pittsburgh was once notorious for its smoke and grime; today, its skies and streets are cleaner than those of many other American cities.

(2) Use semicolon between items in a series when the items contain commas

Chapter 6
Punctuation

(see 6.1):

The tour includes visits to the following art museums: the Prado, in Madrid; the Louvre, in Paris; and the Rijksmuseum, in Amsterdam.

Although productivity per capita in U.S. industry is almost twice that in West European industry, Western Europe has an increasingly well-educated young labor force; and the crucial point is that knowledge, which is transferable between peoples, has become by far the most important world economic resource.

When used transitionally between the clauses of compound sentences, the words *hence*, *however*, *nevertheless*, *indeed*, *so*, *then*, *thus*, and *yet* should be preceded by a semicolon and followed by a comma:

There are those who think of freedom in terms of social and economic egalitarianism; thus, reformist governments of the left are inherently viewed with greater favor than the regimes of the right.

Physical education forms an important part of a university's program; nevertheless, few students and professors clearly recognize its value.

6.3 Colon

The use of the colon (:) in a sentence indicates a discontinuity of grammatical construction greater than that indicated by semicolon. Whereas the semicolon is used to separate parts of a sentence that are of equal significance, colon is used to introduce a clause or phrase that expands, clarifies, or exemplifies the meaning of what precedes it.

(1) Use colon to introduce a list, an elaboration of what was just said, or the formal expression of a rule or principle.

LIST:

The reading list includes three Hemingway's novels: <u>A Farewell to Arms</u>, <u>For Whom the Bell Tolls</u>, and <u>The Old Man and the Sea</u>.

ELABORATION:

The plot is founded on deception: the three main characters have secret identities.

RULE OR PRINCIPLE:

Many books would be briefer if their authors followed the logical principle known as Occam's razor: Explanations should not be multiplied unnecessarily.

(A rule or principle after a colon should begin with a capital letter.)

But a verb or preposition that performs the same introductory function as a colon makes the colon unnecessary.

  The novels on the reading list include <u>A Farewell to Arms</u>, <u>For Whom the Bell Tolls</u>, and <u>The Old Man and the Sea</u>.
  (The verb *include* performs the introductory function.)
  The reading list includes such novels as <u>A Farewell to Arms</u>, <u>For Whom the Bell Tolls</u>, and <u>The Old Man and the Sea</u>.
  (The preposition *as* performs the introductory function.)

(2) Use colon to introduce a quotation that is independent from the structure of the main sentence.

  In <u>The Awakening</u>, Mme Ratignolle exhorts Robert Lebrun to stop flirting with Edna: "She is not one of us; she is not like us."

A quotation that is integral to the sentence structure is generally preceded by no punctuation or, if a verb of saying (*says*, *exclaims*, *notes*, *writes*) introduces the quotation, by a comma.

A colon is used after a verb of saying, however, if the verb introduces certain kinds of formal literary quotations, such as long quotations set off from the main text.

  E. E. Cummings concludes the poem with this vivid description of a carefree scene, reinforced by the carefree form of the lines themselves:
  it's
  spring
  and
    the
      goat-footed
  balloonMan whistles
  far
  and
  wee (16–24)

As noted elsewhere in this book, colon is also used between hours and minutes in notations of time, between the title and subtitle of a book or article, between place and publisher in bibliographical references, and between volume and page numbers in citations, and so forth.

6.4 Dash

Dash (—), which in printing is an elongated hyphen, in typescript consists of

Chapter 6
Punctuation

two hyphens without space between or on either side of them.

A dash or a pair of dashes enclosing a phase may indicate a sudden break in thought that disrupts the sentence structure:

> Rutherford — how could he have misinterpreted the evidence?

> Some of the characters in Tom Jones are "flat" — to use the term E. M. Forster coined — because they unfailingly act in accordance with a set of qualities suggested by a literal interpretation of their names (e.g., Squire Allworthy).

Dash may be used to introduce an element that emphasizes or explains the main clause through repetition of one or more key words:

> He asked where wisdom was to be found — "the wisdom that is above rubies."

> One is expected to cram all this stuff into one's mind — cram it all in, whether it's likely to be useful or not.

Pairs of dashes allow a writer to interrupt a sentence to insert a comment, or to highlight particular material. In contrast to parentheses, dashes give more rather than less emphasis to the material they enclose.

1. Inserting a comment

> The pleasures of reading itself — who doesn't remember? — were like those of Christmas cake, a sweet devouring.

2. Emphasizing explanatory material

> Mr. Angell is addicted to dashes and parentheses — small pauses or digressions in a narrative like those moments when the umpire dusts off home plate or a pitcher rubs up a new ball — that serve to slow an already deliberate movement almost to a standstill.

3. Emphasizing material at the end of a sentence

> In the twentieth century it has become almost impossible to moralize about epidemics — except those which are transmitted sexually.

4. Introducing a summary or explanation

> The status of the man throwing the discus, the charioteer at Delphi, the poetry of Pindar — all show the culmination of the great ideal.

> In walking, the average adult person employs a motor mechanism that weighs about eighty pounds — sixty pounds of muscle and twenty pounds of bone.

5. Indicating hesitation in speech

> As the officer approached his car, the driver stammered, "What — what have I done?"

In introducing a summary or explanation, the difference between a dash and a colon is a subtle one. In general, however, a dash is less formal. In fact you should use dash sparingly, not only because they are somewhat informal but also because they cause an abrupt break in reading. Too many of them create a jerky, disconnected effect that makes it hard for readers to follow your thought.

6.5 Parentheses

The principal uses of parentheses [( )] in the text of a paper are (1) to set off parenthetical elements, (2) to enclose the source of a quotation or other matter when a footnote or endnote is not used for the purpose, and (3) to set off the numbers or letters in an enumeration (as in this sentence).

> Normal children do not confuse reality and fantasy — they confuse them much less often than we adults do (as a certain great fantasist pointed out in a story called "The Emperor's New Clothes").

> Boxing is a purely masculine world. (Though there are female boxers — the most famous is the Black champion Lady Tyger Trimiar with her shaved head and tiger-striped attire — women's role in the sport is extremely marginal.)
>
> — Joyce Carol Oates, *On Boxing*

As the examples above demonstrate, a period may be placed either inside or outside a closing parenthesis, depending on whether the text inside the parentheses is a complete sentence. A comma, on the other hand, is always placed outside a closing parenthesis.

> Gene Tunney's single defeat in an eleven-year career was a flamboyant and dangerous fighter named Harry Greb ("The Human Windmill"), who seems to have been, judging from boxing literature, the dirtiest fighter in history.
>
> — Joyce Carol Oates, *On Boxing*

If the material in parentheses is a question or an exclamation, use a question mark or exclamation mark inside the closing parenthesis.

> Our laughing (so deep was the pleasure!) became screaming.

Use parentheses judiciously, because they break up the flow of a sentence or passage, forcing readers to hold the original train of thought in their minds while considering a secondary one. As a writer, you often have a choice of setting off material in three ways: with comma, with parentheses, or with dashes. The choice is partially one of how interruptive the material is and partially one of personal style. In general, use comma when the material is least interruptive, parentheses when it is more interruptive, and dash when it is the most interruptive. One other consideration is whether the material ends in an exclamation point or question mark; if so, you can use only parentheses or dash.

6.6 Quotation Mark

Quotation marks (" ") tell readers that certain words were spoken or written by someone other than the writer. They signal not only direct quotations but also certain titles, definitions, and words used ironically or invented by the writer.

(1) Use quotation marks to signal direct quotation

> He smiled and said, "Son, this is one incident that I will never forget."

Single quotation marks (' ') enclose a quotation within a quotation. Open and close the passage you are quoting with double quotation marks, and change any quotation marks that appear within the quotation to single quotation marks.

> In "The Uses of the Blues," Baldwin says, "The title 'The Uses of the Blues' does not refer to music; I don't know anything about music."

Do not use quotation marks for indirect quotations, which do not use someone's exact words.

> Father smiled and said that he would never forget the incident.

(2) Use quotation marks to signal an ironical sense.

> Their "friend" brought about their downfall.

Quotation marks are not needed after *so-called*.

> Their so-called friend brought about their downfall.

(3) Use quotation marks to signal a definition or an explanation of a word or phrase that is foreign or invented by the writer.

> The first idiomatic Spanish expression I learned was *irse todo en humo* ("to go up in smoke").

> The French phrase *idée fixe* means literally "fixed idea."

You may use single quotation marks for a translation that follows the original directly, without intervening words or punctuation.

> The word *text* derives from the Latin verb *texere* "to weave."

6.7 Square Bracket

Use square brackets ([ ]) around parenthetical elements within parentheses, so that the levels of subordination can be easily distinguished.

> The sect known as the Jansenists (after Cornelius Jansen [1585-1638]) faced opposition from both the king and the pope.

Use square brackets to insert material within quotations. In the following sentence, the bracketed words replace the words *he* and *it* in the original quotation.

> As Curtis argues, "[Johnson] saw [the war] as a game or wrestling match in which he would make Ho Chi Minh cry 'uncle.'"

In the quotation in the following sentence, the artist Gauguin's name is misspelled. The bracketed word *sic*, which means "so," tells readers that the person being quoted — not the writer — made the mistake.

> One admirer wrote, "She was the most striking woman I'd ever seen — a sort of wonderful combination of Mia Farrow and one of Gaugin's [sic] Polynesian nymphs."

Brackets may be used to enclose the phonetic transcript of a word:

> He attributed the light to the phenomenon called gegenschein [gā-gen-shin?].

6.8 Slash

Slash (/) is used to separate two alternative terms (good/evil, East/West, aged/young), to separate the parts of fractions (½, 3⅖), and to mark line divisions in poetry within text. If more than one line is run into the text, a slash is used, with equal space on either side, to mark the end of one line and the beginning of another. For example,

> Andrew Marvell's praise of John Milton, "Thou hast not missed one thought that could be fit, / And all that was improper dost omit" ("On Paradise Lost"), might well serve as our motto.

> In "Sonnet 29", the persona states, "For thy sweet love rememb'red such wealth brings, / That then I scorn to change my state with kings."

6.9 Period

Period (.) is used at the end of a complete declarative sentence, a moderately

Chapter 6
Punctuation

imperative sentence, and a sentence containing an indirect question.

A comma, not a semicolon, separates an independent clause from a dependent clause or a phrase.

Make sure semicolons are used only between independent clauses or between items in a series.

We all wonder who will win the election.

A period denoting an abbreviation and coming at the end of a sentence may serve also as the closing period of the sentence. If the sentence ends with a question mark or an exclamation point, the abbreviation period is retained:

The meeting adjourned at 5 : 30 P.M.
Was the meeting called for 8 : 00 P.M.?

Periods are omitted at the ends of items in a vertical list or enumeration, unless the items are whole sentences or paragraphs.

The report covers three areas:
1. The securities markets
2. The securities industry
3. The securities industry in the economy

The course has three goals:
1. Emphasis is on the discovery of truth.
2. Emphasis is on the useful.
3. Emphasis is on love of people, especially the altruistic and philanthropic aspects of love.

Periods are omitted at the ends of all the following: ① display headings for chapters, parts, etc.; ② titles of tables; ③ captions of figures, unless the caption consists of more than one sentence; ④ any subheading that is typed on a line by itself; and ⑤ address and date lines in communications, and signatures.

6.10 Question Mark

Question mark (?) is used at the end of a whole sentence containing a query or at the end of a query making up part of sentence:

Would the teacher-transplant idea catch on in countries other than Germany? was the question the finalists were asking.

The question put by the Board was, Would the taxpayers vote another bond issue that

would raise taxes?

The first word of the sentence that asks the question is capitalized, even though it is included in another sentence.

Courtesy disguises as a question such requests as the following, which should end with a period rather than a question mark:

> Will you please submit my request to the appropriate office.

Question in a series may have question marks even when they are not separate sentences.

> I often confronted a difficult choice: should I go to practice? finish my homework? spend time with my friends?

A question mark in parentheses may be used to indicate uncertainty.

> The Italian painter Niccolo dell' Abbate (1512? – 71) assisted in the decorations at Fontainebleau.
>
> The meeting is on Oleonga (?) Street.

Place question mark inside a closing quotation mark if the quoted passage is a question. Place a question mark outside if the quotation ends a sentence that is a question. If a question mark occurs where a comma or period would normally be required, omit the comma or period. Note the use of the question mark and other punctuation marks in the following sentences:

> Whitman asks, "Have you felt so proud to get at the meaning of poems?" (The quoted passage is a question.)
>
> Where does Whitman speak of "the meaning of poems"? (The quotation ends a sentence that is a question.)
>
> "Have you felt so proud to get at the meaning of poems?" Whitman asks. (A comma or period is replaced by the question mark.)

6.11 Exclamation Point

Exclamation point (!) is used to close the sentence that shows surprise or strong emotion: emphatic statements, interjections, and emphatic commands.

> "We shall next be told," exclaims Seneca, "that the first shoemaker was a philosopher!"
>
> What havoc was wrought by hurricane Agnes!
>
> Ouch!

Look out!

Use exclamation points sparingly because they can distract your readers or suggest that you are exaggerating the importance of what you are saying. Do not use them with mild interjections or to suggest sarcasm or criticism. In general, try to create emphasis through diction and sentence structure rather than exclamation points.

6.12 Ellipsis

Ellipsis (...) is used to indicate the omission of a word, phrase, line, paragraph or more from a quoted passage. An ellipsis is made of three ellipsis points which are usually separated from each other and from the text and any contiguous punctuation by a space. Note that whenever you omit words from a quotation, the resulting passage should be grammatically complete and correct.

There are two common methods of using ellipsis points. The first method is to use three ellipsis dots for any omission, regardless of whether it comes in the middle of a sentence or between sentences:

> For instance, consider the rule about ellipses in broken quotations — that when a quoted sentence ends with a period, this period should be printed close up, followed by three dots to show ellipsis ... In my opinion those publishers and journals who have decided to forget about this nicety and now invariably use three dots ... must be congratulated on their common sense.
> (— Eleanor Harman, "A Reconsideration of Manuscript Editing,"
> qtd. in *The Chicago Manual of Style*, 14th ed.: 372)

The second method is preferred by MLA, APA as well as the Chicago Manual of Style. It distinguishes between omissions within a sentence and omissions between sentences.

1. Within a sentence

Three dots indicate an omission within a quoted sentence or fragment of a sentence. Thus the sentence

> Medical thinking, trapped in the theory of astral influences, stressed air as the communicator of disease, ignoring sanitation or visible carriers. (Barbara W. Tuchman, *A Distant Mirror: The Calamitous Fourteenth Century* [1978; New York: Ballantine, 1979] 101-02)

could be shortened to

> Medical thinking ... stressed air as the communicator of disease, ignoring sanitation or visible carriers.

131

Other punctuation may be used on either side of the three ellipsis dots if it helps the sense or better shows what has been omitted.

> To you it is commanded ... that at what time ye hear the sound of the cornet, flute, ... and all kinds of music, ye fall down and worship the golden image ...: and whoso falleth not down and worshippeth shall ... be cast into ... a burning fiery furnace.

2. Between sentences

When the last part of a quoted sentence is omitted and what remains is still grammatically complete, four dots — a period followed by three ellipsis dots — are used to indicate the omission. If the sentence ends with a question mark or an exclamation point, that punctuation replaces the period and is followed by the three ellipsis dots.

> Whether her criticism is valid or not, shall I capitulate to her? ... And shall I be subject to her ridicule the rest of my life! ... I would rather cut off my ears.

Note that there is no space between the period or other terminal punctuation and the preceding word, even though that word does not end the original sentence.

Original text:

> The spirit of our American radicalism is destructive and aimless; it is not loving, it has no ulterior and divine ends; but is destructive only out of hatred and selfishness. On the other side, the conservative party, composed of the most moderate, able, and cultivated part of the population, is timid, and merely defensive of property. It vindicates no right, it aspires to no real good, it brands no crime, it proposes no generous policy, it does not build, nor write, nor cherish the arts, nor foster religion, nor establish schools, not encourage science, nor emancipate the slave, nor befriend the poor, or the Indian, or the immigrant. From neither party, when in power, has the world any benefit to expect in science, art, or humanity, at all commensurate with the resources of the nation. (Emerson, "Politics")

With ellipses:

> The spirit of our American radicalism is destructive and aimless ... the conservative party ... is timid, and merely defensive of property.
>
> American radicalism ... the conservative party ... From neither party ... has the world any benefit ...

If the beginning of the opening sentence of a quotation is deleted, ellipsis dots are usually not necessary and are ordinarily omitted:

> the conservative party ... is timid, and merely defensive of property ...

In a quotation from a modern work, the first word of a sentence following four

Chapter 6
Punctuation

dots may be capitalized even though it is not the first word of the sentence in the original:

> The spirit of our American radicalism is destructive. ... The conservative party ...

But in scholarly works usually and in legal works and textual criticism always, an original lowercase letter following four dots either should not be capitalized or should be capitalized in brackets:

> The spirit of our American radicalism is destructive. ... [T]he conservative party ...

The omission of one full line or several consecutive lines of verse is indicated by one line of dots approximately the length of the line above it (or of the missing line, if that is determinable.)

> I will arise and go now, and go to Innisfree,
> ....
> And live alone in the bee-loud glade.
>
> (W. B. Yeats, *The Lake Isle of Innisfree*)

Unlike APA and the Chicago Manual of Style, MLA requires you to place square brackets around ellipsis points that you add. Leave a space before the second and third periods but no space before the first or after the third.

> The spirit of our American radicalism is destructive and aimless. [...] [T] he conservative party [...] is timid, and merely defensive of property.

If a parenthetical reference follows the ellipsis at the end of your sentence, leave a space before the parenthetical reference, and follow the closing parenthesis immediately with the sentence period.

> In surveying various responses to plagues in the Middle Ages, Barbara W. Tuchman writes, "Medical thinking, trapped in the theory of astral influences, stressed air as the communicator of disease [...]" (101-102).

When omitting a full line or several consecutive lines, position the line of dots within the brackets.

> I will arise and go now, and go to Innisfree,
> [........................]
> And live alone in the bee-loud glade.
>
> (W. B. Yeats, *The Lake Isle of Innisfree*)

Note that you should be consistent in using square brackets if you choose MLA style.

I. **Insert a comma in any of the following sentence where necessary.**

1. "The public be damned" William Henry Vanderbilt was reported to have said. "I'm working for my stockholders."
2. Joseph Epstein admits "I prefer not to be thought vulgar in any wise."
3. Who remarked that "youth is wasted on the young"?
4. "Neat people are lazier and meaner than sloppy people" according to Suzanne Britt.
5. "Who shall decide when doctors disagree?" asked Alexander Pope.

II. **Revise the following sentences to romove the misuse of semicolons.**

1. The new system would encourage high school students to take more academic courses; thus strengthening college preparation.
2. We accept the following forms of payment; cash, check, or credit card.
3. If the North had followed up its victory at Gettysburg more vigorously; the Civil War might have ended sooner.
4. He left a large estate; which was used to endow a scholarship fund.
5. Our uniforms were unbelievably dingy; stained from being splattered with food and often torn here and there.
6. Verbal scores have decreased more than 54 points; while math scores have decreased more than 36.

III. **Revise the following sentences, using quotation marks appropriately to signal titles, definitions, irony, or coinages.**

1. Kowinski uses the term mallarise to mean physical and psychological disturbances caused by mall contact.
2. In Flannery O'Connor's sort story Revelation, colors symbolize passion, violence, sadness, and even God.
3. The little that is known about gorillas certainly makes you want to know more, writes Alan. Moorehead in his essay A Most Forgiving Ape.
4. The fun of surgery begins before the operation ever takes place.
5. Wolfe's article Radical Chic satirized wealthy liberals.

6. Big Bill, the first section of Dos Passos's *U.S.A.*, opens with a birth.
7. Amy Lowell challenges social conformity in her poem Patterns.
8. Pink Floyd's song Time depicts the impact of technology on society.
9. My dictionary defines isolation as the quality or state of being alone.
10. In the episode Driven to Extremes, 48 hours takes a humorous look at driving in New York City.

IV. **Revise the following sentences, deleting quotation marks used inappropriately, moving those placed incorrectly, and using more formal language in place of slang expressions in quotation marks.**

1. In Herman Melville's "Bartleby the Scrivener", Bartleby states "time and again", "I would prefer not to."
2. The grandmother in O'Connor's story shows she is still misguided when she says, "You've got good blood! I know you wouldn't shoot a lady"!
3. What is Hawthorne telling the readers in "Rappaccini's Daughter?"
4. You could hear the elation in her voice when she said, "We did it".
5. This "typical American" is Ruby Turpin, who in the course of the story receives a "message" that brings about a "change" in her life.
6. Being "overweight" is a problem because "excess pounds" are hard to lose and can be "dangerous" to a person's health.
7. One of Jackson's least-known stories is "Janice;" this story, like many of her others, leaves the reader shocked.
8. In his article "The Death of Broadway", Thomas M. Disch writes that "choreographers are, literally, a dying breed[1]".
9. "Know thyself — " this is the quest of the main characters in both Ibsen's *Peer Gynt* and Lewis's *Till We Have Faces*.
10. One thought flashed through my mind as I finished " *In Search of Our Mothers' Gardens:*" I want to read more of this writer's work.

V. **Revise the following sentences using parentheses and brackets correctly.**

1. She was in fourth grade or was it third? when she became blind.
2. One incident of cruelty was brought to public attention by the Animal Liberation Front ALF.
3. During my research, I found that a flat-rate income tax a single-rate tax with

no deductions has its problems.
4. The leaflet urged voters to "defend the rights that are represented by the Statute sic of Liberty."
5. Many researchers used the Massachusetts Multiphasic Personal Inventory the MMPI for hypnotizability studies.
6. Some of the alternatives suggested include 1 tissue cultures, 2 mechanical models, 3 in vitro techniques, and 4 mathematical and electrical models.

VI. Supply commas, periods, question marks, and exclamation points where they are necessary. Try to place punctuation correctly in relation to quotation marks.

1. "Did you know the ending would turn out that way" asked Dr Fisher
2. "No I didn't" she replied
3. The doctor asked her what other movies she had seen lately
4. "Oh not many" she said "Have you seen anything like this before"
5. "What makes you ask that" he replied
6. "Do you know who said 'Movies are getting better'" she asked
7. "Who was it that used to ask 'Why not try a good movie tonight'"
8. "Watch out" he shouted suddenly as they attempted to cross the street in front of the theatre
9. "Wasn't that Mr Wells in his MG Wow That was too close for comfort"
10. "I wonder" he observed "when the streets will ever be safe for pedestrians"

VII. Punctuate the following passage.

an experienced writer works partly by habit, partly by improvising habits vary the testimony in the three volumes of *writers at work* shows a surprising diversity in the ways professional writers incubate ideas. some cant write at all until they have a clear strong conception of what they want to say others have to write in order to find an idea or a plot some make elaborate plans before they begin to write others work out the structure as they go along some write a first draft at top speed paying no conscious attention to matters of sentence structure word choice or punctuation others proceed with the greatest care and deliberation intent on perfecting one sentence before going to the next evidently there is no one method for writing well what works for one writer doesnt work for another the good route for one is anothers dead end but everyone has to find a route and it is altogether likely that for you one way will prove

Chapter 6
Punctuation

easier going than another so experiment try out different approaches settle on the habits of composing that you find most congenial that seem to work best for you most of the time. All the evidence suggests that finding your own characteristic way of handling writing projects will increase both your confidence and your competence. and however successful you are in finding your way you will still have plenty of scope for improvising, for no two writing projects are exactly alike.

Chapter 7
Documentation (1): Modern Language Association (MLA) Style

When you write a research paper, it is important that you credit the scholars and critics who have contributed to your ideas. Using citations and bibliographies in conformity with a certain style is the scholarly method to discharge this important responsibility. It also allows others to access or retrieve this material. When instructors ask you to write in a certain style, for instance, in MLA style, they do not mean writing style. They are referring to the uniformed system of citations in text and reference format established and used by the Modern Language Association in all of the books and journals that it publishes.

Currently, three major styles are usually used to help format citations and bibliographies for most academic papers and research in the humanities, social sciences, and some scientific disciplines: The Modern Language Association (MLA) Style, American Psychological Association (APA) style, and the Chicago Manual style.

The MLA Style is widely used for identifying research sources, which concerns itself with the mechanics of writing, such as punctuation, quotation, and documentation of sources and has been largely adopted by schools, academic departments, and instructors for nearly half a century. Its guidelines are currently used by over 125 scholarly and literary journals, newsletters, and magazines; by hundreds of smaller periodicals; and by many university and commercial presses. MLA style is commonly followed not only in the United States but in Canada and other countries as well; a Chinese translation was published in 1990.

The MLA style requires three methods of acknowledging sources: ① parenthetical citation in the text, ② full documentation in Works Cited, and ③ information notes (either footnotes or endnotes) if needed. Whatever cited in text or mentioned in the content notes must have its correspondence in the Works Cited page(s).

Chapter 7
Documentation (1): Modern Language Association (MLA) Style

7.1　MLA Parenthetical Citation

When you cite a source, whether in the form of direct quotation, paraphrase, or summary, include within the text enough information to identify the source, but no more than necessary. Most parenthetical citations include the name of the author and the page number, without an intervening comma or a *p.*, *pp.* or *pg.* before the page number.

7.1.1　Placement and Punctuation of Citation

The following are the guidelines for parenthetical citations.

(1) Place a parenthetical citation as near as possible to the material without disrupting the flow of the sentence.

(2) When materials from one source and the same page numbers are to be used throughout a paragraph, use one citation at the end of the paragraph rather than a citation at the end of each sentence.

(3) Parenthetical citations usually appear after the closing quotation mark and before the final punctuation mark of the sentence. But in quotes of four or more lines of prose or two or more lines of poetry they are presented as block, or set-off, quotes: that is, they are indented (usually ten spaces) and use no quotation marks. In such cases, place the parenthetical citation after the final punctuation mark.

Here are examples to show the placement and punctuation of parenthetical documentation.

When the author's name appears in the introduction to the material, you need not repeat the name within parentheses.

> Tannen argues that "men and women have different assumptions about the place of talk in relationships" (85).

> "Men and women have different assumptions about the place of talk in relationships," according to Tannen (85).

> What changes in behavior could result from the assumption that, as Tannen puts it, "men and women have different assumptions about the place of talk in relationships" (85)?

If confusion might result about the distinction between your own conclusions and an idea from a source, place the parenthetical reference within a sentence, generally at the end of a clause or phrase.

> Understanding that "men and women have different assumptions about the place of talk in

relationships" (Tannen 85) might help teachers understand their students' comments.

For an ellipsis at the end of a sentence, the parenthetical reference follows three points indicating the omission and precedes the period.

>Schele and Freidel explain that for the Mayas "the Underworld was sometimes called Xibalba ..." (66).

A parenthetical reference at the end of a long, block, or set-off, quotation follows a period and a space.

>According to Schele and Freidel, the Maya represented each point of the compass with a different color.
>
>>East was red and the most important direction since it was where the sun was born. North, sometimes called the "side of heaven," was white and the direction from which the cooling rains of winter came ... West, the leaving or dying place of the sun, was black. South was yellow. (66)

7.1.2 Basic Rules for Print and Electronic Sources

The MLA system of parenthetical citations, which depends heavily on authors' names and page numbers, was created in the early 1980s with print sources in mind. Because some of today's electronic sources have unclear authorship and lack page numbers, they present a special challenge. Nevertheless, the basic rules are the same for both print and electronic sources.

7.1.2.1 Author Named in a Signal Phrase

Introduce the material being cited with a signal phrase that includes the author's name. In addition to preparing readers for the source, the signal phrase will allow you to keep the parenthetical citation brief.

>Christine Haughney reports that shortly after Japan made it illegal to use a handheld phone while driving, "accidents caused by using the phones dropped by 75 percent" (A8).

Notice that the period follows the parenthetical citation. When a quotation ends with a question mark or an exclamation point, leave the end punctuation inside the quotation mark and add a period after the parentheses:

>Johnson was reasonable to raise the question, "What in effect is our true image, our real likeness?" (35).

Chapter 7
Documentation (1): Modern Language Association (MLA) Style

7.1.2.2 Author Named in Parentheses

When you do not name the author in the text, put the author's last name in parentheses along with the page number, without separating them with a comma.

> Most states do not keep adequate records on the number of times cell phones are a factor in accidents; as of December 2000, only ten states were trying to keep such records (Sundeen 2).

7.1.2.3 Author Unknown

For a work listed only by title in your list of works cited, if you do not use the complete title in a signal phrase, use the title in parentheses, shortening it to two or three words. Titles of books are underlined or italicized (*Old Man and the Sea*); titles of articles and other short works are put in quotation marks ("Today's Marketplace"). Your abbreviated title must include the word by which the title is alphabetized in your list. You would not want to abbreviate the title "Today's Marketplace" to "Marketplace", because the entry should be alphabetized by "Today".

> "Hype," by one analysis, is "an artificially engendered atmosphere of hysteria" ("Today's Marketplace" 51).

> As of 2001, at least three hundred towns and municipalities had considered legislation regulating use of cell phones while driving ("Lawmakers" 2).

CAUTION: Before assuming that a Web source has no author, do some detective work. Often the author's name is available but is hard to find. For example, it may appear at the end of the source, in tiny print. Or it may appear on another page of the site, such as the home page.

NOTE: If a source has no author and is sponsored by a corporate entity, such as an organization or a government agency, name the corporate entity as the author (see "Corporate Author" in 7.1.3.4).

7.1.2.4 Page Number Unknown

Give just the author's name in the parenthetical citation when the cited work lacks page numbers, as is the case with many Web sources.

> The California Highway Patrol opposes restrictions on the use of phones while driving,

141

claiming that distracted drivers can already be prosecuted (Jacobs).

When the pages of a Web source are stable (as in PDF files), however, supply a page number in your parenthetical citation.

NOTE: If a Web source uses paragraph or section numbers or screen number, give the abbreviation "par." or "sec." or just "screen" for screen in the parentheses: (Smith, par. 4).

7.1.3 Variations on the Basic Rules

The following are the MLA guidelines for handling a variety of situations not covered by the basic rules just given. Again, these rules on parenthetical citations are the same for both traditional print sources and electronic sources.

7.1.3.1 Two or More Titles by the Same Author

If your list of works cited includes two or more titles by the same author, mention the title of the work in the signal phrase or include a shortened version of the title in the parentheses.

> On December 6, 2000, reporter Jamie Stockwell wrote that distracted driver Jason Jones had been charged with "two counts of vehicular manslaughter ... in the deaths of John and Carole Hall" ("Phone" B1). The next day Stockwell reported the judge's ruling: Jones "was convicted of negligent driving and fined $500, the maximum penalty allowed" ("Man" B4).

Titles of articles and other short works are placed in quotation marks; titles of books are underlined or italicized.

> Shaughnessy points out that "the beginning writer does not know how writers behave" (<u>Errors</u> 79).

> Teachers applauded Shaughnessy's assertion that "teaching them [beginning writers] to write well is not only suitable but challenging work for those who would be teachers and scholars in a democracy" ("Driving In" 68).

In the rare case when both the author's name and a short title must be given in parentheses, separate them with a comma.

> According to police reports, there were no skid marks indicating that the distracted driver who killed John and Carole Hall had even tried to stop (Stockwell, "Man" B4).

7.1.3.2 Two or Three Authors

Name the authors in the signal phrase, as in the following example:

Chapter 7
Documentation (1): Modern Language Association (MLA) Style

Redelmeier and Tibshirani found that "the risk of a collision when using a cellular telephone was four times higher than the risk when a cellular telephone was not being used" (453).

or include their last names in the parenthetical reference:

(Redelmeier and Tibshirani 453)

When three authors are named in the parentheses, separate the names with commas:

(Alton, Davies, and Rice 56)

7.1.3.3 Four or More Authors

Name all of the authors or include only the first author's name followed by "et al." Make sure that your citation matches the entry in the list of works cited.

> The study was extended for two years, and only after results were reviewed by an independent panel did the researchers publish their findings (Blaine et al. 35).

7.1.3.4 Corporate Author

When the author is a corporation or an organization, name the corporate author (if the name is long, give a shortened form) either in the signal phrase or in the parentheses. A page number should be included.

> In fact, one of the leading foundations in the field of higher education supports the recent proposals for community-run public schools (Carnegie Corporation 45).

> Researchers at the Harvard Center for Risk Analysis found that the risks of driving while phoning were small compared with other driving risks (3-4).

In the list of works cited, the Harvard Center for Risk Analysis is treated as the author for the latter case and alphabetized under *H*.

7.1.3.5 Authors with the Same Last Name

If your list of works cited includes works by authors with the same last name, include the author's first name in a signal phrase or first initial in the parentheses.

> Estimates of the number of accidents caused by distracted drivers vary because little evidence is being collected (D. Smith 7).

If the first initials are identical, spell out the first names.

When the two authors are father and son, with the son designated as Jr., include the designation Jr. in the reference, preceded by a comma.

> That book chronicles visionary experiences in early modern Spain (Christian, Jr.).

7.1.3.6 Indirect Sources (Sources Quoted in Other Sources)

When a writer's or a speaker's words are quoted in an other source, begin the citation with the abbreviation "qtd. in". The author and title of the source you actually consulted appear in the list of works cited.

> According to Richard Retting, "As the comforts of home and the efficiency of the office creep into the automobile, it is becoming increasingly attractive as a work space" (qtd. in Kilgannon A23).

> "To be able to see yourself teaching is worth hours of other types of observation" (Bloom, qtd. in Britten and Sow 25).

NOTE: you should use indirect sources as little as possible. Relying too much on the secondary sources will undermine the credibility of your paper.

7.1.3.7 Encyclopedia or Dictionary

Unless an encyclopedia or a dictionary has an author, it will be alphabetized in the list of works cited under the word or entry that you consulted — not under the title of the reference work itself. Either in your text or in your parenthetical reference, mention the word or the entry. No page number is required, since readers can easily look up the word or entry.

> The word crocodile has a surprisingly complex etymology (O.E.D. "Crocodile").

7.1.3.8 Multivolume Work

If your paper cites more than one volume of a multivolume work, indicate which volume you are referring to, followed by a colon and the page number in the parentheses.

> Terman's studies of gifted children reveal a pattern of accelerated language acquisition (2: 279).

If your paper cites only one volume of a multivolume work, you will include the volume number in the list of works cited and will not need to include it in the parentheses.

Chapter 7
Documentation (1): Modern Language Association (MLA) Style

7.1.3.9 Two or More Works (Multiple Citations)

To cite more than one source, separate the citations with a semicolon.

> The dangers of mountain lions to humans have been well documented (Rychnovsky 40; Seidensticker 114; Williams 30).

Multiple citations can be distracting, so you should not overuse the technique. If you want to alert readers to several sources that discuss a particular topic, consider using an information note instead.

7.1.3.10 An Entire Work

To cite an entire work, use the author's name in a signal phrase or a parenthetical reference. There is of course no need to use a page number.

> Slade's revision of Form and Style incorporates changes made in the 1995 edition of the MLA Handbook.

7.1.3.11 Work in an Anthology

Put the name of the author of the work (not the editor of the anthology) in the signal phrase or the parentheses.

> In Susan Glaspell's "A Jury of Her Peers," Mrs. Hale describes both a style of quilting and a murder weapon when she utters the last words of the story: "We call it — knot it, Mr. Henderson" (302).

7.1.3.12 Legal Source

For well-known historical documents, such as articles of the United States Constitution, and for laws in the United States Code, provide a parenthetical citation in the text: (US Const., art. 1, sec. 2) or (12 USC 3412, 2000). There is no need to provide a works cited entry.

7.1.4 Literary Work and Sacred Text

Literary works and sacred texts are usually available in a variety of editions. Your list of works cited will specify which edition you are using, and your in-text citation will usually consist of a page number from the edition you consulted. However, MLA suggests that when possible you should give enough information —

such as book parts, play divisions, or line numbers — so that readers can locate the cited passage in any edition of the work. Note that in your paper you will include the author's name the first time you cite a work, but there is no need to repeat the name later in your paper — as long as your context makes clear what work you are citing.

7.1.4.1 Literary Work without Part or Line Number

Many literary works, such as most short stories and many novels and plays, do not have parts or line numbers that you can refer to. In such cases, simply cite the page number.

> At the end of Kate Chopin's "The Story of an Hour," Mrs. Mallard drops dead upon learning that her husband is alive. In the final irony of the story, doctors report that she has died of a "joy that kills" (25).

7.1.4.2 Verse Play and Poem

For verse plays, MLA recommends omitting page numbers in the parenthetical citation. Instead, include act, scene, and line numbers that can be located in any edition of the work. Use arabic numerals, and separate the numbers with periods.

> In his famous advice to players, Shakespeare's Hamlet defines the purpose of theater, "whose end, both at the first and now, was and is, to hold, as 'twere, the mirror up to nature" (3.2.21-23).

For a poem, cite the part (if there are a number of parts) and the line numbers, separated by a period.

> When Homer's Odysseus comes to the hall of Circe, he finds his men "mild/in her soft spell, fed on her drug of evil" (10.209-11).

For poems that are not divided into parts, use line numbers. For a first reference, use the word "lines": (lines 5-8). Thereafter use just the numbers: (12-13).

7.1.4.3 Novel with Numbered Divisions

When a novel has numbered divisions, put the page number first, followed by a semicolon, and then indicate the book, part, or chapter in which the passage may be found. Use abbreviations such as "bk." and "ch."

> One of Kingsolver's narrators, teenager Rachel, pushes her vocabulary beyond its limits. For example, Rachel complains that being forced to live in the Congo with her missionary

Chapter 7
Documentation (1): Modern Language Association (MLA) Style

family is "a sheer tapestry of justice" because her chances of finding a boyfriend are "dull and void" (117; bk. 2, ch. 10).

7.1.4.4 Sacred Text

When citing a sacred text such as the Bible or the Koran, name the edition you are using in your works cited entry. In your parenthetical citation, give the book, chapter, and verse (or their equivalent), separated by periods. Common abbreviations for books of the Bible are acceptable (e.g. Gen. for Genesis; Matt. for Matthew).

> Consider the words of Solomon: "If your enemies are hungry, give them food to eat. If they are thirsty, give them water to drink" (Holy Bible, Prov. 25.21).

7.2 Information Note

Researchers may use information notes to provide additional material that might interrupt the flow of the paper yet is important enough to include or to refer readers to any sources not discussed in the paper. Information notes may be either footnotes or endnotes. Note that only *one* sentence is used in a note citation, i.e., only *one* period or full stop is used at the end of any note citation.

First footnote or endnote example:

> [2] G. Wayne Miller, <u>King of Hearts: The True Story of the Maverick Who Pioneered Open Heart Surgery</u> (New York: Times, 2000) 245.

Bibliography example:

> Miller, G. Wayne. <u>King of Hearts: The True Story of the Maverick Who Pioneered Open Heart Surgery</u>. New York: Times, 2000.

7.2.1 Use of *ibid.* and *op. cit.*

In his *MLA Handbook for Writers of Research Papers* (6th ed.), Gibaldi does NOT recommend the use of such old-fashioned abbreviations as *ibid.* (from the Latin *ibidem* meaning "in the same place") and *op. cit.* (from the Latin *opere citato* meaning "in the work cited").

For footnote or endnote citations, if you should see the term *ibid.* being used, it just means that the citation is for the second mention of the same work with no intervening entries:

[3] Ibid. 12-15.

More commonly, author and page number(s) are now used instead of *ibid.*, e.g.:

[3] Miller 12-15.

For second or later mention of the same work with intervening entries, where previously *op. cit.* was used, now only the author and page number(s) are used:

[5] Miller 198.

7.2.2 Use of Superscript

Tab or indent footnote and endnote entries 5 spaces from the left margin. Leave one space between the superscript number and the entry. Do not indent second and subsequent lines. Double-space between entries (This is optional. You may ask your instructors for their preference). Number footnotes and endnotes consecutively using a superscript, e.g., [7].

For endnotes, you must use the same superscript number (as in your text) at the beginning of each entry in your *Endnotes* list. Start your list of *Endnotes* on a new page at the end of your essay. Remember to put the *Endnotes* page before the *Bibliography*, or *Works Cited*, or *References* page.

Example in text:

An interesting reference was made to the picking of corn on the Sabbath.[8]

Example of footnote citation:

[8] Matthew 12:1-8.

List under *Works Cited*:

The New Jerusalem Bible: Reader's Edition. New York: Doubleday, 1990.

Do not confuse footnote and endnote citations with explanatory notes that some authors refer to as "endnotes." These notes are not considered to be citations but are used to add comments, explanations, or additional information relating to specific passages in the text. Because long explanatory notes can be distracting to readers, most academic style guidelines (including MLA and APA) recommend limited use of footnotes/endnotes. An exception is the note-bibliography system of Chicago documentary style, which relies on notes for all citations as well as explanatory notes. But even in that case, extensive discursive notes are discouraged. Proper use of notes

Chapter 7
Documentation (1): Modern Language Association (MLA) Style

would only include the following.

(1) Evaluative bibliographic comments, for example:

<blockquote>

¹ See Blackmur, especially chapters three and four, for an insightful analysis of this trend.

² On the problems related to repressed memory recovery, see Wollens pp. 120–35; for a contrasting view, see Pyle.

</blockquote>

(2) Occasional explanatory notes or other brief additional information that would seem digressive if included in the main text but might be interesting to readers, for example:

<blockquote>

³ In a 1998 interview, she reiterated this point even more strongly: "I am an artist, not a politician!" (Weller 124).

</blockquote>

7.3 List of Works Cited

Works Cited is sometimes referred to as References. Both terms mean the same thing — an alphabetical list of works you have cited or made reference to in the text. The title "Works Cited" is generally used when citing sources using MLA style, while "References" is used when citing sources using APA style.

Bibliography, however, is different from Works Cited and References. In a *Bibliography* you may list all the materials you have consulted in preparing your essay even though you did not cite them in the text at all.

Entries in Works Cited, References, or Bibliography are all put in alphabetical order by last names of authors, editors, translators, etc. or by first words of titles when no author's name found. In deciding whether to place a translator's or editor's name first rather than the author's name, for example, you need to know the purpose for which you will cite the work in your paper. If your text will refer primarily to the decisions made by a translator, the translator's name should appear first in the entry. If, on the other hand, you plan to discuss only the original work, the author's name should appear first and the name of the translator should follow the title.

When an entry begins with a title, if the first word of the title is "The", "A", or "An", and the word is being used as an article, e.g., in the title: *The Little Book of Irish Clans*, the entry is placed under "Little" and the article "The" is ignored. In the title *A Is for Apple*, however, the entry is placed under A because A is used as a noun, not as an article.

Sometimes the article "The" is used as part of the name of a company or magazine or journal for emphasis, e.g., *The Champ*, or *The Sports Network*. For

Internet sites, use the URL (Uniform Resource Locator or electronic address) as a guide. If "The Yellow Pages" is used in the URL, treat "The" as part of the title, and list "The Yellow Pages" alphabetically under "The". If "Edge" and not "The Edge" is used in the URL, list the magazine title "The Edge" under "Edge" and treat "The" as an article and ignore it.

Where appropriate, a cross reference may be used to direct readers to the proper location, e.g. *Yellow Pages, The.* See *The Yellow Pages.*

Remember:

(1) Do not number entries.

(2) Do not list citations separately by categories. All references are placed in one alphabetical list by first words of citations, regardless of where citations come from.

(3) Begin on a new page. Start on the second line from the top [or 1″ (2.54 centimeters) down from the top of the paper], center, and type one of the following titles: Works Cited, References, or Bibliography. Double space after the title. List all entries in alphabetical order by the first word, taking into consideration the rules governing titles that begin with articles.

(4) Begin the first line of each entry flush at the left margin. Keep typing until you run out of room at the end of the line. Indent 5 spaces for second and subsequent lines of the same entry. Double-space all lines, both within and between entries. (This is a guideline adapted from the *MLA Handbook*. You are advised to follow the style preferred by your instructor. To save space, illustrations of the entries of the works cited would all be single-spaced.)

(5) When listing an online source originally printed in a book, journal, or other printed format, use the general guidelines you would use to cite the printed form, followed by the online citation.

(6) Web sites should have author (if given), title (underlined), date of publication or update (if available), originator (if available), date of access, and the URL.

(7) Articles from library subscription services (databases) are cited just like the print version with the addition of the name of the database underlined, the name of the service, the library, the date of access, and URL if known.

7.3.1 Author

Alphabetize entries in the list of works cited by authors' last names (if a work

Chapter 7
Documentation (1): Modern Language Association (MLA) Style

has no author, alphabetize it by its title). The author's name is important because citations in the text of the paper refer to it and readers will be looking for it at the beginning of an entry in the alphabetized list. For example, if you cite the name in text: According to Matt Sundeen, ... you will begin the entry in the works cited list:

> Sundeen, Matt.

7.3.1.1 Single Author

For a work with one author, begin the entry with the author's last name, followed by a comma; then give the author's first name, followed by a period.

> Tannen, Deborah.

7.3.1.2 Multiple Authors

For works with two or three authors, name the authors in the order in which they are listed in the source. Reverse the name of only the first author.

> Walker, Janice R., and Todd Taylor.

> Wilmut, Ian, Keith Campbell, and Colin Tudge.

For a work with four or more authors, either name all of the authors or name the first author, followed by "et al." (See also 7.1.3.)

> Sloan, Frank A., Emily M. Stout, Kathryn Whetten-Goldstein, and Lan Liang.

or

> Sloan, Frank A., et al.

7.3.1.3 Corporate Author

When the author of a print document or Web site is a corporation, a government agency, or some other organization, begin your entry with the name of the group. (See also 7.1.3.)

> First Union.

> United States Census Bureau.

> American Automobile Association.

When the corporate author is also the publisher, the name is not repeated.

> American Museum of Natural History. <u>Annual Report, 1993-1994</u>. New York, 1995.

7.3.1.4　Unknown Author

When the author of a work is unknown, begin with the work's title (see also 7.1.2). Titles of articles and other short works, such as brief documents from Web sites, are put in quotation marks. Titles of books and Web sites are underlined. (See also 5.3, 5.9.3, 5.9.4.) Before concluding that the author of a Web source is unknown, check carefully. Also remember that an organization may be the author.

7.3.1.5　Two or More Works by the Same Author

If your list of works cited includes two or more works by the same author, use the author's name only for the first entry. For other entries use three hyphens followed by a period. The three hyphens must stand for exactly the same name or names as in the first entry. List the titles in alphabetical order.

>　　Atwood, Margaret. <u>Alias Grace: A Novel</u>. New York: Doubleday, 1996.
>
>　　———. <u>The Robber Bride</u>. New York: Doubleday, 1993.

7.3.2　Books

For most books, arrange the information into three units, each followed by a period and one space:

(1) The author's name

(2) The title and subtitle, underlined

(3) The place of publication, the publisher, and the date

>　　Tan, Amy. <u>The Bonesetter's Daughter</u>. New York: Putnam, 2001.

Take the information about the book from its title page and copyright page. Use a short form of the publisher's name; omit terms such as *Press*, *Inc.*, and *Co.* except the university presses (Harvard UP, for example). If the copyright page lists more than one date, use the most recent one.

7.3.2.1　Author with an Editor

Begin with the author and the title, followed by the name of the editor. The abbreviation "Ed." means "Edited by," so it is the same for one or multiple editors.

>　　Kerouac, Jack. <u>Atop an Underwood</u>. Ed. Paul Marion. New York: Penguin, 2000.

Chapter 7
Documentation (1): Modern Language Association (MLA) Style

7.3.2.2 Author with a Translator

Begin with the name of the author. After the title, write "Trans." for "Translated by" and the name of the translator.

> Allende, Isabel. <u>Daughter of Fortune</u>. Trans. Margaret Sayers Peden. New York: Harper, 2000.

If the translation rather than the text is the main concern, the translator would come first.

> Lattimore, Richard, trans. <u>The Iliad</u>, by Homer. Chicago: Univ. of Chicago Press, 1962.

7.3.2.3 Editor

An entry for a work with an editor is similar to that for a work with an author except that the name is followed by a comma and the abbreviation "ed." for "editor" or "eds." for "editors".

> Craig, Patricia, ed. <u>The Oxford Book of Travel Stories</u>. Oxford: Oxford UP, 1996.

> Steinbeck, Elaine, and Robert Wallsten, eds. <u>Steinbeck: A Life in Letters</u>. New York: Viking, 1975.

7.3.2.4 Work in an Anthology

Give the elements in this order:

(1) The name of the author of the selection (not the name of the editor of the anthology);

(2) The title of the selection in quotation marks;

(3) The title of the anthology underlined;

(4) The name of the editor, preceded by "Ed.";

(5) Publication information;

(6) The pages on which the selection appears.

> Desai, Anita. "Scholar and Gypsy." <u>The Oxford Book of Travel Stories</u>. Ed. Patricia Craig. Oxford: Oxford UP, 1996. 251–73.

When two or more works from the same anthology or collection are cited, they are cross-referenced to the editor of the larger work. Give only the editor's surname after the name of the author and title of the work. No punctuation is needed between the editor's name and the page numbers for the cited work. Omit *ed.* or other

153

descriptive words in the cross-reference.

> Craig, Patricia, ed. The Oxford Book of Travel Stories. Oxford: Oxford UP, 1996.
> Desai, Anita. "Scholar and Gypsy." Craig 251-73.
> Malouf, David. "The Kyogle Line." Craig 390-96.

Alphabetize the entry for the anthology under the name of its editor (Craig); alphabetize the entries for the selections under the names of the authors (Desai, Malouf). The in-text citation for these would be: (Desai 256); (Malouf 390-91).

7.3.2.5 Edition Other Than the First

If you are citing an edition other than the first, include the number of the edition after the title (or after the names of any translators or editors that appear after the title): 2nd ed., 3rd ed., and so on.

> Auletta, Ken. The Underclass. 2nd ed. Woodstock, NY: Overlook, 2000.

7.3.2.6 Multivolume Work

Include the total number of volumes before the city and publisher, using the abbreviation "vols."

> Conway, Jill Ker, ed. Written by Herself. 2 vols. New York: Random, 1996.

If your paper cites only one of the volumes, give the volume number before the city and publisher and give the total number of volumes after the date.

> Conway, Jill Ker, ed. Written by Herself. Vol. 2. New York: Random, 1996. 2 vols.

When each volume has a separate title, you may cite the work without referring to the other volumes or you may include the title of the particular volume along with that of the complete volumes. If the volumes were published over a period of years, give the first and last years.

> Freehling, William W. The Road to Disunion. New York: Oxford UP, 1991.

or

> Freehling, William W. The Road to Disunion. New York: Oxford UP, 1991. Vol. 1 of
>   Secessionists at Bay, 1776-1854. 2 vols. 1991-92.

7.3.2.7 Encyclopedia or Dictionary Entry

When an encyclopedia or a dictionary is well known, simply list the author of

Chapter 7
Documentation (1): Modern Language Association (MLA) Style

the entry (if there is one), the title of the entry, the title of the reference work, the edition number (if any), and the date of the edition.

> Posner, Rebecca. "Romance Languages." The New Encyclopaedia Britannica: Macropaedia. 15th ed. 1987.
>
> "Sonata." The American Heritage Dictionary of the English Language. 4th ed. 2000.

Volume and page numbers are not necessary because the entries in the source are arranged alphabetically and therefore are easy to locate.

If a reference work is not well known, provide full publication information as well.

> Brasingly, C. Reginald. "Birth Order." Encyclopedia of Psychology. Ed. Raymond J. Corsini. New York: Wiley, 1984.

7.3.2.8 Foreword, Introduction, Preface, or Afterword

Begin with the author of the foreword or other book part, followed by the name of that part. Then give the title of the book; the author of the book, preceded by the word "By"; and the editor of the book (if any). After the publication information, give the page numbers for the part of the book being cited.

> Morris, Jan. Introduction. Letters from the Field, 1925-1975. By Margaret Mead. New York: Perennial-Harper, 2001. xix-xxiii.

If the book part being cited has a title, include it immediately after the author's name.

> Ozick, Cynthia. "Portrait of the Essay as a Warm Body." Introduction. The Best American Essays 1998. Ed. Ozick. Boston: Houghton, 1998. xv-xxi.

7.3.2.9 Book with a Title within Its Title

If the book title contains a title normally underlined, neither underline the internal title nor place it in quotation marks, but underline the punctuation that is part of the longer title (e.g. Doris Lessing's The Four-Gated City: The Summer before the Dark).

> Vanderham, Paul. James Joyce and Censorship: The Trials of Ulysses. New York: New York UP, 1997.

If the title within the title is normally put in quotation marks, retain the quotation marks and underline the entire title.

Faulkner, Dewey R., ed. Twentieth Century Interpretations of "The Pardoner's Tale." Englewood Cliffs: Prentice, 1973.

7.3.2.10 Book in a Series

When the title page indicates that a book is part of a series, give the series title and number before the city of publication.

Malena, Anne. The Dynamics of Identity in Francophone Caribbean Narrative. Francophone Cultures and Lits. Ser. 24. New York: Lang, 1998.

7.3.2.11 Republished Book

After the title of the book, cite the original publication date, followed by the current publication information. If the republished book contains new material, such as an Introduction or Afterword, include information about the new material after the original date.

Hughes, Langston. Black Misery. 1969. Afterword Robert O'Meally. New York: Oxford UP, 2000.

7.3.2.12 Publisher's Imprint

If a book is part of an imprint, a name given to a group of books within a company's publications, the name of the imprint comes first, followed by a hyphen and the name of the publishing company.

Truan, Barry. Acoustic Communication. Westport: Ablex-Greenwood, 2000.

7.3.2.13 Book in a Foreign Language

If you wish to clarify any portion of the entry with an English translation, place it in brackets immediately following the original language version, which should be punctuated and capitalized according to rules for the particular language.

Buendía, Delicidad. Libros de caballerías espa noles [Spanish Novels of Chivalry]. Madrid: Aguilar, 1960.

If you quote from a book written in Chinese, write the author's name in *Pinyin* followed by the Chinese characters and a period. For the title of the book, write it in this order: *Pinyin*, the Chinese characters, and the English translation in parentheses, followed by a period. You do not need to give the Chinese characters for the city in

Chapter 7
Documentation (1): Modern Language Association (MLA) Style

which the book is published and for the name of the publisher.

> Liu Jianbo 刘洊波. <u>Nanfang Shiluo de Shijie: Fu Ke Na Xiaoshuo Yanjiu</u> 南方失落的世界——福克纳小说研究 (The Fallen World in the South: A Study of Faulkner's Novels). Chongqing: Southwest China Normal University Press, 1999.

7.3.3 Magazine and Journal

For articles appearing on consecutive pages, provide the range of pages, such as 121-29 or 298-310. When an article does not appear on consecutive pages, give the number of the first page followed by a plus sign: 32+.

7.3.3.1 Magazine

List the following elements, in order, separated by periods:
(1) The author's name;
(2) The title of the article in quotation marks;
(3) The title of the magazine underlined;
(4) The date and the page numbers separated by a colon.

Abbreviate the names of the months except May, June, and July. If the magazine is issued monthly, give just the month and year.

> Kaplan, Robert D. "History Moving North." <u>Atlantic Monthly</u> Feb. 1997: 21+.

If the magazine is issued weekly, give the exact date.

> Lord, Lewis. "There's Something about Mary Todd." <u>US News and World Report</u> 19 Feb. 2001: 53.

7.3.3.2 Journal Paginated by Volume and by Issue

Many scholarly journals continue page numbers throughout the year instead of beginning each issue with page 1; at the end of the year, the issues are collected in a volume. To find an article, readers need only the volume number, the year (in parentheses), and the page numbers.

> Ryan, Katy. "Revolutionary Suicide in Toni Morrison's Fiction." <u>African American Review</u> 34 (2000): 389-412.

If each issue of the journal begins with page *1*, you need to indicate the number of the issue. After the volume number, put a period and the issue number.

> Wood, Michael. "Broken Dates: Fiction and the Century." <u>Kenyon Review</u> 22.3 (2000): 50

-64.

When a journal numbered by issue rather than by volume, treat the issue number like a volume number.

> Nwezeh, C. E. "The Comparative Approach to Modern African Literature." <u>Yearbook of General and Comparative Literature</u> 28 (1979): 22-30.

7.3.4 Daily Newspaper

Begin with the name of the author, if there is one, followed by the title of the article. Next give the name of the newspaper, the date, and the page number (including the section letter). Use a plus sign "+" after the page number if the article does not appear on consecutive pages.

> Murphy, Sean P. "Decisions on Status of Tribes Draw Fire." <u>Boston Globe</u> 27 Mar. 2001: A2.

If the section is marked with a number rather than a letter, handle the entry as follows:

> Wilford, John Noble. "In a Golden Age of Discovery, Faraway Worlds Beckon." <u>New York Times</u> 9 Feb. 1997, late ed., sec. 1: 1+.

When an edition of the newspaper is specified on the masthead, name the edition after the date and before the page reference (eastern ed., late ed., and so on), as in the example just given.

If the city of publication is not obvious (neither included in the title nor widely known), include it in brackets after the name of the newspaper: <u>City Paper</u> [Washington, DC].

7.3.5 Book or Film Review

Name the reviewer and the title of the review, if any, followed by the words "Rev. of" and the title and author or director of the work reviewed. Add the publication information for the publication in which the review appears.

> Gleick, Elizabeth. "The Burdens of Genius." Rev. of <u>The Last Samurai</u>, by Helen DeWitt. <u>Time</u> 4 Dec. 2000: 171.

> Kienitz, Gail M. Rev. of <u>Tennyson and the Doom of Romanticism</u>, by Herbert F. Tucker. <u>Religion and Literature</u> 24 (Spring 1992): 87-90.

> Denby, David. "On the Battlefield." Rev. of <u>The Hurricane</u>, dir. Norman Jewison. <u>New

Chapter 7
Documentation (1): Modern Language Association (MLA) Style

Yorker 10 Jan. 2000: 90-92.

7.3.6 Electronic Sources

The minimum information for an electronic source includes the author, if any; the title of the section you used, in quotation marks; the title of the entire source, underlined; volume or issue number; year or date of publication (in parentheses); number of pages (if applicable); a description of the medium (CD-ROM, diskette, etc.); the name of the computer network or vendor and, if it is not well known, an address preceded by the word *Available*; the date of electronic publication; if necessary for your purpose, the equipment required to run it; and, in the case of on-line or e-mail materials, the date you accessed the source. You may supply the electronic address or path at the end of the entry. If you cannot locate some of the required information, cite whatever you do have.

Note that when a Web address in a works cited entry must be divided at the end of a line, MLA recommends that you break it after a slash. Do not insert a hyphen.

7.3.6.1 An Entire Website

Give as many of the following elements as apply and as are available:

(1) The name of the author or corporate author (if known);
(2) The title of the site, underlined;
(3) The names of any editors;
(4) The date of publication or last update;
(5) The name of any sponsoring organization;
(6) The date of access, not followed by a period;
(7) The URL in angle brackets (< >), followed by a period.

In the following example, not all items apply.

1. With author

Peterson, Susan Lynn. The Life of Martin Luther. 1999.9 Mar. 2001 <http://pweb.netcom. com/~supeters/luther.htm>.

2. With corporate (group) author

United States. Environmental Protection Agency. Values and Functions of Wetlands. 25 May 1999. 24 Mar. 2001 <http://www.epa.gov-owow/wetlands/facts/fact2.html>.

159

3. Author unknown

Margaret Sanger Papers Project. 18 Oct. 2000. History Dept., New York U. 3 Apr. 2001 <http://www.nyu.edu/projects/sanger/>.

4. With editor

Exploring Ancient World Cultures. Ed. Anthony F. Beavers. 1997. U of Evansville. 12 Mar. 2001 <http://eawc.evansville.edu/index.htm>.

If the site has no title, substitute a description, such as "Home page," for the title. Do not underline the words or put them in quotation marks.

Block, Marylaine. Home page. 5 Mar. 2001. 12 Apr. 2001 <http://www.marylaine.com>.

7.3.6.2 Short Work from a Website

For a short work from a Web site, include as many of the following elements as apply and as are available:

(1) Author's name;
(2) Title of the short work in quotation marks;
(3) Title of the site underlined;
(4) Date of publication or last update;
(5) Sponsor of the site (if not named as the author or given as the title of the site);
(6) Date you accessed the source;
(7) The URL in angle brackets (< >) followed by a period.

Usually at least some of these elements will not apply or will be unavailable. In the following example, no sponsor or date of publication was available. (The date given is the date on which the researcher accessed the source.)

1. With author

Shiva, Vandana. "Bioethics: A Third World Issue." Nativeweb. 15 Sept. 2001. <http://www.nativeweb.org/pages/legal/shiva.html>.

2. Author unknown

"Media Giants." Frontline: The Merchants of Cool. 2001. PBS Online. 7 Mar. 2001 <http://www.pbs.org/wgbh/pages/frontline/shows/cool/giants>.

When the URL for a short work from a Web site is very long, you may give the URL for the home page and indicate the path by which readers can access the source.

160

Chapter 7
Documentation (1): Modern Language Association (MLA) Style

"Obesity Trends among U.S. Adults between 1985 and 2001." <u>Centers for Disease Control and Prevention</u>. 3 Jan. 2003. 17 Feb. 2003 <http://www.cdc.gov>. Path: Health Topics A-Z: Obesity Trends; U.S. Obesity Trends 1985 to 2001.

7.3.6.3 Online Book

When a book or a book-length work such as a play or a long poem is posted on the Web as its own site, give as much publication information as is available, followed by the date of access and the URL.

    Rawlins, Gregory J. E. <u>Moths to the Flame</u>. Cambridge: MIT P, 1996. 3 Apr. 2001 <http://mitpress.mit.edu/e-books/Moths/contents.html>.

If the book-length work is posted on a scholarly Web site, provide information about that site.

    Jacobs, Harriet Ann. <u>Incidents in the Life of a Slave Girl</u>. Boston, 1861. <u>Documenting the American South: The Southern Experience in Nineteenth-Century America</u>. Ed. Ji-Hae Yoon and Natalia Smith. 1998. Academic Affairs Lib., U of North Carolina, Chapel Hill. 14 Mar. 2001 <http://docsouth.unc.edu/jacobs/jacobs.html>.

If what you have cited is a part of an online book, place the part title before the book's title. If the part is a short work such as a poem or an essay, put its title in quotation marks. If the part is an introduction, a preface, or other division of the book, do not use quotation marks.

    Adams, Henry. "Diplomacy." <u>The Education of Henry Adams</u>. Boston: Houghton, 1918. <u>Bartleby.com: Great Books Online</u>. 1999. 17 Feb. 2003 <http://bartleby.com/159/8.html>.

    Bryan, William S., and Robert Rose. Preface. <u>A History of the Pioneer Families of Missouri</u>. St. Louis: Bryan, 1876. <u>University of Missouri Digital Library</u>. 2002. 20 Feb. 2003 <http://digital.library.umsystem.edu/cgi-bin/Ebind2h3/umkc3>.

7.3.6.4 Online Periodical

When citing online articles, follow the guidelines for printed articles, giving whatever information is available in the online source. End the citation with the date of access and the URL.

In some online articles, paragraphs are numbered. For such articles, include the total number of paragraphs in your citation.

1. From an online scholarly journal

Belau, Linda. "Trauma and the Material Signifier." <u>Postmodern Culture</u> 11.2 (2001): 37 pars. 30 Mar. 2001 <http://jefferson.village.virginia.edu/pmc/current.issue/11.2belau.html>.

2. From an online magazine

Morgan, Fiona. "Banning the Bullies." <u>Salon.com</u> 15 Mar. 2001. 2 Apr. 2001 <http://www.salon.com/news/feature/2001/03/15/bullying/index.html>.

3. From an online newspaper

Whillon, Phil. "Ready or Not." <u>Los Angeles Times</u> 2 Dec. 2001. 3 Dec. 2001 <http://www.latimes.com/news/la-foster-special.special>.

7.3.6.5 CD-ROM

Treat a CD-ROM as you would do with any other source, but name the medium before the publication information.

"Pimpernel." <u>The American Heritage Dictionary of the English Language</u>. 4th ed. CD-ROM. Boston: Houghton, 2000.

Wattenberg, Ruth. "Helping Students in the Middle." <u>American Educator</u> 19.4 (1996): 2-18. <u>ERIC</u>. CD-ROM. SilverPlatter. Sept. 1996.

7.3.6.6 E-mail

To cite an e-mail, begin with the writer's name and the subject line. Then write "E-mail to" followed by the name of the recipient. End with the date of the message.

O'Donnell, Patricia. "Re: Interview Questions." E-mail to the author. 15 Mar. 2001.

7.3.7 Multimedia Source

Multimedia sources include visuals (such as works of art), audio works (such as sound recordings), audiovisuals (such as films), and live events (such as the performance of a play).

When citing multimedia sources that you retrieved online, consult the appropriate model in this section and give whatever information is available for the online source; then end the citation with the date of access and the URL.

7.3.7.1 Work of Art

Cite the artist's name, followed by the title of the artwork, usually underlined,

Chapter 7
Documentation (1): Modern Language Association (MLA) Style

and the institution and city in which the artwork can be found. If you want to indicate the work's date, include it after the title. For a work of art you viewed online, end your citation with your date of access and the URL.

> Constable, John. Dedham Vale. Victoria and Albert Museum, London.
>
> van Gogh, Vincent. The Starry Night. 1889. Museum of Mod. Art, New York. 3 Feb. 2003 < http://moma.org/collection/depts/paint_sculpt/blowups/ paint_sculpt_003.html>.

7.3.7.2 Advertisement

Name the product or company being advertised, followed by the word "Advertisement." Give publication information for the source in which the advertisement appears.

> Truth by Calvin Klein. Advertisement. Vogue Dec. 2000: 95-98.

7.3.7.3 Map or Chart

Cite a map or chart as you would do with a book or a short work within a longer work. Add the word "Map" or "Chart" following the title.

> Serbia. Map. 2 Feb. 2001. 17 Mar. 2003 <http://www.biega.com/serbia.html>.
>
> Joseph, Lori, and Bob Laird. "Driving While Phoning Is Dangerous." Chart. USA Today 16 Feb. 2001: 1A.

7.3.7.4 Musical Composition

Cite the composer's name, followed by the title of the work. Underline the title of an opera, a ballet, or a composition identified by name, but do not underline or use quotation marks around a composition identified by number or form.

> Ellington, Duke. Conga Brava.
>
> Haydn, Franz Joseph. Symphony no. 88 in G.

7.3.7.5 Sound Recording

Begin with the name of the person you want to emphasize: the composer, conductor, or performer. For a long work, give the title, underlined, followed by names of pertinent artists (such as performers, readers, or musicians) and the orchestra and conductor (if relevant). End with the manufacturer and the date.

163

Bizet, Georges. <u>Carmen</u>. Perf. Jennifer Laramore, Thomas Moser, Angela Gheorghiu, and Samuel Ramey. Bavarian State Orch. and Chorus. Cond. Giuseppe Sinopoli. Warner, 1996.

For a song, put the title in quotation marks. If you include the name of the album, underline it.

Chapman, Tracy. "Paper and Ink." <u>Telling Stories</u>. Elektra, 2000.

7.3.7.6 Film or Video

Begin with the title, underlined. For a film, cite the director and the lead actors or narrator ("Perf." or "Narr."), followed by the name of the distributor and the year of the film's release. For a videotape or DVD, add "Videocassette" or "DVD" before the name of the distributor.

<u>Chocolat</u>. Dir. Lasse Hallstr. Perf. Juliette Binoche, Judi Dench, Alfred Molina, Lena Olin, and Johnny Depp. Miramax, 2001.

<u>High Fidelity</u>. Dir. Stephen Frears. Perf. John Cusack, Iben Hjejle, Jack Black, and Todd Louiso. 2000. Videocassette. Walt Disney Video, 2001.

7.3.7.7 Radio or Television Program

Begin with the title of the radio segment or television episode (if there is one) in quotation marks, followed by the title of the program, underlined. Next give relevant information about the program's writer ("By"), director ("Dir."), performers ("Perf."), or host ("Host"). Then name the network, the local station (if any), and the date the program was broadcast.

"Monkey Trial." <u>American Experience</u>. PBS. WGBH, Boston. 18 Mar. 2003.

"Live in 4A: Konstantin Soukhovetski." <u>Performance Today</u>. Natl. Public Radio. 2 May 2002. 10 May 2002 <http://www.npr.org/programs/pt/features/4a/soukhovetski.02.html>.

If there is a series title, include it after the title of the program, neither underlined nor in quotation marks.

<u>Mysteries of the Pyramids</u>. On the Inside. Discovery Channel. 7 Feb. 2001.

7.3.7.8 Lecture or Public Address

Cite the speaker's name, followed by the title of the lecture (if any), the organization sponsoring the lecture, the location, and the date.

Chapter 7
Documentation (1): Modern Language Association (MLA) Style

Cohran, Kelan. "Slavery and Astronomy." Adler Planetarium, Chicago. 21 Feb. 2001.

7.3.7.9 Personal Interview

Begin with the name of the person you interviewed. Then write "Personal interview," followed by the date of the interview.

Shaikh, Michael. Personal interview. 22 Mar. 2001.

7.3.8 Other Sources

7.3.8.1 Government Publication

Treat the government agency as the author, giving the name of the government followed by the name of the agency.

United States. Natl. Council on Disability. Promises to Keep: A Decade of Federal Enforcement of the Americans with Disabilities Act. Washington: GPO, 2000.

For government documents published online, give as much publication information as is available and end your citation with the date of access and the URL.

United States. Dept. of Transportation. Natl. Highway Traffic Safety Administration. An Investigation of the Safety Implications of Wireless Communications in Vehicles. Nov. 1999. 20 May 2001 <http://www.nhtsa.dot.gov/people/injury/research/wireless>.

7.3.8.2 Pamphlet

Cite a pamphlet as you would a book.

Commonwealth of Massachusetts. Dept. of Jury Commissioner. A Few Facts about Jury Duty. Boston: Commonwealth of Massachusetts, 1997.

7.3.8.3 Dissertation

Begin with the author's name, followed by the dissertation title in quotation marks, the abbreviation "Diss.," the name of the institution, and the year the dissertation was accepted.

Jackson, Shelley. "Writing Whiteness: Contemporary Southern Literature in Black and White." Diss. U of Maryland, 2000.

For dissertations that have been published in book form, underline the title. After

the title and before the book's publication information, add the abbreviation "Diss.," the name of the institution, and the year the dissertation was accepted.

> Damberg, Cheryl L. <u>Healthcare Reform: Distributional Consequences of an Employer Mandate for Workers in Small Firms</u>. Diss. Rand Graduate School, 1995. Santa Monica: Rand, 1996.

7.3.8.4 Published Proceedings of a Conference

Cite published conference proceedings as you would do with a book, adding information about the conference after the title.

> Kartiganer, Donald M., and Ann J. Abadie. <u>Faulkner at 100: Retrospect and Prospect</u>. Proc. of Faulkner and Yoknapatawpha Conf., 27 July-1 Aug. 1997, U of Mississippi. Jackson: UP of Mississippi, 2000.

7.3.8.5 Published Interview

Name the person interviewed, followed by the title of the interview (if there is one). If the interview does not have a title, include the word "Interview" followed by a period after the interviewee's name. Give publication information for the work in which the interview was published.

> Renoir, Jean. "Renoir at Home: Interview with Jean Renoir." <u>Film Quarterly</u> 50.1 (1996): 2-8.

If the name of the interviewer is relevant, include it after the name of the interviewee.

> Prince. Interview with Bilge Ebiri. <u>Yahoo! Internet Life</u> 7.6 (2001): 82-85.

7.3.8.6 Personal Letter

Begin with the writer's name and add the phrase "Letter to the author," followed by the date.

> Coggins, Christopher. Letter to the author. 6 May 2001.

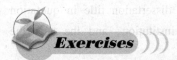

Exercises

I. Decide which one is the proper parenthetical citation for the given materials.

1. A. Branscomb argues that "it's a good idea to lurk (i.e., read all the

Chapter 7
Documentation (1): Modern Language Association (MLA) Style

  messages without contributing anything) for a few weeks, to ensure that you don't break any of the rules of etiquette" (7) when joining a listserv.
- B. "It's a good idea to lurk (i.e., read all the messages without contributing anything) for a few weeks, to ensure that you don't break any of the rules of etiquette (Branscomb, 7)" when joining a listserv.
- C. Branscomb argues that "it's a good idea to lurk (i.e., read all the messages without contributing anything) for a few weeks, to ensure that you don't break any of the rules of etiquette" (p. 7) when joining a listserv.
- D. Branscomb argues that "it's a good idea to lurk (i.e., read all the messages without contributing anything) for a few weeks, to ensure that you don't break any of the rules of etiquette (7)" when joining a listserv.

2. A. The modern world requires both the ability to concentrate on one thing and the ability to attend to more than one thing at a time: "Ideally, each individual would cultivate a repertoire of styles of attention, appropriate to different situations, and would learn how to embed activities and types of attention one within another" (Bateson, 97).
- B. The modern world requires both the ability to concentrate on one thing and the ability to attend to more than one thing at a time: "Ideally, each individual would cultivate a repertoire of styles of attention, appropriate to different situations, and would learn how to embed activities and types of attention one within another" (Bateson 97).
- C. The modern world requires both the ability to concentrate on one thing and the ability to attend to more than one thing at a time: "Ideally, each individual would cultivate a repertoire of styles of attention, appropriate to different situations, and would learn how to embed activities and types of attention one within another (Bateson 97)".
- D. The modern world requires both the ability to concentrate on one thing and the ability to attend to more than one thing at a time: "Ideally, each individual would cultivate a repertoire of styles of attention, appropriate to different situations, and would learn how to embed activities and types of attention one within another". (Bateson 97)

3. A. Bolles argues that the most effective job hunting method is what he calls the creative job hunting approach:

  Figuring out your best skills, and favorite knowledge, and then researching any

employer that interests you, before approaching that organization and arranging, through your contacts, to see the person there who has the power to hire you for the position you are interested in. This method, faithfully followed, leads to a job for 86 out of every 100 job-hunters who try it. (57)

B. Bolles argues that the most effective job hunting method is what he calls the creative job hunting approach:

"Figuring out your best skills, and favorite knowledge, and then researching any employer that interests you, before approaching that organization and arranging, through your contacts, to see the person there who has the power to hire you for the position you are interested in. This method, faithfully followed, leads to a job for 86 out of every 100 job-hunters who try it". (57)

C. Bolles argues that the most effective job hunting method is what he calls the creative job hunting approach:

"Figuring out your best skills, and favorite knowledge, and then researching any employer that interests you, before approaching that organization and arranging, through your contacts, to see the person there who has the power to hire you for the position you are interested in. This method, faithfully followed, leads to a job for 86 out of every 100 job-hunters who try it" (57).

D. Bolles argues that the most effective job hunting method is what he calls the creative job hunting approach:

Figuring out your best skills, and favorite knowledge, and then researching any employer that interests you, before approaching that organization and arranging, through your contacts, to see the person there who has the power to hire you for the position you are interested in. This method, faithfully followed, leads to a job for 86 out of every 100 job-hunters who try it (57).

II. Complete the parenthetical references according to the given information about the cited sources.

1. In their Preface, the authors point out that "Learning Hypertext Markup Language (HTML) and Extensible Hypertext Markup Language (XHTML) is like learning any new language, computer or human" (   ).

    The work cited (page xi):

    Musciano, Chuck, and Bill Kennedy. HTML and XHTML: The Definitive Guide. 4th ed. Sebastopol, CA: O'Reilly, 2000.

2. In traditional British East Africa, between the time of puberty and marriage, a young Akamba girl must maintain an avoidance relationship with her own

Chapter 7
Documentation (1): Modern Language Association (MLA) Style

father (   ).

The work cited (page 17):

Freud, Sigmund. <u>Totem and Taboo</u>. New York: Random, 1918.

3. The Occultopedia also points out that taboo is found among many other cultures including the ancient Egyptians, Jews and others (   ).

The work cited (no available page number):

"Taboo." <u>Occultopedia: Encyclopedia of Occult Sciences and Knowledge</u>. Site created and designed by Marcus V. Gay. 18 Jan. 2005 <http://www.occultopedia.com/t/taboo.htm>.

4. Mangrove forests are part of the coastal environment and stretch throughout the tropics and sub-tropics of the world (   ).

The works cited (the first on page 89, the second on pages 45-46):

Tomlinson, P. B. <u>The Botany of Mangroves</u>. Cambridge: Cambridge University Press, 1994.

Hogarth, P.J. <u>The Biology of Mangroves</u>. Oxford: Oxford University Press, 1999.

5. Video imagery has been described as a "tool of the mind" (   ) that has the potential to help children relive their experiences and process them in deeper, more focused, and more detailed ways.

The work cited (page 15):

Murphy, Karen L., Roseanne DePasquale, and Erin McNamara. "Meaningful Connections: Using Technology in Primary Classrooms." <u>Young Children</u> 58.6 (2003): 12-18.

6. On May 2, 2002, some 4 500 students wrote the difficult University of Waterloo, Physics Department, Sir Isaac Newton (SIN) Examination. Amazingly, there were three perfect papers! Two team members from Don Mills Collegiate Institute broke Waterloo's SIN record not so much for finishing First Place but both students on the team had perfect exams (   ).

The work cited (no page number given):

"SIN 2002 Book Prize Winners." U of Waterloo. 3 Nov. 2002 <http://www.science.uwaterloo.ca/physics/sin/prizewin.html>.

III. **Give appropriate explanation to the boldfaced parts in the following items.**

Kasson, **John.**[1] <u>Civilizing the Machine: Technology and Republican Values in</u>

America 1776-1900. New York: **Penguin**,[2] 1976.

Lopate, Philip, **ed.**[3] The Art of the Personal Essay: An Anthology from the Classical Era to the Present. **New York**:[4] Anchor-Doubleday, 1994.

Zola, Irving Kenneth.[5] "Medicine as an Institution of Social Control." The American Health Empire: Power, Profits, and Politics. Ed. **Barbara Ehrenreich and John Ehrenreich.**[6] New York: Vintage, 1971. 80-100.

Garvey, Lawrence. "**El Paso, Illinois.**"[7] Encyclopedia Americana. 1982 **ed.**[8]

Warner, Megan B. **et al.**[9] "The Longitudinal Relationship of Personality Traits and Disorders." Journal of Abnormal Psychology 113 (2004): **217-27.**[10]

IV. Correct the mistake(s) in each of the following items.

1. Ficaro, Barbara. "Canterbury's First Dean." Sixteenth Century Journal 18 1987: 343-46.

2. Frost, Robert. Letter to Editor of the Independent. 28 Mar. 1894. Selected Letters of Robert Frost. Ed. Lawrance Thompson. New York: Holt, 1964. 19.

3. Said, Edward. "Through Gringo Eyes." Harper's 1988 Apr.: 70-72.

4. Holden, Ted. "Campbell's Taste of the Japanese Market is Mm-Mm Good." Business Week 28 of Mar. 1988: 42.

5. Vanderham, Paul. James Joyce and Censorship: The Trials of Ulysses. New York: New York UP, 1997.

6. Fee, Elizabeth, and Fox, Daniel M. ed. Aids: The Burdens of History. Berkeley: University of California Press, 1988.

7. Daches, David. "W. H. Auden: The Search for a Public". Poetry 54 (1939). 148-56. Rpt. in Poetry Criticism. Robyn V. Young. Ed. Vol. 1. Detroit: Gale, 1991. pp. 332-33.

8. Majid, Anouar. "Living with Ismam." The Chronicle of Higher Education 14 Mar. 2003. 27 Oct. 2003. <http://chronicle.com/prm/weekly/v49/i27/27b01001.htm>.

9. Whillon, Phil. Ready or Not. Los Angeles Times 2 Dec. 2001. 3 Dec. 2001 <http://www.latimes.com/news/la-foster-special.special>.

10. Zamora, Martha. 1990. Frida Kahlo: The Brush of Anguish. Marilyn Sode Smith. Trans. San Francisco: Chronicle.

Chapter 7
Documentation (1): Modern Language Association (MLA) Style

V. Read the materials and answer the questions that follow.

1. "When somebody is destroyed everybody finally contributes to it, but in Willy's case, the end product would be virtually the same" (Arthur, qtd. in Martin and Meyer 375).

   How do you interpret the elements in the parentheses: Arthur, qtd. in, Martin and Meyer, and 375? What do they respectively stand for?

2. Herrera indicates that Kahlo believed in a "vitalistic form of pantheism" (328).

   From whom is the phrase "vitalistic form of pantheism" quoted?

3. "Hype," by one analysis, is "an artificially engendered atmosphere of hysteria" ("Today's Marketplace" 51).

   Why is the title of the article — rather than the name of the author — given in the parentheses?

4. Hall, Stuart. "Cold, Comfort, Farm." <u>New Socialist</u> Nov. 1985: 10–12.

   ---. "Thatcherism: A New Stage?" <u>Marxism Today</u> Feb. 1980: 22–27.

   What do the three hyphens stand for? In what occasion are they used?

5. A team can be defined as "a small number of people with complementary skills who are committed to a common purpose, performance goals, and approach for which they hold themselves mutually accountable" (M. Booth 45).

   Why is the author's first initial given in the parenthetical citation?

6. In his famous advice to players, Shakespeare's Hamlet defines the purpose of theater, "whose end, both at the first and now, was and is, to hold, as'twere, the mirror up to nature" (3.2.21–23).

   How do you interpret the Arabic numerals in the parentheses? What do they respectively refer to?

Chapter 8

Documentation (2): The American Psychological Association (APA) Style

APA style refers to the uniformed system of citations in text and reference format established and used by the American Psychological Association in all of the books and journals it publishes. Many others working in the social and behavioral sciences have adopted this style as their standard as well.

APA style requires two elements for citing outside sources: reference citations in text, and a reference list.

8.1 Reference Citation in Text

In APA style, citations to sources are placed in the text of the paper in order to briefly identify sources for readers and enable them to locate the source of the cited information in the Reference List. These parenthetical references include the author's last name and the year of publication enclosed in parentheses. The parenthesized author name and year of publication are punctuated by a comma. Citations are placed within sentences and paragraphs so that it is clear what information is being quoted or paraphrased and whose information is being cited.

8.1.1 Work by a Single Author

The last name of the author and the year of publication are inserted in the text at the appropriate point.

> In a recent study of reaction times (Walker, 2000) ...

If the name of the author appears as part of the narrative, cite only the year of publication in parentheses.

> Walker (2000) compared reaction times ...

Chapter 8
Documentation (2): The American Psychological Association (APA) Style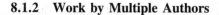

8.1.2 Work by Multiple Authors

When a work has two authors, always cite both surnames. In parenthetical material join the names with an ampersand (&).

> As has been shown (Joreskog & Sorbom, 1989) ...

In the narrative text, when the authors' names are part of the sentence, join the names with the word "and."

> As Nightlinger and Littlewoord (1993) demonstrated ...

When a work has three, four, or five authors, cite all authors' surnames for the first reference.

> Wasserstein, Zappulla, Rosen, Gerstman and Rock (1994) found ...

However, in all subsequent citations per paragraph, include only the surname of the first author followed by "et al." and the year of publication.

> Wasserstain et al. (1994) found ...

8.1.3 Work by Associations, Corporations, Government Agencies, Etc.

The names of groups that serve as authors (corporate authors) are usually written out each time they appear in a text reference, as in

> (National Institute of Mental Health [NIMH], 1999)

8.1.4 Work by Unknown Author

When a work has no author, use the first two or three words of the work's title (omitting any initial articles) as your text reference, capitalizing the initial letter of each word.

> the book *College Bound Seniors* (1979)

Place the title in quotation marks if it refers to an article or chapter of a book, or italicize it if it refers to a book, periodical, brochure, or report. For example, a synonymously published article can be cited as

> ... study finds ("On Free Care," 1982)

8.1.5 Work from Electronic Source

To cite a specific part of a source, indicate the page, chapter, figure, table, or equation at the appropriate point in text. Always give page numbers for quotations. Note that the words page and chapter are abbreviated to "p." and "chap." in text citations.

> ... as is indicated (Cheek & Buss, 1981, p. 332)

> ... the author argued (Shimamura, 1989, chap. 3)

For electronic sources that do not provide page numbers, use the paragraph number, if available, preceded by the paragraph symbol ¶ or the abbreviation *para*. If neither paragraph nor page numbers are visible, cite the heading and the number of the paragraph following it to direct the reader to the location of the material.

> (Myers, 2000, ¶ 5)

> (Beutler, 2000, Conclusion section, para. 1)

8.2 References Cited

References cited in the text of a research paper must appear in a Reference List or Bibliography. This list provides the information necessary to identify and retrieve each source. A thorough understanding of the following guidelines is most desirable before you proceed on to the details.

(1) Start on a new page. Center the word *References* at the top. As usual, the entire reference section is double spaced.

(2) Any citations made in the manuscript must be presented in this section and vice versa. That is, if something is not cited in the text, it should not appear in this section.

(3) In any of the previous sections, whenever you say something like "studies have shown …", you must provide a citation. This section tells the reader where they can find these parenthetical citations.

(4) Capitalize only the first word of a title and subtitle (if any), and any proper names that are part of a title.

(5) This section is arranged alphabetically according to the surname, or last name of authors, or the surname of the first author involved in the study. Sources without authors are arranged alphabetically by title within the same list.

(6) The first line of the entry is flush with the left margin. Hanging indents are used starting with the second line of each reference (five space indented).

(7) For each author, give the last name followed by a comma and the first (and

Chapter 8
Documentation (2): The American Psychological Association (APA) Style

middle) initials followed by periods.

(8) For articles with more than six authors, give the last names and initials of the first six authors, followed by "et al." (note the period after *al*).

(9) Separate multiple authors with commas and the last author with the ampersand "&" rather than the word "and."

(10) After the author(s) comes the year (in parentheses, followed by a period).

(11) It is appropriate to use italics instead of underlining for titles of books and journals.

In short, a reference should be able to supply the detailed information of a corresponding parenthetical citation, for readers to locate and retrieve a source. It answers, almost in a sequential order, basically such questions as "who at what time published what article with what title at what place and was published by whom."

8.2.1 Book

References to an entire book or a periodical must, if possible, include the following elements: author(s) or editor(s), date of publication, title, place of publication, and the name of the publisher.

1. No author or editor

For anonymously published books, put the book title and the edition number before the year of publication. Note also that the title of the book should be italicized and the edition number should be put in the parentheses.

> *Merriam-Webster's collegiate dictionary* (10th ed.). (1993). Springfield, MA: Merriam Webster.

2. One author

> Baddeley, A. D. (1999). *Essentials of human memory*. Hove, England: Psychology Press.

3. Two authors

> Beck, C. A. J., & Sales, B. D. (2001). *Family mediation: Facts, myths, and future prospects*. Washington, DC: American Psychological Association.

4. Corporate author, author as publisher

> Australian Bureau of Statistics. (1991). *Estimated resident population by age and sex in statistical local areas, New South Wales, June 1990* (no. 3209.1). Canberra, Australian Capital Territory: Author.

In the above entry, "Author" after the place of publication indicates that the author is also the publisher.

5. Edited book

Gibbs, J. T., & Huang, L. N. (Eds.). (1991). *Children of color: Psychological interventions with minority youth*. San Francisco: Jossey-Bass.

8.2.2 Essay or Chapter in Edited Book

When you refer to a specific essay or chapters in an edited book, you must include the following elements: essay or chapter authors, date of publication, essay or chapter title, book editor(s), book title, essay or chapter page numbers, place of publication, and the name of the publisher.

Massaro, D. (1992). Broadening the domain of the fuzzy logical model of perception. In H. L. Pick Jr., P. van den Broek, & D. C. Knill (Eds.), *Cognition: Conceptual and methodological issues* (pp. 51-84). Washington, DC: American Psychological Association.

When there are more than one editors, ampersand (&) is used. (See also the above example.)

Bjork, R. A. (1989). Retrieval inhibition as an adaptive mechanism in human memory. In H. L. Roediger III & F. I. M. Craik (Eds.), *Varieties of memory & consciousness* (pp. 309–330). Hillsdale, NJ: Erlbaum.

8.2.3 Encyclopedia or Dictionary and Entry in an Encyclopedia

References for encyclopedias must include the following elements: author(s) or editor(s), date of publication, title, place of publication, and the name of the publisher.

1. Encyclopedia set or dictionary

When you refer to an encyclopedia set or dictionary, you must include the name of the editors or compilers, as well as the edition number and volume numbers.

Sadie, S. (Ed.). (1980). *The new Grove dictionary of music and musicians* (6th ed., Vols. 1–20). London: Macmillan.

2. Encyclopedia article

No names of the editors or compliers are mentioned when a specific article is mentioned. The name of the article author is included instead.

Chapter 8
Documentation (2): The American Psychological Association (APA) Style

Bergman, P. G. (1993). Relativity. In *The new encyclopedia Britannica* (Vol. 26, pp. 501-508). Chicago: Encyclopedia Britannica.

8.2.4 Journal, Magazine, and Newspaper

References to periodical articles must include the following elements: author(s), date of publication, article title, journal title, volume number, issue number (if applicable), and page numbers.

1. Journal article, one author

Mellers, B. A. (2000). Choice and the relative pleasure of consequences. *Psychological Bulletin*, 126, 910-924.

2. Journal article, two or more authors

Klimoski, R., & Palmer, S. (1993). The ADA and the hiring process in organizations. *Consulting Psychology Journal: Practice and Research*, 45 (2), 10-36.

Saywitz, K. J., Mannarion, A. P., Berliner, L., & Cohen, J. A. (2000). Treatment for sexually abused children and adolescents. *American Psychologist*, 55, 1040-1049.

3. Magazine article, chapter in a volume in a series

Kandel, E. R., & Squire, L. R. (2000, November 10). Neuroscience: Breaking down scientific barriers to the study of brain and mind. *Science*, 290, 1113-1120.

Maccoby, E. E., & Martin, J. (1983). Socialization in the context of the family: Parent-child interaction. In P. H. Mussen (Series Ed.) & E. M. Hetherington (Vol. Ed.), *Handbook of child psychology: Vol. 4. Socialization, personality, and social development* (4th ed., pp. 1-101). New York: Wiley.

In the above entry, Mussen is the series editor of the magazine, *Handbook of Child Psychology*, whereas Hetherington is the editor of the fourth volume.

4. Newspaper article

Include the author name (if any and necessary), article name, date of publication, newspaper name, and page number.

New drug appears to sharply cut risk of death from heart failure. (1993, July 15). *The Washington Post*, p. A12.

If the cited article is on discontinuous pages, include at the end of your entry all the related page numbers, separated with a comma.

Schwartz, J. (1993, September 30). Obesity affects economic, social status. *The Washington*

Post, pp. A1, A4.

8.2.5 Thesis or Dissertation

For an unpublished thesis or dissertation, the word *unpublished* is necessary. Location or sponsoring body or both should appear as well, with a date if possible.

> Almeida, D. M. (1990). Fathers' participation in family work: Consequences for fathers' stress and father-child relations. Unpublished master's thesis, University of Victoria.

A dissertation issued on microfilm is treated as a published work. If the citation is an abstract published in *Dissertation Abstracts International*, the form may be as follows:

> Bower, D. L. (1993). Employee assistant programs supervisory referrals: Characteristics of referring and nonreferring supervisors. *Dissertation Abstracts International*, 54 (01), 534B. (UMI No. 9315947).

8.2.6 Technical and Research Report

References to a report must include the following elements: author(s), date of publication, title, place of publication, and name of publisher. If the issuing organization assigned a number (e.g., report number, contract number, or monograph number) to the report, give that number in parentheses immediately after the title.

> U. S. Department of Health and Human Services. (1992). *Pressure ulcers in adults: Prediction and prevention* (AHCPR Publication No. 92-0047). Rockville, MD: Author.

8.2.7 Audio-Visual Media

References to audio-visual media must include the following elements: name and function of the primary contributors (e.g., producer, director), date, title, the medium in brackets, location or place of production, and name of the distributor. If the medium is indicated as part of the retrieval ID, brackets are not needed (see example for "Audio recording").

1. Videocassette

> Garmon, L. (Producer and Director), & Apsell, P. (Executive Producer). (1994). *Secret of the wild child* [Videocassette]. Boston, MA: WGBH Educational Foundation.

2. Audio recording

> Costa, P. T., Jr. (Speaker). (1988). *Personality, continuity, and changes of adult life*

Chapter 8
Documentation (2): The American Psychological Association (APA) Style

(Cassette Recording No. 207-433-88A-B). Washington, DC: American Psychological Association.

3. Motion picture

Scorsese, M. (Producer), & Lonergan, K. (Writer/Director). (2000). *You can count on me* [Motion Picture]. United States: Paramount Pictures.

4. Television broadcast

Crystal, L. (Executive Producer). (1993, October 11). *The MacNeil/Lehrer news hour* [Television Broadcast]. New York and Washington, DC: Public Broadcasting Service.

5. Television series

Miller, R. (Producer). (1989). *The mind* [Television series]. New York: WNET.

6. Music recording

Shocked, M. (1992). Over the waterfall: On *Arkansas traveler* [CD]. New York: PolyGram Music.

8.2.8 Article from Electronic Source

When referring to electronic sources, you must include the following elements: author(s), date of publication, essay title, book title, date of retrieval, and the website. Variations are made when necessary.

When an online article has a printed version, no reference to the website is needed, but "[Electronic version]" must be used to indicate that it is the online version that you referred to.

VandenBos, G., Knapp, S., & Doe, J. (2001). Role of reference elements in the selection of resources by psychology undergraduates [Electronic version]. *Journal of Bibliographic Research*, 5, 117-123.

1. Internet-only journal

Fredrickson, B. L. (2000, March 7). Cultivating positive emotions to optimize health and well-being. *Prevention & Treatment*, 3, Article 0001a. Retrieved November 20, 2000, from http://journals.apa.org/prevention/volume3/pre0030001a.html

2. Online encyclopedia

Bergman, P. G. & Editors of Encyclopedia Britannica Online. (1994-1999). Relativity. *Encyclopedia Britannica Online*. Retrieved August 4, 1999, from Encyclopedia Britannica Online on the World Wide Web: http://search.eb.com/bol/topic? eu =

117376&sctn=1

3. Professional website

American Psychological Association. (1999, June 1). Electronic preference formats recommended by the American Psychological Association. Retrieved July 18, 1999, from the World Wide Web: http://www.apa.org/journals/webref.html

4. Document available on university program or department site

Chou, L., McClintock, R., Moretti, F., & Nix, D. H. (1993). *Technology and education: New wine in new bottles: Choosing pasts and imagining educational futures.* Retrieved August 24, 2000, from Columbia University, Institute for Learning Technologies Web site: http://www.ilt.columbia.edu/publications/papers/newwine1.html

5. Internet-only newsletter

Glueckauf, R. L., Whitton, J., Baxter, J., Kain, J., Vogelgesang, S., Hudson, M., et al. (1998, July). Videocounseling for families of rural teens with epilepsy — Project update *Telehealth News,* 2 (2). Retrieved May 23, 1999, from http://www.telehealth.net/subscribe/newslettr4a.html1

6. Electronic copy of a journal article, three to five authors, retrieved from database

Borman, W. C., Hanson, M. A., Oppler, S. H., Pulakos, E. D., & White, L. A. (1993). Role of early supervisory experience in supervisor performance. *Journal of Applied Psychology,* 78, 443-449. Retrieved October 23, 2000, from PsycARTICLES database.

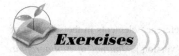

I. Answer the following questions.

1. In what disciplines are APA style most used?
2. What are the major components of an APA parenthetical citation?
3. In what order are the major elements of an APA reference entry arranged?

II. Fill in the blanks with the appropriate information.

1. APA style requires two elements for citing outside sources: _____ and

2. In-text citations are put in _____ and usually include two elements,

Chapter 8
Documentation (2): The American Psychological Association (APA) Style

  _____ and _____. They are usually separated with a _____.

3. The References page in APA style lists any citation in the manuscript. The page is headed with the word _____, which is centered and start _____. The entire Reference page is _____ spaced.

4. A reference supplies the details of a source. The elements are arranged in such an order to answer questions like _____.

5. Only the _____ and _____ are capitalized, and any proper names that are part of a title.

6. Entries in References are arranged _____ according to the _____ of the author, or the _____. Sources without authors are arranged alphabetically by the _____.

7. The first line of the entry is flush with _____. _____ are used starting with the second or subsequent lines of each reference.

8. In APA style, you do not need footnotes or endnotes to cite your sources. The only reasons for you to use footnotes are for _____ or _____, or sponsorship.

9. References to periodical articles must include the following elements: author (s), _____, _____, _____, _____, _____, and page numbers.

10. Quotation marks are not needed when a quotation has been _____ from the text.

III. Correct the mistakes in each of the following entries.

1. Berndt, T. J. (2002). Friendship Quality and Social Development. *Current Directions in Psychological Science*, 11, 7–10.

2. Wegener, D. T., and Petty, R. E. (1994). Mood management across affective states: The hedonic contingency hypothesis. *Journal of personality & social psychology*, 66, 1034–1048.

3. Henry, W. A., III. Making the grade in today's schools. *Time*, 135, 28–31. (1990, April 9).

4. Gibbs, J. T., & Huang, L. N. (1991). (Eds.). *Children of color: Psychological interventions with minority youth*. San Francisco: Jossey-Bass.

5. Bjork, R. A. (1989). Retrieval inhibition as an adaptive mechanism in human memory. H. L. Roediger III & F. I. M. Craik (Eds.). Varieties of memory & consciousness (pp. 309–330). Hillsdale, NJ: Erlbaum.

181

6. New drug appears to sharply cut risk of death from heart failure. *The Washington Post*, p. A12. (1993, July 15).

7. Fandangos, G., Knapp, S., & Doe, J. (2001). Role of reference elements in the selectionof resources by psychology undergraduates. *Journal of Bibliographic Research*, 5, 117-123. (Electronic version).

8. Fredrickson, B. L. (2000, March 7). Cultivating positive emotions to optimize health and well-being. *Prevention & Treatment*, 3, Article 0001a. Retrieved November 20, 2000. (http://journals.apa.org/prevention/volume3/pre0030001a.html).

IV. **Create a parenthetical citation and the corresponding Reference entry with the formation in each situation.**

1. A 1996 journal article co-authored by Jason Murzynski and David Degelman, titled Body Language of Women and Judgments of Vulnerability to Sexual Assault. The article appeared in the 26th volume of the journal, *Journal of Applied Social Psychology*, page range 1617-1626.

2. A book titled Invitation to the Psychology of Religion by Raymond F. Paloutzian, second edition, published in Boston by Allyn and Bacon Press in 1996.

3. An article titled A Closer Look at the Drug Abuse-maternal Aggression Link from *journal of Interpersonal Violence*, volume 15, page 503 – 522, published in 2000. The article was retrieved on May 20, 2000, from ProQuest database. The article was co-authored by Dassen Hien and Tim Honeyman.

4. A Chapter by James D. Shea in 1992, titled Religion and Sexual Adjustment. It was from the book Religion and Mental Health, edited by Jeofery F. Schumaker, page range 70-84. The book was published in New York by Oxford University Press.

5. An article titled Achoo! Published in 1999 by Roger Sahelian from Better Nutrition, volume 61, page 24. The article was electronically retrieved from the Academic Index on September 17, 2001.

6. An article from an electronic journal. The title of article is Reflections on determining authorship credit and authorship order on faculty-student collaborations, from page 1141 to 1147 in the 48th volume of the ejournal *American Psychologist*. The article was retrieved on June 7, 1999, from http://www.apa.org/journals/amp/kurdek.html.

Chapter 9
Documentation (3): The Chicago Manual Style

Most history instructors and some humanities instructors require you to document sources with footnotes or endnotes based on the Chicago style. The Chicago manual style is also generally known as the Turabian style, named after a Chicago professor who made tremendous contributions in formulating the Chicago documentary style. Traditionally, the Chicago documentary style is thought of as a note system, for unlike MLA and APA styles, it places bibliographic citations at the bottom of a page (footnotes) or at the end of a paper (endnotes). However, *The Chicago Manual of Style*, 15th ed. (Chicago: University of Chicago Press, 2003) also offers guidelines for parenthetical documentation and reference lists. Therefore, when you are required to write in the Chicago style, you will actually have to make a decision to choose between two sub-documentary systems — the traditional note-bibliography system and the modern author-date system.

9.1 Note-Bibliography System

9.1.1 General Guidelines: Creating Chicago Notes

The functions of Chicago documentary style are three-fold. The first is to acknowledge gratitude to the authors for their works from which a writer borrowed wisdom. The second is to help the potential readers locate and retrieve the works which may also seem interesting to them. The third function is to back up the writer's statement or claims. The Chicago style has standardized the ways in which a note should be created. Here are the general guidelines.

(1) Citations in footnotes may appear in a full form, or in a shortened form.

(2) All notes are numbered consecutively in Arabic numerals.

(3) For each entry the author's surname or family name comes after the given name. There is no punctuation whatsoever between the two names.

(4) The location of publication, publisher, and year of publication are put in parentheses for books.

(5) Commas are used to separate items.

(6) Specific pages from which you took information are listed.

(7) For each entry the first line is indented 5 spaces; subsequent lines are not.

However, due to the complicated nature of the sources a writer may refer to, variations are made to cater for the different types of sources.

As mentioned above, bibliographic citations in footnotes may appear in a full form, or in a shortened form. The basic elements of a full-form note are author(s), date, book/article, journal title, volume, pages, place of publication, publisher, and other information. The full form is usually used the first references. Any further or subsequent references to this work in the footnotes are presented as shortened citations. A shortened citation consists of the author's family name, and the title of the work, shortened if more than four words.

However, if your bibliography includes all works cited in your notes, it is suggested that even those notes which contain the first citation of a particular work may be in shortened form. In this section, full citations are used for the first reference, and shortened citations are used for further or subsequent references.

9.1.2 General Guidelines: Creating Chicago Bibliography

The bibliography provides approximately the same citation details with the Chicago notes. However, there are several significant differences between them.

(1) All works in the bibliography should be alphabetized according to the author's last name; if it is not given, simply go on to the next item in order (the title of the book or article, for example) and use that to alphabetize the entry.

(2) For each entry the author's surname or family name comes before the given name, with a comma in between.

(3) The location of publication, publisher, and year of publication are not put in parentheses.

(4) Periods are used to separate items.

(5) For each entry the first line is not indented; subsequent lines are indented 5 spaces.

Chapter 9
Documentation (3): The Chicago Manual Style

9.1.3 Examples: Creating Chicago Notes and Bibliography

The sources that a writer refers to in his/her article may include books, book chapters, journal articles, newspaper articles, conference papers, government publications, encyclopaedia, dictionaries, theses, websites, and website documents. Creating documentary citations in the Chicago style concerning these sources will be presented in detail in the following pages. For each source, the ways to create the first reference, subsequent reference, and bibliography are briefly presented in the form of a formula.

9.1.3.1 Book

1. One author

1) Formula

First reference:

Author Name Surname, *Title of Book* (Place of publication: Name of Publisher, Year of publication), page number.

Subsequent reference:

Author Surname, *Title of Book*, page number.

In the above formula, the title of book can be shortened if it is more than four words.

Bibliography:

Author Surname, Author Name. *Title of Book*. Place of publication: Name of Publisher, Year of publication.

2) Example

First reference:

1. Joseph Migga Kizza, *Computer Network Security and Cyberethics* (Jefferson, N.C.: McFarland, 2002), 35.

Subsequent reference:

2. Kizza, *Computer Network Security*, 39.

Bibliography:

Kizza, Joseph Migga. *Computer Network Security and Cyberethics*. Jefferson, N.C.: McFarland, 2002.

2. Second or subsequent edition

1) Formula

First reference:

Author Name Surname, *Title of Book*, number ed. (Place of publication: Name of Publisher, Year of publication), page number.

Subsequent reference:

Author Surname, *Title of Book* (shortened if more than 4 words), page number.

Bibliography:

Author Surname, Author Name. *Title of Book*. Number ed. Place of publication: Name of Publisher, Year of publication.

2) Example

First reference:

1. Alan Fenna, *Australian Public Policy*, 2nd ed. (Frenchs Forest, N.S.W.: Pearson Education Australia, 2004), 42.

Subsequent reference:

2. Fenna, *Australian Public Policy*, 47.

Bibliography:

Fenna, Alan. *Australian Public Policy*. 2nd ed. Frenchs Forest, N.S.W.: Pearson Education Australia, 2004.

3. Two or three authors

For a book by two authors, the word "and" is used between the authors' full names. For a book by three authors, the first two authors' full names are separated by a comma, and the third author is jointed with the word "and."

1) Formula

First reference:

Author Name Surname and Author Name Surname, *Title of Book* (Place of publication: Name of Publisher, Year of publication), page number.

Subsequent reference:

Author Surname and Author Surname, *Title of Book* (shortened if more than 4 words), page number.

Chapter 9
Documentation (3): The Chicago Manual Style

Bibliography:

Author Surname, Author Name and Author Name Surname. *Title of Book*. Place of publication: Name of Publisher, Year of publication.

2) Example
First reference:

1. Ken Coates and Carin Holroyd, *Japan and the Internet Revolution* (New York: Palgrave Macmillan, 2003), 15.

Subsequent reference:

2. Coates and Holroyd, *Japan and the Internet*, 19.

Bibliography:

Coates, Ken and Carin Holroyd. *Japan and the Internet Revolution*. New York: Palgrave, 2003.

4. Four or more authors

While creating a note, for a book by four or more authors, entry only the first author's name, follow it up by the word "et al." There is no need to mention all the authors in the notes. However, all the authors' names should be mentioned in full in the bibliography.

1) Formula
First reference:

Author Name Surname et al., *Title of Book*, number ed. (Place of publication: Name of publisher, Year of publication), page number.

Subsequent reference:

Author Surname et al., *Title of Book* (shortened if more than 4 words), page number.

Bibliography:

Author Surname, Author Name, Author Name Surname, Author Name Surname and Author Name Surname. *Title of Book*. Number ed. Place of publication: Name of Publisher, Year of publication.

2) Example
First reference:

1. David Besanko et al., *Economics of Strategy*, 3rd ed. (New York: J. Wiley, 2003), 23.

Subsequent reference:

2. Besanko et al., *Economics of Strategy*, 37.

Bibliography:

Besanko, David, David Dranove, Mark Shanley and Scott Schaefer. *Economics of Strategy*. 3rd ed. New York: J. Wiley, 2003.

5. One volume of a multi-volume work

Sometimes the source is from one volume of a multi-volume work. Write down the name of author or editor (indicated by "ed") of the volume, the volume number, and the title of the volume.

1) Formula

First reference:

Author Name Surname, *Title of Book*, volume number, *Title of volume* (Place of publication: Name of Publisher, Year of publication), page number.

Subsequent reference:

Author Surname, *Title of Book* (shortened if more than 4 words), *Title of volume*, page number.

Bibliography:

Author Surname, Author Name. *Title of Book*. Volume No., *Title of volume*. Place of publication: Name of Publisher, Year of publication.

2) Example

First reference:

1. J. William Pfeiffer, ed., *Theories and Models in Applied Behavioral Science*, vol. 4, *Organizational* (San Diego: Pfeiffer, 1991), 34.

Subsequent reference:

2. Pfeiffer, *Theories and Models*, *Organizational*, 42.

Bibliography:

Pfeiffer, J. William. *Theories and Models in Applied Behavioural Science*. Vol. 4, *Organizational*. San Diego: Pfeiffer, 1991.

6. An edited book

1) Formula

First reference:

Editor Name Surname, ed., *Title of Book* (Place of publication: Name of Publisher, Year of publication), page number.

Subsequent reference:

    Editor surname, *Title of Book* (shortened if more than 4 words), page number.

Bibliography:

Editor Surname, Editor Name, ed. *Title of Book*. Place of publication: Name of Publisher, Year of publication.

2) Example

First reference:

    1. Margit Misangyi Watts, ed., *Technology: Taking the Distance Out of Learning* (San Francisco: Jossey-Bass, 2003), 73.

Subsequent reference:

    2. Watts, *Technology*, 96.

Bibliography:

Watts, Margit Misangyi, ed. *Technology: Taking the Distance Out of Learning*. San Francisco: Jossey-Bass, 2003.

7. Unknown author

When the author of a book is not given, start your entry with the italicized book title.

1) Formula

First reference:

    Title of Book, number ed. (Place of publication: Name of Publisher, Year of publication), page number.

Subsequent reference:

    Title of Book (shortened), page number.

Bibliography:

Title of Book. Number ed. Place of publication: Name of Publisher, Year of publication.

2) Example

First reference:

    1. *Style Manual for Authors, Editors and Printers*, 5th ed. (Canberra: Australian Government Publishing Service, 1996), sec. 57.

Subsequent reference:

    2. *Style Manual*, 59.

Bibliography:

Style Manual for Authors, Editors and Printers. 5th ed. Canberra: Australian Government Publishing Service, 1996.

8. Corporate author

1) Formula

First reference:

Name of Organization, *Title of Book*, number ed. (Place of publication: Name of Publisher, Year of publication), page number.

Subsequent reference:

Name of Organization (shortened if appropriate), *Title of Book* (shortened), page number.

Bibliography:

Name of Organization. *Title of Book*. Number ed. Place of publication: Name of Publisher, Year of publication.

2) Example

First reference:

1. National Gallery of Australia, *The Eye of the Storm: Eight Contemporary Indigenous Artists*, 2nd ed. (Canberra: National Gallery of Australia, 1997), 15.

Subsequent reference:

2. National Gallery of Australia, *Eye of the Storm*, 19.

Bibliography:

National Gallery of Australia. *The Eye of the Storm: Eight Contemporary Indigenous Artists*. 2nd ed. Canberra: National Gallery of Australia, 1997.

9. Indirect source

Indirect citations occur when you choose to cite the work of an author using a reference/citation made by another author, i.e., you do not examine the original work. Details of both the original and secondary sources must be listed.

Secondary source cited in note:

1. Sheila Allen, "Some Theoretical Problems in the Study of Youth," *Sociological Review* 16, no. 3 (1968): 1, quoted in Johanna Wyn and Rob White, *Rethinking Youth* (St Leonards, N.S.W.: Allen & Unwin, 1997), 8.

Chapter 9
Documentation (3): The Chicago Manual Style

Bibliography:

Allen, Sheila. "Some Theoretical Problems in the Study of Youth." *Sociological Review* 16, no. 3 (1968): 1. Quoted in Johanna Wyn and Rob White. *Rethinking Youth*. St Leonards, N.S.W.: Allen & Unwin, 1997, 8.

10. Same first author, published in the same year

Robbins, Stephen P. *Organizational Behaviour*. 11th ed. Upper Saddle River, N.J.: Prentice Hall, 2004.

Robbins, Stephen P. and David A. DeCenzo. *Fundamentals of Management: Essential Concepts and Applications*. 5th ed. Upper Saddle River, N.J.: Prentice Hall, 2004.

11. Same author, published in the same year

In your bibliography, order these works alphabetically according to the title of the work. Ignore any initial "The", "A" or "An" in the title. A dash replaces the repeated author name.

Blainey, Geoffrey. *Black Kettle and Full Moon: Daily Life in a Vanished Australia*. Camberwell, Victoria: Penguin/Viking, 2003.

———. *The Rush the Never Ended: A History of Australian Mining*. 5th ed. Carlton, Victoria: Melbourne University Press, 2003.

12. Citing more than one author at one point in the text

Sometimes similar statements may have been made on a certain topic by more than one author, and you need to cite them all at one point in the text. In that case, you can include several citations in a single footnote, separated by a semi-colon.

Multiple references cited in note:

1. Zygmunt Bauman, *Globalization and Culture* (Oxford: Polity Press, 1999), 6; John Tomlinson, *Globalization: The Human Consequences* (London: Routledge, 1999), 11.

Note that the multiple references appear as one entry in the notes, but separate ones in the bibliography.

Multiple references cited in bibliography:

Bauman, Zygmunt. *Globalization and Culture*. Oxford: Polity Press, 1999.

Tomlinson, John. *Globalization: The Human Consequences*. London: Routledge, 1999.

9.1.3.2 Book Chapter

Sometimes you need to cite from chapters in a book or an edited book. Different

requirements are laid for them accordingly.

1. Chapter in a book

1) Formula

First reference:

    Author Name Surname and Author Name Surname, "Title of Chapter," in *Title of Book* (Place of publication: Name of Publisher, Year of publication), page number.

In the above formula, "and" indicates the book has more than one author, and "in" indicates the book name.

Subsequent reference:

    Author Surname and Author Surname, "Title of Chapter (shortened)," page number.

Bibliography:

Author Surname, Author Name and Author Name Surname. "Title of Chapter." In *Title of Book*. Place of publication: Name of Publisher, Year of publication.

2) Example

First reference:

    1. Johanna Wyn and Rob White, "The Concept of Youth," in *Rethinking Youth* (Sydney: Allen and Unwin, 1997), 11.

Subsequent reference:

    2. Wyn and White, "The Concept of Youth," 17.

Bibliography:

Wyn, Johanna and Rob White. "The Concept of Youth." In *Rethinking Youth*. Sydney: Allen and Unwin, 1997.

2. Chapter in an edited book

1) Formula

First reference:

    Author of chapter Name Surname, "Title of Chapter," in *Title of Book*, ed. Editor Name Surname, page number (Place of publication: Name of Publisher, Year of publication).

Subsequent reference:

    Author of chapter Surname, "Title of Chapter (shortened)," page number.

Bibliography:

Author of chapter Surname, Name. "Title of Chapter." In *Title of Book*, edited by Editor Name Surname. Place of publication: Name of Publisher, Year of publication.

It needs to be pointed out that in both the notes and bibliography, the editors' first name is put before the surname. In addition, unlike in the previous examples, the page reference is inserted before the publishing details.

2) Example

First reference:

1. Barry M. Maid, "No Magic Answer," in *Technology: Taking the Distance Out of Learning*, ed. Margit Mesangyi Watts, 21 (San Francisco: Jossey-Bass, 2003).

Subsequent reference:

2. Maid, "No Magic Answer," 24.

Bibliography:

Maid, Barry M. "No Magic Answer." In *Technology: Taking the Distance Out of Learning*, edited by Margit Mesangyi Watts. San Francisco: Jossey-Bass, 2003.

9.1.3.3 Journal Article

Journal articles can be accessed from many different ways. Apart from the conventional print version, they can nowadays be accessed from database, website, and many other channels.

There are several things to pay attention to when citing a journal article in the Chicago notes and bibliography. Firstly, title of article is put before title of journal. Secondly, both the volume number and issue number can be mentioned when they are available. Thirdly, the only item that is put in parenthesis is the year of publication.

1. Print version

1) Formula

First reference:

Author Name Surname and Author Name Surname, "Title of Article," *Title of Journal* volume number, no. issue number (Year of publication): page number.

Subsequent reference:

    Author Surname, "Title of Article (shortened)," page number.

Bibliography:

Author Surname, Name and Author Name Surname. "Title of Article." *Title of Journal* volume number, no. issue number (Year of publication): page range of article.

2) Example

First reference:

    1. Mihir Parikh and Sameer Verma, "Utilizing Internet Technologies to Support Learning: An Empirical Analysis," *International Journal of Information Management* 22, no. 1 (2002): 31.

Subsequent reference:

    2. Parikh and Verma, "Utilizing Internet Technologies," 43.

Bibliography:

Parikh, Mihir and Sameer Verma. "Utilizing Internet Technologies to Support Learning: An Empirical Analysis." *International Journal of Information Management* 22, no. 1 (2002): 27-46.

2. Accessed from database in the same format as the original (PDF)

First reference:

    1. Jeff Bennett, "Environmental Values and Water Policy," *Australian Geographical Studies* 41, no. 3 (2003): 239, http://www.catchword.com/.

Subsequent reference:

    2. Bennett, "Environmental Values," 247.

Bibliography:

Bennett, Jeff. "Environmental Values and Water Policy." *Australian Geographical Studies* 41, no. 3 (2003): 237-250. http://www.catchword.com/.

Note: Provide the URL of the main entrance to the database service. An access date may be added in parentheses at the end of the citation.

3. Accessed from a website in the same format as the original (PDF)

First reference:

    1. Tim Sprod, "Philosophy, Young People and Well-being," *Youth Studies Australia* 18, no. 2 (1999): 13, http://www.acys.utas.edu.au/ysa/articles/ysa_pdfs/ysa-v18n2pp12-

16.pdf.

Subsequent reference:

    2. Sprod, "Philosophy, Young People," 15.

Bibliography:

Sprod, Tim. "Philosophy, Young People and Well-being." *Youth Studies Australia* 18, no. 2 (1999): 12-16. http://www.acys.utas.edu.au/ysa/articles/ysa_pdfs/ysa-v18n2pp12-16.pdf.

4. Accessed from a website in a format different from the print version

Sometimes a journal article may be accessed from a website in a format different from the print version, and may not give page numbers, or page range. In that case, a subheading can be used as a locator within the article for the first reference. For subsequent reference and bibliography, no locator is needed.

First reference:

    1. Deborah Valentine, "Access to Higher Education: A Challenge to Social Work Educators," *Journal of Social Work Education* 40, no. 2 (2004), under "Effects and Consequences," http://www.cswe.org/publications/jswe/04-2editorial.html.

In the above example, "Effects and Consequences," is the subheading used as a locator under which the citation can be retrieved.

Subsequent reference:

    2. Valentine, "Access to Higher Education."

Bibliography:

Valentine, Deborah. "Access to Higher Education: A Challenge to Social Work Educators." *Journal of Social Work Education* 40, no. 2 (2004). http://www.cswe.org/publications/jswe/04-2editorial.html.

5. Article by the same first author

Sometimes you may cite from an author's article as well as articles he/she collaborated with others. In that case, single author entries come first in the bibliography.

Bessant, Judith. "The Question of Public Trust and the Schooling System." *Australian Journal of Education* 45, no. 2 (2001): 207-226.

Bessant, Judith and Ruth Webber. "Policy and the Youth Sector: Youth Peaks and Why We Need Them." *Youth Studies Australia* 20, no. 1 (2001): 43-47.

6. Article by the same author

When you cite more than one article in your essay, create the note by alphabetically listing the titles by the same author under different entries.

  1. Jocelynne A. Scutt, "Future Access: Discrimination and the Disability Discrimination Act," *Access* 5, no.3 (2003): 6-10.

  2. Jocelynne A. Scutt, "Without Precedent: Sex/Gender Discrimination in the High Court," *Alternative Law Journal* 28, no. 2 (2003): 74-77.

9.1.3.4 Newspaper Article

1) Formula

First reference:

  Author Name Surname, "Title of Article," *Newspaper Name* (City of publication), Month day, Year of publication, edition number.

Subsequent reference:

  Author Surname, "Title of Article (shortened)."

Bibliography:

  Author Surname, Name. "Title of Article." *Newspaper Name* (City of publication), Month day, Year of publication, edition number.

2) Example

First reference:

  1. Stephen Cauchi, "World's Green Markers on the Brink," *Age* (Melbourne), October 16, 2004, first edition.

Subsequent reference:

  2. Cauchi, "World's Green Markers."

Note: Because there may be several editions of the paper on one day, with items moved or eliminated, page numbers are best omitted. Adding the name of the newspaper section, and the edition, may be useful.

Bibliography:

  Cauchi, Stephen. "World's Green Markers on the Brink." *Age* (Melbourne), October 16, 2004, first edition.

Notes: An initial "The" in the newspaper title is omitted. Unless it is obvious from the newspaper name, the city of publication should be added, in parentheses, after the newspaper title.

Chapter 9
Documentation (3): The Chicago Manual Style

When the newspaper article is accessed from a database, include the URL of the main entrance of the database service, as well as edition and section details.

Example:

1. Henry Gee, "A Breed Apart," *Age* (Melbourne), October 29, 2004, first edition, A3. http://global.factiva.com.

Bibliography:

Gee, Henry. "A Breed Apart." *Age* (Melbourne), October 29, 2004, first edition, A3. http://global.factiva.com.

9.1.3.5 Conference Paper

1. Published conference paper

1) Formula

First reference:

Author Name Surname, "Title of Paper," in *Conference Proceedings Name* (Place of publication: Name of Publisher, Year of publication), page number.

Subsequent reference:

Author Surname, "Title of Paper (shortened)," page number.

Bibliography:

Author Surname, Name. "Title of Paper." In *Conference Proceedings Name*. Place of publication: Name of Publisher, Year of publication.

2) Example

First reference:

1. Mick Common, "The Role of Economics in Natural Heritage Decision Making," in *Heritage Economics: Challenges for Heritage Conservation and Sustainable Development in the 21st Century: Proceedings of the International Society for Ecological Economics Conference, Canberra, 4 July 2000* (Canberra: Australian Heritage Commission, 2001), 22.

Subsequent reference:

2. Common, "Role of Economics," 22.

Bibliography:

Common, Mick. "The Role of Economics in Natural Heritage Decision Making." In *Heritage Economics: Challenges for Heritage Conservation and Sustainable Development in the 21st Century: Proceedings of the International Society for Ecological Economics Conference, Canberra, 4 July 2000*. Canberra: Australian Heritage Commission, 2001.

2. Unpublished conference paper

For an unpublished paper, the details are put in the parentheses for the first reference.

1. Anna Byas, "Family Law: Old Shadows and New Directions" (paper presented to the 8th Australian Institute of Family Studies Conference, Melbourne, February 12–14, 2003).

Bibliography:

Byas, Anna. "Family Law: Old Shadows and New Directions." Paper presented to the 8th Australian Institute of Family Studies Conference, Melbourne, February 12–14, 2003.

9.1.3.6 Statistics from Agency Database

1) **Formula**

First reference:

Author Agency Name, *Title of Publication*, Catalogue number, Place of publication, Year of publication, page number, name of database URL.

Subsequent reference:

Author Agency Name, *Title of Publication* (shortened), page number.

Bibliography:

Author Agency Name. *Title of Publication*. Catalogue number. Place of publication, Year of publication. Name of database URL.

2) **Example**

First reference:

1. Australian Bureau of Statistics, *Social Trends in Australia 2004*, Cat. no. 4120.0, Canberra, *2004*, 192, AusStats http://www.abs.gov.au.

Note: The name of the AusStats database is given, as subscription to it provides access to ABS publications not freely available on their public website at the same URL. The name of the publisher is omitted, as it is the same as the authoring agency.

Subsequent reference:

2. ABS, *Social Trends*, 193.

Note: If you use an acronym, include a cross-reference in your bibliography.

Bibliography (Cross references in your bibliography):

ABS. *See* Australian Bureau of Statistics

Australian Bureau of Statistics. *Social Trends in Australia 2004*. Cat. no. 4120.0. Canberra,

2004. AusStats http://www.abs.gov.au.

9.1.3.7 Encyclopedia and Dictionary

References to well-known encyclopedia and dictionaries are normally cited in notes, and not in the bibliography. References to an alphabetically arranged work do not cite the volume or page number. Instead they cite the item, preceded by *s.v.* (Latin "under the word").

While creating a note, omit the details of publication, but specify the edition, if it is not the first.

    1. *Encyclopedia Britannica*, 15th ed., *s.v.* "Salvation."

Other reference works may be listed with their publication details:

    1. *International Encyclopedia of Business and Management*, 2nd ed., ed. Malcolm Warner (London: Thomson Learning, 2002), *s.v.* "Educational Marketing."

9.1.3.8 Thesis/Dissertation

Theses or dissertations are also important sources of citation. They may appear in the printed form or the electronic form.

1. Print version

1) Formula

First reference:
    Author Name Surname, "Title of Thesis" (Award/type of thesis, Name of academic institution under whose auspices study was taken, Year of preparation), page number.

Subsequent reference:
    Author Surname, "Title of Thesis (shortened)," page number.

Bibliography:
    Author Surname, Name. "Title of Thesis." Award/type of thesis, Name of academic institution, Year of preparation.

2) Example

First reference:
    1. Maritza Ivonne Byrne, "Self-talk and Test Anxiety" (PhD thesis, Monash University, Melbourne, 1996), 7.

Subsequent reference:

    2. Byrne, "Self-talk," 10.

Bibliography:

Byrne, Maritza Ivonne. " Self-talk and Test Anxiety." PhD thesis, Monash University, Melbourne, 1996.

2. Electronic version
1) Formula
First reference:

    Author Name Surname, "Title of Thesis" (Award/type of thesis, Name of academic institution under whose auspices study was taken, Year of preparation), page number, URL.

Subsequent reference:

    Author Surname, "Title of Thesis (shortened)," page number.

Bibliography:

Author Surname, Name. "Title of Thesis." Award/type of thesis, Name of academic institution, Year of preparation. URL.

2) Example
First reference:

    1. Timothy Robert Kurz, " A Psychology of Environmentally Sustainable Behaviour" (PhD thesis, Murdoch University, Perth, 2003), 9, http://wwwlib.murdoch.edu.au/adt/browse/view/adt-MU20040428.152013.

Subsequent reference:

    2. Kurz, "Psychology," 13.

Bibliography:

Kurz, Timothy Robert. " A Psychology of Environmentally Sustainable Behaviour." PhD thesis, Murdoch University, Perth, 2003. http://wwwlib. murdoch. edu. au/adt/browse/view/adt-MU20040428.152013.

3. Website

When citing a website, in addition to the URL, the date of access is included if the site is likely to have substantive updates, or includes information which may be time-sensitive, e.g. medical or legal advice.

1) Formula

First reference:

Agency Author of Content, "Title of Page," Owner of the site, URL (date of access).

Subsequent reference:

Agency, "Title of Page."

Bibliography:

Agency Author of Content. "Title of Page." Owner of the site. City. URL.

2) Example

First reference:

1. Therapeutic Goods Administration, "Recalls & Alerts," Department of Health and Ageing, Canberra, http://www.tga.gov.au/recalls/index.html (accessed December 13, 2004).

Second reference:

2. Therapeutic Goods Administration, "Recalls & Alerts."

Bibliography:

Therapeutic Goods Administration. "Recalls & Alerts." Department of Health and Ageing. Canberra. http://www.tga.gov.au/recalls/index.html.

9.1.3.9 Website Document

1) Formula

First reference:

Author Name Surname, "Title of Document/page," Owner of site, URL (date of access).

Subsequent reference:

Author Surname, "Title of Document/page (shortened)."

Bibliography:

Author Surname, Name. "Title of Document/Page." Owner of site. URL.

2) Example

First reference:

1. Bruce McGregor, "History of Creek Activism," Friends of Merri Creek, http://home.vicnet.net.au/~fomc/ (accessed December 12, 2004).

Subsequent reference:

2. McGregor, "History of Creek Activism."

Bibliography:

McGregor, Bruce. "History of Creek Activism." Friends of Merri Creek. http://home.vicnet. net.au/~fomc/.

9.2 The Author-Date System

In comparison with the note-bibliography system, the author-date system is economical in space, in time (for author, editor, and typesetter), and in cost (to publisher and public). The author-date system of documentation comprises two indispensable parts: the text citation, usually enclosed in parentheses, and the list of sources cited, often called the reference list. Unlike the humanities style of documentation, in which full bibliographic information may be given in both notes and bibliography, the author-date system provides brief identifying information in the text citation and reserves full documentation for the list of references.

9.2.1 Author-Date Text Citation

9.2.1.1 Basic Form

The basic form of the author-date citation in running text or at the end of a block quotation consists of the author's last, or family, name and the year of publication of the work. No punctuation is used between the author's name and the date in the text citation. Where the reference list includes two or more works by different authors with the same last name and the same date, it is necessary to include the authors' initials in the text citations.

1. One author

(Blinksworth 1987)
(Tao 2000)
(EPA 1986)
(P. Brown 1991)

Note: Reference list entries providing complete information for the author-date citations given above might be as follows:

Chapter 9
Documentation (3): The Chicago Manual Style

Blinksworth, Roger. 1987. *Converging on the evanescent.* San Francisco: Threshold Publications.

Tao, Jie, ed. 2000. Selected Readings in American Literature. Beijing: Higher Education Press.

Environmental Protection Agency (EPA). 1986. *Toxicology handbook.* Rockville, Md.: Government Institutes.

2. Two or three authors

For works by tow or three authors, all last names are included (use *and*, not an ampersand "&"):

(Finburn and Cosby 1990)

(Smith, Wessen, and Gunless 1988)

In a reference to a work by two family members with the same last name, the name is repeated:

(Weinberg and Weinberg 1980)

The plural of the name may be used in the text when the reference is to the persons rather than the work:

The Weinbergs (1980) maintain that Darrow ...

3. More than three authors

For more than three authors, use the last name of the first author followed by *et al.* or *and others.*

(Zipursky et al. 1959)

(Zipursky and others 1959)

9.2.1.2 Page or Other Specific Reference

1. Page reference

A specific page section, figure, or other division or element of the cited work follows the date and is preceded by a comma. Unless confusion would result, the abbreviation for *page* or *pages* is omitted. Abbreviations for other elements or divisions should be included.

(Blindsworth 1987, 125)

(Foley 1955, 23, 43, 46-51)

(McAndrew 1989, 246 n. 4)

2. Volume and page number

When reference to both volume and page number is required, a colon will distinguish between them, and the abbreviations *vol.* and *p.* or *pp.* are omitted:

(Wazinski 1989, 3: 114)

If more than one volume of the author's work is referred to in the same reference, the volumes are separated by commas:

(Garcia 1987, 2: 168, 3: 119-23)

When a volume is referred to as a whole, without page number, the abbreviation *vol.* is required for clarity:

(Garcia 1987, vol. 2)

9.2.1.3 Multiple References

When two or more references are given together in one parenthetical citation, they are separated by semicolons:

(Light 1972; Light and Wang 1975; Rooster 1976)

(Whipsmith 1988, 34; Larisch 1987, 2: 150; Ohmstead 1990, 28)

Additional works by the same author are indicated in the citation by date only, the dates being separated by commas. If two or more of the works by a single author or team of authors have the same date of publication, additional alphabetical identifiers must be given:

(Keller 1896a, 1896b, 1907)

(Knight and Belinsky 1987a, 1987b)

9.2.2 Reference List

To complete the brief form of the text citations that it employs, the author-date system requires detailed list of sources in which full bibliographic information is given. Such a list of sources may be called Works Cited, Literature Cited, Sources Cited, or simply References. All sources cited in the text must be included in the reference list.

When the author-date system of documentation is used, the reader is best served by references arranged in a single alphabetical list. There is rarely a need to divide the list into sections. Observe the following principles.

(1) A single-author entry comes before a multiauthor entry beginning with the

same name.

Ramos, Frank P. 1990. Deconstructing the deconstructionists. *Eolian Quarterly* 11(spring): 41-58.

Ramos, Frank P., John R. Wizmont, and Clint T. O'Finnery. 1987. *Texts and nontexts*. Philadelphia: Whynot Press.

(2) All works attributed to one author, editor, translator, or compiler should be listed together in chronological order. The chronological arrangement facilitates location from the author-date citation.

Alcazar, W. C., ed. 1966. *Microphysiology: New frontiers*. Seattle: Warburton.

―――. 1967. Dysfunction in pseudopodia. *Bacteriological Quaterly* 17 (winter): 16-21.

Two or more works by the same author or authors published in the same year are distinguished by roman letters, in alphabetical sequence, following the date without intervening space. The works published in one year are alphabetized by title:

Langston, W., Jr., 1965a. Fossil crocodilians from Colombia and the Cenozoic history of the Crocodilia in South America. *Univ. Calif. Publ. Geol. Sci.* 52:1-157.

―――. 1965b. *Oedaleops campi* (Reptilia: Pelycosauria): A new genus and species from the Lower Permian of New Mexico, and the family Eothyrididae. *Bull. Tex. Mem. Mus.* E9: 1-47.

9.2.2.1 Book

1. Author

In reference list entries, authors' names should be given as they appear on the title pages of their books, except that, especially in scientific works, initials often replace first and middle names, even when the full forms appear on the title page. (Note that space is added between initials.) Whether one elects to present all names exactly as they appear on the title page, to use initials for given names, or to use full given names, one should observe consistency as far as possible, unless authors' preferences require variation.

1) One author

In the reference list, where entries are arranged alphabetically by authors' last names, the name is inverted, last name first:

Woodthrush, Julian R. 1985. *Birdsong and mating behavior*. New Haven, Conn.: George and Lilian Fromson.

2) Two or three authors

The name of the first author is inverted, that of the other author(s) is given in its natural order, and conjunction is preceded by a comma:

> Weinberg, Arthur, and Lila Weinberg. 1980. *Clarence Darrow: A sentimental rebel*. New York: Putnam's Sons.

> Brett, P. D., S. W. Johnson, and C. R. T. Bach. 1989. *Mastering string quartets*. San Francisco: Amati Press.

3) More than three authors

When referring to a work by more than three authors, the text citation should give the last name of the first author followed by *et al.* or *and others* without intervening punctuation. In the reference list entry, it is customary to give all of the authors, in the order in which they appear on the title page.

> (Sanders et al. 1989)

> Sanders, G. S., T. R. Brice, V. L. deSantis, and C. C. Ryder. 1989. *Prediction and prevention of famine*. Los Angeles: Timothy Peters.

4) Anonymous work

If the authorship of a work is known but not revealed on the title page, the name is given in brackets:

> [Doe, Jane]. 1948. *The burden of anonymity*. Nowhere: Nonesuch Press.

If the identity of the author is merely surmised, a question mark follows the name before the closing bracket:

> [Doe, Jane?]. 1948. *The burden of anonymity*. Nowhere: Nonesuch Press.

The text citation in both cases should give the name in brackets. In the latter case a question mark may be included if desired.

> ([Doe] 1948)

> ([Doe?] 1948)

If the name of the author is unascertainable, the reference entry should begin with the title of the work. The date follows the title.

> *The burden of anonymity*. 1948. Nowhere: Nonesuch Press.

In alphabetizing the entry, the initial article is discounted. The article may be transposed to the end of the title, following a comma:

Burden of anonymity, The.

The text reference for such an entry may substitute the title, or a shortened version of the title, for the author:

(*Burden of anonymity* 1948)

or

(*Burden* 1948)

5) Editor, compiler, or translator

The name of the editor, compiler, or translator takes the place of the author when no author is listed on the title page. In the reference list, the abbreviation *ed./ eds., comp./comps.*, or *trans.* follows the name and is preceded by a comma.

> Wiley, Bell I., ed. 1980. *Slaves no more: Letters from Liberia, 1833–1869.* Lexington: University Press of Kentucky.

> McBurney, William Harlin, comp. 1960. *A check list of English prose fiction, 1700–1739.* Cambridge: Harvard University Press.

6) Editor, compiler, or translator with an author

The edited, compiled, or translated work of an author indicated on the title page is normally listed under that author's name rather than the name of the editor, compiler, or translator. In the reference list the name of the editor, compiler, or translator is part of a new element following the title and a period. The new element is introduced by *Edited by*, *Compiled by*, or *Translated by*. The abbreviations *Ed.*, *Comp.*, and *Trans.* may also be used, but in this case they stand for *Edited by*, *Translated by*, and so forth, and therefore the plural abbreviations *Eds.* and *Comps.* should not be used.

> Pound, Ezra. 1953. *Literary essays.* Edited by T. S. Eliot. New York: New Directions.

Or, to shorten this entry:

> Pound, Ezra. 1953. *Literary essays.* Ed. T. S. Eliot. New York: New Directions.

When matters of editing and compiling are more complicated, they may need to be clarified in the reference list:

> *Chaucer life-records.* 1966. Edited by Martin M. Crow and Clair C. Olson from materials compiled by John M. Manly and Edith Rickert, with the assistance of Lilian J. Redstone and others. London: Oxford University Press.

If the editor or translator is more germane to the discussion than is the author, the editor's name is given first in the reference list and alone in the text citation. Thus, in a work on T. S. Eliot, the citation and reference list entry for the work list

> Pound, Ezra. 1953. *Literary essays*. Edited by T. S. Eliot. New York: New Directions.

would be as follows:

(Eliot 1953)

> Eliot, T. S., ed. 1953. *Literary essays*, by Ezra Pound. New York: New Directions.

7) Author of foreword or introduction

If the foreword or introduction is the item cited, the entry is listed under the name of the author of the foreword or introduction. The author of the work itself is given after the title of the work, from which it is separated by a comma and the word *by*:

> Namsorg, Nodj. 1990. Foreword to *the psychodynamics of chronic stress*, by Salvador Mensana. New York: Isadore O'Malley and Son.

The text citation uses the name of the author of the foreword or introduction:

(Namsorg 1990)

2. Part of a Book

When a chapter or other titled part of a book is cited, that title is given in roman type, with sentence capitalization, without quotation marks. The title ends with a period and is followed by *In* and the title of the book. If the part is identified by type and number ("Chap. 8 in," "Pt. 1 of"), this information replaces *In* preceding the book title.

> Kaiser, Ernest. 1964. The literature of Harlem. In *Harlem: A community in transition*, edited by J. H. Clarke. New York: Citadel Press.

The citations to such titled parts may include the page reference, but the part is unnecessary:

(Kaiser 1964, 48, 54)

1) Chapter originally published elsewhere

The text citation should refer only to the publication listed first.

(Fromson 1990, 134)

> Fromson, Orlando. 1990. Progressives in the late twentieth century. In *To left and right: Cycles in American politics*, edited by Wilmer F. Turner (Boston: Lighthouse Press). First published in *North American political Review* 18 (fall 1988): 627-42.

2) Preface, foreword, introduction, and similar parts of a book

Jacobs, James B. 1989. Introduction to *Drunk driving: An American dilemma*. Chicago: University of Chicago Press.

Zimring, Franklin E. 1989. Foreword to *Drunk driving: An American dilemma*. Chicago: University of Chicago Press.

3) Letter, memoranda, and similar communication in published collection

The text citation:

In a letter to Charles Milnes Gaskell from London, 30 March 1868, Henry Adams wrote ... (Adams 1930, 141).

Reference list entry:

Adams, Henry. 1930. *Letters of Henry Adams, 1858-1891*. Edited by Worthington Chauncey Ford. Boston: Houghton Mifflin.

3. Edition

1) Subsequent edition

Smart, Ninian. 1976. *The religious experience of mankind*. 2nd ed. New York: Scribner's Sons.

2) Modern edition of the classics

When classics are referred to by page number, the edition must be cited:

Horace. 1932. *Satires, epistles, and Ars poetica*. Loeb Classical Library.

(Horace 1932, 146)

Maimonides. 1965. *The code of Mainmonides, Book 5: The book of holiness*. Translated and edited by Louis I. Rabinowitz and Philip Grossman. Yale Judaica Series. New Haven: Yale University Press.

(Maimonides 1965, 98)

4. Multivolume Works

1) Citing the work as a whole

Wright, Sewall. 1968-1978. *Evolution and the genetics of populations*. 4 vols. Chicago: University of Chicago Press.

2) Citing a particular volume

Farmwinkle, William. 1983. *Humor of the American Midwest*. Vol. 2 of *Survey of American humor*. Boston: Plenum Press.

3) One volume in two or more books

Skelton, Margaret. 1988. *A critical history of modern dance*. Vol. 2, bk. 1. Chicago: Terpsichore Press.

Lach, Donald F. 1977. *Asia in the making of Europe*. Vol. 2, *A century of wonder*. Bk. 2, *The literary arts*. Chicago: University of Chicago Press.

or

Lach, Donald F. 1977. *The literary arts*. Bk. 2 of *A century of wonder*. Vol. 2 of *Asia in the making of Europe*. Chicago: University of Chicago Press.

5. Series

Reference list entries for works in a series include, between the book title and the place of publication, the title of the series, in roman type and headline capitalization; series editor, though this is usually omitted; series number, if other than the first; and volume number and subsidiary number, if these apply.

Wattle, Ralph. 1989. *Economic aspects of professional sports in America*. Vol. 2, *Player salaries and bargaining power*. Trends in American Economy, no. 11. Boston: Flummery Press.

or

Wattle, Ralph. 1989. *Player salaries and bargaining power*. Vol. 2 of *Economic aspects of professional sports in America*. Trends in American Economy, no. 11. Boston: Flummery Press.

Boxer, Charles R., ed. 1953. *South China in the sixteenth century*. Hakluyt Society Publications, 2nd ser., vol. 106. London.

9.2.2.2 Periodical

In general, the data included in reference list entries for articles in periodicals are as follows:

(1) author's name;

(2) year;

(3) title of article;

(4) title of periodical;

(5) issue information (volume, issue number, month or season);

(6) page reference.

The names of the authors of articles in periodicals are inverted in reference

Chapter 9
Documentation (3): The Chicago Manual Style

lists — last name first. In reference lists, however, initials often replace all given names. Whether full given names or initials are used, consistency should be observed if possible, but it is also acceptable to mix the two practices in order to accommodate the preferences of the cited authors.

Titles of articles are given sentence capitalization and are set in roman type without quotation marks. Subtitles may be omitted, if this is done consistently, and it is also acceptable to omit the whole title, leaving the reader to find the article in the cited volume or issue of the periodical.

The titles of the periodicals themselves are italicized and given headline, or regular title, capitalization. Periodical titles are sometimes abbreviated, especially in the sciences.

Issue information includes volume and issue number, when applicable, and sometimes the month and day, the month alone, or the season. The year is omitted from the issue information, since it has already appeared after the author's name. Arabic numerals are used for both volume and issue numbers.

1. Journal

1) Article title and journal title

Banks, William. 1958. A secret meeting in Boise. *Midwestern Political Review* 6: 26-31.

Bennett, J. W. 1946. The interpretation of Pueblo culture. *Southwestern Journal of Anthropology* 2: 361-74.

or

Bennett, J. W. 1946. *Southwestern Journal of Anthropology* 2: 361-74.

2) Title within article title

Lofton, Peter. 1989. Reverberations between wordplay and swordplay in *Hamlet*. *Aeolian Studies* 2: 12-29.

Loomis, C. C., Jr. 1960. Structure and sympathy in Joyce's "The dead." *PMLA* 75: 149-51.

3) Quotation within article title

Arbogast, Melvin. 1988. Meeting "a nicens little boy named baby tuckoo": Joyce observed. *Fictive Reviews* 2: 23-31.

4) Title ending with question mark or exclamation point

Starczak, E. S. 1986. At last! Patience rewarded. *Esoterica* 13: 42-49.

Quimber, Collie. 1977. Did Babbington disclose more than was necessary? *Political Review* 16: 71-78.

211

5) Month and season

Orsansky, Mollie. 1965. Counting the poor: Another look at the poverty profile. *Social Security Bulletin* 28 (January): 3-29.

Martin, Albro. 1979. Uneasy partners: Government-business relations in twentieth-century American history. *Prologue* 11 (summer): 91-105.

2. Magazine

Karen, Robert. 1990. Becoming attached. *Atlantic*, February, 35-70.

Caspari, E. W., and R. E. Marshak. 1965. The rise and fall of Lysenko. *Science*, 16 July, 275-78.

9.2.2.3 Newspaper

Finnonian, Albert. 1990. The Iron Curtain rises. *Wilberton Journal*, 7 February, final edition.

Philadelphia inquirer. 1990. Editorial, 30 July.

9.2.2.4 Interview

Citations to interviews are best made in running text in the author-date system, but if the author wishes, they may also be listed in the reference list or in an appendix.

Published:

Bundy, McGeorge. 1990. Interview by Robert MacNeil. *MacNeil/Lehrer news hour*. Public Broadcasting System, 7 February.

Unpublished:

Peterson, Tim G. 1989. Interview by author. Long Beach, Calif., 1 August.

9.2.2.5 Secondary Source

When reference is made to the work of one author as quoted in the work of another author, the reference list entry should include both works. If the discussion emphasizes the original work, that comes first in the entry. If the emphasis is on the use of the original source by the author of the secondary source, the secondary source should be listed first.

Zukofsky, Louis. 1931. Sincerity and objectification. *Poetry* 37 (February): 269. Quoted in Bonnie Costello, *Marianne Moore: Imaginary possessions* (Cambridge: Harvard

Chapter 9
Documentation (3): The Chicago Manual Style

University Press, 1981), 78.

or

Costello, Bonnie. 1981. *Marianne Moore: Imaginary possessions*, 78. Cambridge: Harvard University Press. Quoting Louis Zukofsky, Sincerity and objectification, *Poetry* 37 (February 1931): 269.

9.2.2.6 Thesis, Dissertation and Other Unpublished Work

The title of an unpublished paper is treated like the title of an article or other short work. In the reference list, it is set in roman type and given sentence capitalization, but it is not enclosed in quotation marks.

(King 1976, 32-37)

King, Andrew J. 1976. Law and land use in Chicago: A pre-history of modern zoning. Ph.D. diss., University of Wisconsin.

(Ross n.d., 142-55)

Ross, Dorothy. n.d. The Irish-Catholic immigrant, 1880-1900: A study in social mobility. Master's thesis, Columbia University.

9.2.2.7 Paper Read at Meeting

(Royce 1988)

Royce, John C. 1988. Finches of Du Page County. Paper read at 22nd Annual Conference on Practical Bird Watching, 24-26 May, at Midland University, Flat Prairie, Illinois.

9.2.2.8 Sound Recording

Recordings of drama, prose or poetry readings, lectures and the like, which often carry the name and location of the publisher and the date of publication or copyright, may be cited as follows in parenthetical text references and reference list.

(*Genesis of a novel* 1969)

Genesis of a novel: A documentary on the writing regimen of Georges Simenon. 1969. Tucson, Ariz.: Motivational Programming Corp. Sound cassette.

(Senn 1974)

Senn, M. J. E. 1974. *Masters and pupils*. Audiotapes of lectures by Lawrence S. Kubie, Jane Loevinger, and M. J. E. Senn presented at meeting of the Society for Research in Child Development, Philadelphia, March 1973. Chicago: University of Chicago Press.

If the date is unavailable, the recording is mentioned in the running text, and full documentation, minus the date, is given in the reference list entry:

Thomas, Dylan. *Under Milk Wood*. Performed by Dylan Thomas and others. Caedmon TC-2005. Audiocassette.

Thomas, Dylan. *Under Milk Wood*. Performed by Dylan Thomas and others. Caedmon TC-2005. Compact disk.

9.2.2.9 Slide, Film, and Videocassette

(*Greek and Roman World* 1977)

The Greek and Roman World. 1977. Chicago: Society for Visual Education. Filmstrip.

(Mihalyi 1975)

Mihalyi, Louis J. 1975. *Landscapes of Zambia, Central Africa*. Santa Barbara, Calif.: Visual Education. Slides.

(*Itzak Perlman* 1985)

Itzak Perlman: *In my case music*. 1985. Produced and directed by Tony Denonno. 10 min. DeNonno Pix. Videocassette.

9.2.2.10 Electronic Document

"Acquired Immunodeficiency Syndrome." 1990. In MESH vocabulary file [database online]. Dethesda, Md.: National Library of Medicine, 1990 [cited 3 October 1990]. Identifier no. D000163. [49 lines.]

Belle de jour. 1990. In Magill's Survey of the Cinema [database online]. Pasadena, Calif.: Salem Press, ca. 1989- [cited 1 January 1990]. Accession no. 50053. P. 2 of 4. Available from DIALOG Information Services, Inc., Palo Alto, Calif.

"Jericho's Walls." 1990. In History Log9008 [electronic bulletin board]. S. 1. 27 August 1990- [cited 15 December 1990]. Available from listserv@ FINHUTC.BITNET.

KULIKOWSKI, Stan. 1989. "Readability Formula." In NL-KR (Digest vol.5, no.10) [electronic bulletin board]. Rochester, N.Y., 1988 [cited 31 January 1989]. Available from nl-kr@ cs.rochester.edu; INTERNET.

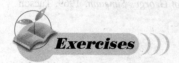

I. Answer the following questions.

1. What are the major differences between the notes and the bibliography?

Chapter 9
Documentation (3): The Chicago Manual Style

2. What changes do you make to convert a note entry into a bibliographic one?
3. What are the indispensable parts of the author-date system the Chicago style?
4. What are the similarities and differences between the note-bibliography system and the author-date system in documentation?

II. Fill in the blanks with the appropriate information.

1. Chicago style is traditionally a system of _____ and _____. It is most frequently used in the field of _____ and _____.
2. The Chicago documentary style consists of three elements, citation markers, _____, and _____. Notes are _____ numbered by Arabic _____. Footnotes are placed at the _____ of a page, and bibliography is _____ listed on a new page following the end of the text.
3. The first line of the note is indented _____; subsequent lines are flush _____. They are _____ spaced.
4. The bibliography begins on a _____ page and the word Bibliography is usually used as its _____.
5. While creating a note, for a book by four or more authors, enter only the _____ author's name, follow it up by the word _____. There is no need to mention all the authors in the notes. However, all the authors' names should be mentioned in full in the _____.
6. Most of the words in each entry are capitalized, with the exception of _____, _____, _____ and the infinitive _____. But any of these words may be capitalized when occur as the _____ or _____ word of a title or subtitle.
7. In the Chicago style, you may use either _____ or _____ for emphasis and title of books. You can not use them alternatively. You have to be _____ in your choice. But titles of _____ like the Koran or Bible (and all books therein) are not underlined or italicized.
8. If the foreword is the item cited, the entry is listed under the name of the author of the _____. The author of the _____ itself is given _____ the title of the work, from which it is separated by a comma and the word _____.
9. The names of the authors of articles in periodicals are _____ in reference lists. In reference lists, however, initials often replace all _____. Whether full given names or _____ are used, consistency should be

observed if possible, but it is also acceptable to _____ the two practices in order to accommodate the preferences of the cited authors.

10. When reference to both volume and page number is required, a _____ will distinguish between them, and the abbreviations *vol* and *p.* or *pp.* are _____. If more than one volume of the author's work is referred to in the same reference, the volumes are separated by _____. When a volume is referred to as a whole, without page number, the abbreviation *vol.* is _____ for clarity.

III. Decide whether the following entries are correct CHICAGO NOTE ENTRIES or not (N for NO, Y for YES).

1. David, Daiches, *Moses: The Man and his Vision* (New York: Praeger Publishers, 1975).( )

2. Jeff Bennett, "Environmental Values and Water Policy," *Australian Geographical Studies* 41, no. 3 (2003): 239, http://www.catchword.com/.( )

3. Julia Reinhard Lupton, "Creature Caliban," Shakespeare Quarterly 51.1 (2000): 17.( )

4. Matthew Arnold, "The Scholar-Gipsy," in *Poetry and Criticism of Matthew Arnold*, ed. A. Dwight Culler (Boston: Houghton-Mifflin, 1961): 151. ( )

5. American Political Science Association, *APSANET: The American Political Science Association Online*, 1 July 2000, <http://apsanet.org/> (23 August 2000).( )

6. "A Right to Discriminate?" *Washington Post*, B6, 20 August 2000.( )

7. Teresa del Valle, ed., *Gendered Anthropology* London and New York: Routledge, 1993.( )

8. Michael Harvey, *The Nuts and Bolts of College Writing* (Indianapolis: Hackett, 2000), <http://www.nutsandboltsguide.com/> (15 September 2000).( )

9. Jakob Burckhardt, *Fortune Is a Woman: Gender and Politics in the Thought of Nicole Machiavelli*, quoted in Hanna Fenichel Pitkin, (Berkeley: University of California Press, 1984), 25.( )

10. "Cuckoo Song," in *The Oxford Book of English Verse*, 1250–1900, ed. Arthur Thomas Quiller-Couch (1919; online edition, Bartleby.com, 1999),

Chapter 9
Documentation (3): The Chicago Manual Style

<http://.www.bartleby.com/101/1.html> (16 August 2000).( )

IV. **Decide whether the following entries are correct CHICAGO BIBLIOGRAPHY ENTRIES or not (N for NO, Y for YES).**

1. William H Rehnquist. *The Supreme Court: A History*. New York: Knopf, 2001. (   )
2. Kramer, Heinz. *A Changing Turkey: The Challenge to Europe and the United States*. Washington, DC: Brookings Press, 2000. http://brookings.nap.edu/books/0815750234/html/index.html. (   )
3. Rolle, Andrew F. *California: A History*. 5th ed. Wheeling, IL: Harlan Davidson, 1998. (   )
4. Zimmerman, Jonathan. "Ethnicity and the History Wars in the 1920s." *Journal of American History* 87, no. 1 (2000): 92–111. (   )
5. Pryce-Jones, David. "The Great Sorting Out: Postwar Iraq." *National Review*, May 5, 2003, 17 – 18. http://newfirstsearch.oclc.org. (   )
6. Budin, Stephanie Lynn. "The Origins of Aphrodite (Greece)." PhD diss., University ofPennsylvania, 2000. (   )
7. Willon, Phil. "Ready or Not." *Los Angeles Times*, December 2, 2001. http://www.latimes.com/news/la-foster-special.special.(   )
8. Tonya Browning, "Embedded Visuals: Student Design in Web Spaces," *Kairos: A Journal for Teachers of Writing in Webbed Environments* 3, no. 1 (1997), <http://english.ttu.edu/kairos/2.1/features/browning/index.html> (21 October 1999). (   )
9. U.S. Department of State. *Foreign Relations of the United States: Diplomatic Papers*, 1943. Washington, DC: GPO, 1965. (   )
10. Stephen Cauchi, "World's Green Markers on the Brink," *Age* (Melbourne), October 16, 2004, first edition. (   )

V. **With the information given in each situation, create (1) a note and the corresponding bibliography entry in the note-bibliography system; (2) an author-date citation and the corresponding reference entry in author-date system. Which one is more economical?**

1. *Paradise Lost* by John Milton, edited by Scott Elledge, published by W. W. Norton Press in New York in 1975.

2. An article by J. Schwarts, titled "Obesity Affects Economic, Social Status" published in the newspaper *The Washington Post*, September 30, 1993, the first edition.

3. Page 159 from the book *Femininity and Masculinity at the Movies: Impossible Bodies* by Chris Holmlund, published by Routledge in New York in 2002.

4. A chapter titled "What is a 'Religious War'?" page 324 of the book *Politics and Society in Reformation Europe*, co-edited by E. I. Kouri and Tom Scott, the book published by Macmillan Press in London in 1987.

5. An article titled "The Beguiled: Misogynyist Myth or Feminist Fable?" by Gina Herring from the journal *Literature Film Quarterly*. The article is in the 26th volume of the journal and the third issue of 1998. The page range of the article is 214–219.

6. An article "Pols on Film" by David Edelstein in an online magazine "Slate Magazine", published on August 18, 2000, from the website http://slate.msn.com/MovieReview/00-08-18/MovieReview.asp> and is accessed on August 20, 2006.

7. The PDF version of an article titled "Environmental Values and Water Policy" by Jeff Bennett from the 41st volume of the databank *Australian Geographical Studies* on page 239. The main entrance to the database is http://www.catchword.com/.

8. A reference to *If you want to write* by Brenda Uelang published by G. P. Putnam's Sons in New York in 1938, which was reprinted by Graywolf in St. Paul, MN, with the page range 15–16. The quoted part was from page 2 of the book *Becoming Expert: Writing and Learning in the disciplines* by Stuart C. Brown, Robert K. Mittan, and Duane H. Roen published by Kendall/Hunt Publishing Company at Dubuque, Iowa in 1990.

Appendix A
General Exercises for MLA, APA and Chicago Manual (Author-Date System) Styles

Write the parenthetical citation and the reference list entry in MLA, APA and Chicago author-date style respectively, according to the given information about the cited work.

1. John Oller called it a "formidable technical problem" (   ).
   Author: John W. Oller, Jr.
   Book title: Language tests at school
   Place of publication: London
   Time of publication: 1979
   Publisher: Longman
   Page number: 233

2. Most processes, actions, and entities, or conversely as themselves being constituent parts of larger ones (   ).
   Authors: A. J. Sanford and S. C. Garrod
   Book title: Understanding Written Language
   Place of publication: Chichester
   Time of publication: 1981
   Publisher: Wiley
   Page number: 30

3. The order of information in each utterance may be conceived as the answer to an imagined question, in which, as a general rule, known information is fronted and unknown information forced to the end, following the principle of "end focus" (   ).
   Authors: R. Quirk, S. Greenbaum, G. N. Leech, and J. Svartvik
   Book title: A Comprehensive Grammar of the English Language

Place of publication: London

Time of publication: 1985

Publisher: Longman

Page number: 1360-2

4. "Kiss" — as Barr and Feigenbaum observe — is not the same as "MOVE lips to lips" (   ).

Authors: A. Barr, and E. A. Feigenbaum

Book title: The Handbook of Artificial Intelligence (Vol. 2. of 3 vols)

Place of publication: Los Altos, Calif.

Time of publication: 1981

Publisher: William Kaufman

Page number: 214

5. In 1820, one master baker, at the opening of an apprentice's library, asked of the assembled, "Who can tell how many Franklins may be among you?" (   ).

Speaker: Mercein

Quoted Source (book title): Keepers of the Revolution: New Yorkers at Work in the Early Republic

Editors: Paul A. Gilje, and Howard B. Rock

Place of publication: Ithaca

Time of publication: 1992

Publisher: Cornell UP

Page number: 53

6. Initial work in AI concentrated almost exclusively on text comprehension rather than generation, sometimes with the vague and naïve assumption that human text generation is simply comprehension in reverse (   ).

Authors: J. Pitrat

Book title: An Artificial Intelligence Approach to Understanding Natural Language

Translated by: E. F. Harding

Place of publication: London

Time of publication: 1988

Publisher: North Oxford

Page number: 93

7. He cried out to his wife, "Faith! Faith! Look up to heaven and resist the wicked one" (   ), making his last effort in order to retain his hope.

Appendix A
General Exercises for MLA, APA and Chicago Manual (Author-Date System) Styles

Authors: Nathaniel Hawthorne
Title of the selection: Young Goodman Brown
Title of the anthology: The Norton Anthology of American Literature 3rd ed. Shorter
Editor of the anthology: Nina Baym
Place of publication: New York
Time of publication: 1989
Publisher: W. W. Norton and Company, Inc.
Page number on which the words quoted: 181
The pages on which the selection appears: 165-89

8. "Lacking a collective memory of the past, we lapse into a kind of amnesia, unaware of the human condition and the long struggles of men and women everywhere to deal with the problems of their day and to create a better society" ( ).

    Authors: Gary B. Nash, and Julie Roy Jeffrey
    Cited source: Preface of The American People: Creating a Nation and a Society (vol.1 of two vols.) Brief 3rd edition
    Editors of the book: Nash Gary B., et al.
    Place of publication: New York
    Time of publication: 2000
    Publisher: Longman
    Page number on which the words quoted: xvii
    The pages on which the preface appears: xvii-xxii

9. Building on work by Oskaarson, Joanna Lewis has written a delightful article about the use of self-assessment, also based on adult learners in Australia.
    Information for work 1:
    Author: Matts Oskaarson
    Article: Self-assessment of Language Proficiency: Rationale and Applications
    Source journal: Language Testing (6th volume, 1st issue)
    Year of publication: 1989
    Page numbers: 1-25
    Information for work 2:
    Author: Joanna Lewis
    Article: Self-assessment in the Classroom: A Case Study
    Source book: The second language curriculum in action (edited by Geoff

Brindley)

Year of publication: 1990

Page numbers: 187-213

Place of publication: Sydney

Publisher: Macquarie University, National Centre for English Language Teaching and Research

10. Liz Hamp-Lyons and Barbara Kroll explain the dilemma this way:

    The first requirement of any assessment of any assessment measure is stability: The goalposts, whatever they may be, must be the same for all persons being assessed and for all persons asked to make judgments. But a portfolio by its nature permits each writer to create a personal portrait, a personal record, which is in important ways different from the portrait or record created by every other writer. The force of the portfolio is in the sense of uniqueness it gives each writer. (   )

    Author: Liz Hamp-Lyons, and Barbara Kroll

    Article: Issues in ESL Writing Assessment: An Overview

    Source journal: College ESL (6th volume, 1st issue)

    Year of publication: 1996

    Page number for cited part: 67

    Page numbers on which the article appears: 52-72

11. The general conclusion was "the Jewish community has overreacted and Falwell may be a genuine ally of the Jews" (   ).

    Author: Phil Jacobs

    Article: Have We Been Misleading Jerry Falwell?

    Source newspaper: The Jewish News

    Date of publication: 21 Mar. 1986

    Page number: A16

12. As shown by Mendoza-Denton, taking into account the beliefs and attitudes of marginalized ethnic groups like the Lumbee about their own language variation augments traditional speech community studies.

    Author: Norma Catalina Mendoza-Denton

    Ph. D. dissertation: Chicana/Mexicana Identity and Linguistic Variation: An Ethnographic and Sociolinguistic Study of Gang Affiliation in an Urban High School

    Year accepted: 1997

Appendix A
General Exercises for MLA, APA and Chicago Manual (Author-Date System) Styles

Name of the institution: Stanford U

13. "The Events of War are uncertain: We cannot insure Success, but We can deserve it" (   ).

    Author: John Adams

    Letter: Letter to Abigail Adams

    Date: 18 Feb. 1776

    Printed in (book title): Reading the American Past Vol. 1

    Editor of the book: Michael P. Johnson

    Time of publication: 1998

    Place of Publication: Boston

    Publisher: Bedford

    Page number: 106

14. The three major ethnic groups in the county are American Indians (38.0%), Anglo Americans (30.8%), and African Americans (25.1%) (   ).

    Corporate author: Bureau of the Census.

    Title of the work: 2000 Census of Population and Housing: North Carolina

    Web site: Profiles of General Demographic Characteristics, 2000

    Date the work issued: May 2001

    Date the source accessed: 19 Apr. 2002

    URL: http://www.census.gov/prod/cen2000/dp1/2kh37.pdf

    Page number for the cited content: 79

15. "President Vladimir Putin believes that a powerful, state-controlled energy sector is the key to Russia's economic future, even if he has to strong-arm foreign investors to get it" (   ).

    Title of the editorial: The Kremlin's Shell Game

    Online newspaper: New York Times

    Date of publication: 19 Dec. 2006

    Date of access: 20 Dec. 2006

    URL: http://www.nytimes.com/2006/12/19/opinion/19tuc1.html

16. "While in Japanese culture, ambiguous terminology is typical of their language. Indirect and vague expression is more acceptable than direct and specific references" (   ).

    Author: Cheng Qiang

    Article: The Impact of Cultural Factors on Trans-cultural Negotiation

Printed in Journal: US-China Foreign Language (3rd volume, 4th issue)
Year of publication: 2005
Page number for cited part: 43
Page numbers on which the article appears: 42–44
Date of access: 20 Dec. 2006
URL: http://www.linguist.org.cn/doc/uc200504/uc20050407.doc

Appendix B
Samples

Sample 1　Title Page

A Preliminary Study of Heathcliff's
Humanity in *Wuthering Heights*(**Title of the Thesies**)

By
×××(**Anthor's Name**)

A Thesis Submitted to
Department of Foreign Languages and Literature
In Partial Fulfillment of the Requirements
For the Degree of B.A. in English
At ×× University

Under the Supervision of ××× (Instructor's Name)

(Completion Date)

Sample 2-1 Outline Page (in number-letter style)

Outline

Title: Microcomputer Programs and the Process of Writing

Thesis statement: Microcomputer programs can have a positive effect on students' writing if both the potentials and limitations of the programs are understood.

I. Major Steps in the writing process
   A. Organizing
   B. Writing the first draft
   C. Evaluating
   D. Revising

II. Writing programs for the microcomputer
   A. Types of programs and their relationship to the writing process
      1. Thought
         a. Use in organizing
         b. Use in revising
      2. Word processors
         a. Use in writing the first draft
         b. Use in revising
      ...
   B. Positive and Negative Aspects of Computer Writing Programs
      1. Positive features
         a. Less time spent on repetitive or mechanical writing tasks
         b. Greater flexibility and versatility in writing process
         ...
      2. Negative features
         a. The increased time spent on learning software programs and computers
         b. The availability of hardware and software
         c. The unrealistic expectations of users
            (1) A cure-all for writing problems
            (2) A way to avoid learning correct grammar/syntax/spelling
         ...

III. Future Possibilities of Computer Programs for Writing
   A. Rapid change
   B. Improved programs
   C. Increased use and availability
   D. More realistic assessment of value-critical work

...

Sample 2-2　Outline Page (in decimal style)

Outline

Title: Microcomputer Programs and the Process of Writing
Thesis: Microcomputer programs can have a positive effect on students' writing if both the potentials and limitations of the programs are understood.

1. Major Steps in the writing process
    1.1 Organizing
    1.2 Writing the first draft
    1.3 Evaluating
    1.4 Revising

2. Writing programs for the microcomputer
    2.1 Types of programs and their relationship to the writing process
        2.1.1 Thought
            2.1.1.1 Use in organizing
            2.1.1.2 Use in revising
        2.1.2 Word processors
            2.1.2.1 Use in writing the first draft
            2.1.2.2 Use in revising
        ...
    2.2. Positive and Negative Aspects of Computer Writing Programs
        2.2.1 Positive features
            2.2.1.1 Less time spent on repetitive or mechanical writing tasks
            2.2.1.2 Greater flexibility and versatility in writing process
            ...
        2.2.2 Negative features
            2.2.2.1 The increased time spent on learning software programs and computers
            2.2.2.2 The availability of hardware and software
            2.2.2.3 The unrealistic expectations of users
                2.2.2.3.1 A cure-all for writing problems
                2.2.2.3.2 A way to avoid learning correct grammar/syntax/spelling
            ...

3. Future Possibilities of Computer Programs for Writing
    3.1 Rapid change
    3.2 Improved programs
    3.3 Increased use and availability
    3.4 More realistic assessment of value-critical work
...

(Online Writing Lab qtd. in Liu Jianbo 35-36 — adapted)

Sample 3   Table of Contents

Contents

Introduction ·· 1

Chapter I. The Causes for Heathcliff's Distortion ················· 2

    A. Heathcliff's Personal background ··· 3

    B. Injustice of Society ··· 5

    C. Blow of the Betrayed Love ·· 7

Chapter II. The Manifestation of Heathcliff's Distortion ········· 8

    A. Merciless Revenge ··· 8

    B. Sadistic Abuse ··· 10

Chapter III. The Result of Heathcliff's Distortion ··············· 12

    A. Destructiveness to Other Characters ······································· 13

    B. Self-destructiveness of His Own Life ······································· 14

Conclusion ··· 16

Notes ··· 17

Works Cited ·· 18

(qtd. in Tian Guisun and Duan Xiaoying 127)

Appendix B
Samples

Sample 4 List of Tables

Tables

1. Smokers and Non-smokers, by Sex 2

2. Smokers and Non-smokers, by Age 3

3. Smoking among Adult Chinese, by Type of Background, Urban or Rural 8

4. Smoking among University Students, by Type of Background, Family-Supported or Self-Supported 13

5. Effect of Smoking on University Students during Four Year's Life at Campus 15

Appendix C
Revision Symbols

abb	incorrect abbreviation
act	use active voice
agr	faulty subject-verb agreement
awk	awkward expression
bf	set in boldface type
bib	bibliographic form incorrect
cap	use capital letter
ce	chinese english
cit	citation missing or incorrect
co	use correct coordination
coh	lack of coherence
cs	comma splice
d	use appropriate diction
dang	dangling modifier
dev	development needed
div	improper word division
emph	emphasis unclear
ex	example needed
fig	faulty figure of speech
frag	sentence fragment
fs	fused sentence
gd	good word or sentence
gr	error in grammar
hyph	hyphen
id	unidiomatic expression
ital	use italics
lc	use a lowercase letter

Appendix C
Revision Symbols

log	faulty logic
mm	misplaced modifier
mng	meaning unclear
ms	improper manuscript form
no ,	no comma
no cap	capital letter not needed
no ¶	new paragraph not needed
p	error in punctuation
pl	error in plural use
pro	error in pronoun use
red	redundant
ref	faulty pronoun reference
rep	needless reputation
rev	revise
run-on	run-on sentence
sexist	sexist language
shift	confusing shift
slang	slang
sp	spelling error
sub	subordination
sum	summarize
t	error in verb tense
tr	transpose
trans	transition required
trite	trite expression
u	unity
vague	vague statement
vb	error in verb form
vo	error in voice
wrdy	wordy
wv	weak verb
ww	wrong word
⌣	close up space (vertical)
⌢	close up space (horizontal)
⌇	delete

英语专业毕业论文写作教程
Writing Thesis in English *A Course in Writing for English Majors*

∧	something missing, insert something
¶	start new paragraph
#	insert space
?	unclear
⟂	indent
⊙	insert period
∽	invert

Bibliography

Booth, Wayne C., Gregory G. Colomb, and Joseph M. Williams. *The Craft of Research*. Chicago: The University of Chicago Press, 1995.

Brown, Stuart C., Robert K. Mittan, and Duane H. Roen. *Becoming Expert: Writing and Learning in the Disciplines*. Dubuque, Iowa: Kendall/Hunt Publishing Company, 1990.

Cheng Aimin, and Qi Shouhua. *Effective Academic Writing in English: An Essential Guide*. Shanghai: Shanghai Foreign Education Press, 2005.

The Chicago Manual of Style. 14th ed. Chicago: The University of Chicago Press, 1993.

Devlin, Brian. *International Standards for Students' Writing*. Beijing: Qinghua University Press, 2003.

Ding Wangdao, Wu Bing, Zhong Meisun, and Guo Qiqing. *A Basic Course in Writing*. Beijing: Higher Education Press, 1998.

Fabb, Nigel, and Alan Durant. *How to write Essays, Dissertations and Theses in Literary Studies*. Chengdu: Sichuan University Press, 2003.

Feng Cuihua. *Essential Strategies for English Academic Writing*. Shanghai: Shanghai Foreign Language Education Press, 2003.

Gao Fen 高奋. *Waiyu Lei Xuesheng Biye Lunwen Xiezuo Zhidao* 外语类学生毕业论文写作指导 (Thesis Writing Guide for Students of Foreign Languages). Hangzhou: Zhejiang University Press, 2004.

Gibaldi, Joseph. *MLA Handbook for Writers of Research Papers*. 5th ed. New York: MLA, 1999.

---. *MLA Handbook for Writers of Research Papers*. 6th ed. New York: MLA, 2003.

Hashimoto, Irvin Y., Barry M. Kroll, and John C. Schafer. *Strategies for Academic Writing: A Guide for College Students*. The University of Michigan Press, 1982.

Huang Guowen, Ge Daxi, and Zhang Meifang. *How to Write a Research Paper*. Chongqing: Chongqing University Press, 2004.

Li Zhengshuan 李正栓. *Yingyu Zhuanye Benke Biye Lunwen Sheji Yu Xiezuo Zhidao*

英语专业本科毕业论文设计与写作指导(Thesis Design and Writing Guide for English Majors). Beiing：Beijing University Press, 2006.

Lindemann, Erika. *A Rhetoric for Writing Teachers*. New York：Oxford University Press, 1982.

Liu, Jianbo, ed. *Writing English Research Papers：A Handbook for English Majors*. Beijing：Higher Education Press, 2004.

Liu Xinmin 刘新民. *Yingyu Lunwen Xiezuo Guifan* 英语论文写作规范(Standard Formats for English Research Papers). Beijing：Higher Education Press, 2003.

Lunsford, Andrea, and Robert Connors. *The St. Martin's Handbook*. 2nd ed. New York：ST. Martin's Press, 1992.

Mu Shixiong 穆诗雄. *Yingyu zhuanye biye lunwen xiezuo* 英语专业毕业论文写作 (Paper Writing：A Guide for English Majors). Beijing：Foreign Language Teaching and Research Press, 2002.

Seyfer, Harlen, and Wu Guhua. *English Academic Paper Writing*. Beijing：Higher Education Press, 1998.

Shi Jian, and Shuai Peitian. *English Essay Writing*. Chengdu：Sichuan People's Press, 2005.

Slade, Carole. *Form and Style：Research Papers, Reports and Thesis*. 10th ed. Beijing：Foreign Language Teaching and Research Press & Thomson Learning Asia Houghton Mifflin Company, 2000.

Sun Xiaoling, Ren Suihu 孙晓玲,任遂虎. *Biye Lunwen Xiezuo fangfa Jingyao* 毕业论文写作方法精要 (Essentials of Thesis Writing). Lanzhou：Lanzhou University Press, 2005.

Swales, John M., and Christine B. Feak. *Academic Writing for Graduate Students：Essential Tasks and Skills*. The University of Michigan Press, 1994.

Tian Guisen, and Duan Xiaoying. *Writing Graduation Thesis*. Beijing：Beijing Institute of Technology Press, 2006.

Turabian, Kate L. *Student's Guide for Writing College Papers*. 3rd ed. Chicago：The University of Chicago Press, 1976.

---. *A Manual for Writers of Term Papers, Thesis, and Dissertations*. 5th ed. Rev. & Exp. Bonnie Birtwistle Honigsblum. Chicago：The University of Chicago Press, 1987.

Voss, Ralph F., and Michael L. Keene. *The Heath Guide to College Writing*. Lexington, MA：D.C. Heath and Company, 1992.

Wang Jialing 王嘉陵. *Biye Lunwen Xiezuo Yu Dabian* 毕业论文写作与答辩(Thesis

Bibliography

Writing and Oral Defense). Chengdou: Sichuan University Press, 2003.

Wen Qiufang. *Applied Linguistics: Research Methods and Thesis Writing.* Beijing: Foreign Language Teaching and Research Press, 2001.

Zhang Xiuguo. *English Rhetoric.* Beijing: Qinghua University Press, and Beijing Jiaotong University Press, 2005.

Zhou Kaixin. *A Handbook of Academic Research Paper Writing for English Majors.* Beijing: Foreign Language Teaching and Research Press, 2006.

Guffey, Mary Ellen. *MLA Style Electronic Format.* 25 Aug. 2001. 2 Mar. 2006 <http://www.westwords.com/guffey/mla.html>.

Hacker, Diana. *Research and Documentation on Line.* Feb. 2006. 2 Mar. 2006 <http://www.dianahacker.com/resdoc/home.html>.

Honolulu Community College Library. *MLA Citation Examples.* 20 Sep. 2004. 20 Feb. 2006 <http://honolulu.hawaii.edu/legacylib/mlahcc.html>.

Kilborn, Judith. *MLA Parenthetical Documentation.* 16 Mar. 2004. 12 Feb. 2006 <http://leo.stcloudstate.edu/research/mlaparen.html>.

Lee, I. *A Research Guide for Students.* 24 Mar. 2005. 10 Dec. 2005 <http://www.aresearchguide.com/index.html>.

MLA Style Guide. 1 Mar. 2006. 2 Mar. 2006 <http://www.lib.usm.edu/research/guides/mla.html>.

Index

abbreviations 3. 1. 9; 5. 2; 5. 2. 1-6; 5. 8. 1; 5. 8. 6; 7. 1. 4. 3-4; 7. 2. 1; 9. 2. 1. 2

abstract

    in Chinese 3. 1. 4

    in English 3. 1. 3

appendix 3. 3. 2; 5. 1; 5. 9. 4; 5. 11. 1; 5. 11. 3; 5. 15; 9. 2. 2. 4

approach 1. 2; 2. 3. 2; 3. 1. 3

argument 2. 3; 2. 3. 2-3; 2. 3. 5. 2; 2. 4; 2. 5. 1. 2; 2. 6; 3. 1. 5; 3. 2. 1. 1; 3. 2. 3; 4. 2; 4. 6; 4. 6. 1; 4. 13; 5. 11; 5. 11. 2; 5. 11. 4

background 3. 2; 3. 2. 1; 3. 2. 1. 1

    general 2. 2. 1. 1

    information 2. 2. 2; 2. 6; 3. 2. 1. 1

    material 2. 2. 1. 1; 3. 2. 1. 1

    publication 2. 3. 2

bibliography 3. 3. 1; 5. 1; 5. 9; 5. 15; 7. 2; 7. 2. 2; 7. 3; 8. 2; 9. 1. 1-3

    working 1. 2; 2. 2. 1. 6; 2. 3; 2. 3. 1; 3. 3. 1

capitalization 2. 7; 2. 7. 3; 3. 1. 1; 3. 1. 6; 5. 1; 5. 8. 7; 5. 9

    headline-style 5. 1

    sentence-style 5. 1

caption 3. 1. 7; 5. 11. 2; 5. 11. 4; 6. 9

CD-ROM 2. 2. 1. 4; 2. 2. 1. 5; 7. 3. 6; 7. 3. 6. 5

checker

    spell 2. 7. 2

    grammar 2. 7. 2

citation 2. 3. 1; 5. 15; 6. 3; 7. 2; 7. 3; 7. 3. 1; 7. 3. 6. 4; 7. 3. 7; 7. 3. 7. 1; 7. 3. 8. 1; 8. 1; 8. 1. 2; 8. 1. 5; 8. 2; 8. 2. 5; 9. 1. 1-3; 9. 1. 3. 1-4; 9. 1. 3. 8; 9. 2; 9. 2. 1-2; 9. 2. 2. 1; 9. 2. 2. 4

    note 7. 2

    parenthetical 2. 3. 5; 7. 1; 7. 1. 1-4; 8. 2; 9. 2. 1. 3

    placement of 7. 11

Index

punctuation of 7. 11
coherence 2. 5. 1. 2 ; 2. 7. 3 ; 4. 8 ; 4. 10 ; 4. 11 ; 4. 13
conference paper 9. 1. 3
    published 9. 1. 3. 5
    unpublished 9. 1. 3. 5
consistency 5. 4 ; 9. 2. 2. 1 ; 9. 2. 2. 2
    logical 4. 9
copyright 2. 3. 1
    page 2. 3. 1 ; 7. 3. 2
dash 5. 1 ; 5. 15 ; 5. 16. 1 ; 6. 4 ; 6. 5 ; 9. 1. 3. 1
data 1. 2 ; 2. 1. 2. 2 ; 2. 1. 3 ; 2. 2 ; 2. 3. 1 ; 2. 3. 4. 1 ; 2. 6 ; 3. 1. 3 ; 3. 1. 5 ; 5. 11 ;
    5. 11. 1−2 ; 9. 2. 2. 2
data-analysis 3. 2. 2
data-collection 3. 2. 2
database 2. 2 ; 2. 2. 1. 4−5 ; 2. 3. 1 ; 7. 3 ; 9. 1. 3. 3 ; 9. 1. 3. 4 ; 9. 1. 3. 6
date
    of access 2. 2. 1 ; 7. 3 ; 7. 3. 6. 1 ; 7. 3. 6. 3 ; 7. 3. 6. 4 ; 7. 3. 7 ; 7. 3. 7. 1 ; 7. 3. 8. 1 ;
    9. 1. 3. 8 ; 9. 1. 3. 9
    of edition 7. 3. 2. 7
    of publication 3. 3. 1 ; 7. 3 ; 7. 3. 2. 11 ; 7. 3. 6 ; 7. 3. 6. 1−2 ; 8. 2. 1−4 ; 8. 2. 4. 4 ;
    8. 2. 6 ; 8. 2. 8 ; 9. 2. 1. 3 ; 9. 2. 2. 8
decimal 5. 8. 1−2 ; 5. 8. 4
    pattern 2. 5. 2
    point 5. 8. 2
    outline format 2. 5. 2
diction 2. 7. 3 ; 4. 1 ; 6. 11
division 2. 5. 2 ; 2. 7. 1 ; 5. 1 ; 5. 3 ; 5. 9. 4 ; 5. 18 ; 5. 18. 2 − 3 ; 7. 1. 4 ; 7. 1. 4. 3 ;
    7. 3. 6. 3 ; 9. 2. 1. 2
    of letter 5. 17. 2
    of lines of text 5. 17. 2
    of number 5. 17. 2
    of word 5. 17. 1
double-space 3. 1. 6 ; 3. 1. 7 ; 3. 1. 8 ; 3. 1. 9 ; 3. 3. 2 ; 5. 12 ; 5. 15 ; 5. 18. 3 ; 7. 2. 2 ;
    7. 3
economy 4. 4

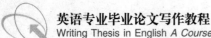

editing 2.7; 2.7.1-2; 4.12; 9.2.2.1
ellipsis 6.12; 7.1.1
enumeration 4.10; 5.10; 6.5; 6.9
exclamation points 6.11
experiment 2.1.3; 2.2; 3.2.1.1; 3.2.2; 4.5
figure 3.1; 3.1.7; 3.3.2; 4.13; 5.1; 5.8.1-5; 5.8.7; 5.8.9; 5.11; 5.11.3;
    5.18.3; 6.9; 8.1.5; 9.2.1.2
  placement of 5.11.5
  relation of figures and text 5.11.4
foreign word 5.3; 5.6
fraction 5.8.1; 5.8.3; 6.8
grammar 2.3.4.2; 2.7.2; 6.1
heading 2.5.1; 2.5.1.2; 2.5.2; 3.1.2; 3.1.6; 3.1.9; 4.8; 4.9; 5.9; 5.16.4;
    5.18; 5.18.2-3; 6.9; 8.1.5
hyphenation 5.4; 5.7
hypothesis 2.1; 3.2.3
illustration 3.1.7; 3.3.2; 5.2; 5.11.3; 7.3
indentation 5.10; 5.15; 5.16.3; 5.18.3
index 2.2.1.2; 2.3.1
  book 2.2; 2.2.1.3
  electronic 2.2.1.5
  periodical 2.1.2.1; 2.2; 2.2.1.4
italic 5.3; 5.6; 8.2
judgment 1.2; 2.1.1; 2.3.5.2; 4.2; 5.15
literary work 7.1.4; 7.1.4.1
literature review 3.2; 3.2.2
manageability 2.1; 2.1.2; 2.4
margin 5.10; 5.11.5; 5.12; 5.15; 5.16.2-4; 5.17.1-2; 5.18.3; 7.2.2; 7.3;
    8.2
method 1.2; 2.1.2.1; 2.1.2.2; 2.3.4.1; 2.4; 3.1.3; 3.3.2; 4.10; 6.12
motivation 3.1.3
number
  chapter 3.1.6; 5.18.2
  figure 3.1.7; 5.11.4
  inclusive 5.8.8

Index

    note 5. 15
    part 3. 1. 6; 5. 18. 2
    plurals of 5. 8. 9
    punctuation of 5. 8. 2
    superscript 7. 2. 2
    table 3. 18; 5. 11. 2
number-letter sequence 2. 5. 2
numerals 2. 5. 2; 5. 2. 4; 5. 8. 1; 5. 8. 3; 5. 8. 5–6; 5. 10; 5. 12; 5. 18. 2
    arabic 3. 1. 7; 3. 3. 3; 5. 8. 10; 5. 10; 5. 12; 7. 1. 4. 2; 9. 1. 1; 9. 2. 2. 2
    roman 3. 1. 6; 5. 8. 10; 5. 12
objectivity 2. 3. 2
outline 2. 3. 4. 1; 2. 4; 2. 5; 2. 6; 4. 8; 4. 9; 5. 8. 10; 5. 15
    page 3. 1; 3. 1. 2
    paragraph 2. 5. 1. 3; 3. 1. 2
    sentence 2. 5. 1. 2; 4. 8
    style 2. 5. 2
    topic 2. 5. 1; 2. 5. 1. 1; 3. 1. 2
    types of 2. 5. 1
paragraph
    constructing 4. 13
    structure of 4. 13
    transitional 2. 7. 1; 4. 11
    unity 4. 10
parentheses
    use of 6. 5
part
    of speech 5. 9. 1
    title 3. 1. 6; 7. 3. 6. 3
percentage 5. 8. 1; 5. 8. 4
period
    internal 5. 2. 1
    leaders 3. 1. 6; 3. 1. 7
    use of 5. 2. 1
plagiarism 2. 3. 5
    deliberate 2. 3. 5

unintended 2.3.5; 2.3.5.3
plural 4.3; 4.12; 5.5; 5.8.9; 9.2.1.1; 9.2.2.1
proofreading 1.2; 2.6; 2.7; 2.7.1; 2.7.3
punctuation
    marks 5.16.1; 6.10
    of citation 7.1.1
    of number 5.8.2
quotation
    direct 2.3.4.2; 2.3.5; 2.3.5.2-3; 5.3; 6.6; 7.1
    indirect 6.6
reference
    book 2.2
    cross 7.3; 9.1.3.6
    list 3.3; 3.3.1; 5.1; 5.2.3; 5.9; 5.10; 8.1; 8.2; 9.2; 9.2.1.1; 9.2.2;
        9.2.2.1; 9.2.2.2; 9.2.2.4-6; 9.2.2.8
    parenthetical 3.3.3; 5.1; 5.2.3; 5.15; 6.12; 7.1.1; 7.1.3.2; 7.1.3.7;
        7.1.3.10; 8.1
    works 2.2.1; 2.3.2; 9.1.3.7
research
    field 2.2; 2.3.5.1-2
    primary 2.2
    secondary 2.2
resource 2.1.3; 2.2.1.6
revising 2.6; 2.7; 2.7.1; 4.12
revision 1.1; 2.7.1; 2.7.3; 3.3.1; 4.4
signal phrase 2.3.4.2; 7.1.2.1; 7.1.2.3; 7.1.3.1-2; 7.1.3.4-5; 7.1.3.10-11
single-space 3.1.6-9; 5.15
slash 5.15; 6.8; 7.3.6
source
    electronic 2.3.1; 7.1.2-3; 7.3.6; 8.1.5; 8.2.8
    multimedia 7.3.7
    print 7.1.2-3
spacing 3.1.1; 3.3.2; 5.8.3; 5.16.1
specificity 2.4
spelling 2.7; 5.1; 5.4

Index

square bracket 6. 7; 6. 12
subject 1. 1; 1. 2; 2. 1; 2. 1. 1; 2. 1. 2. 1 – 2; 2. 2. 1. 1; 2. 2. 1. 3; 2. 2. 1. 5 – 6; 2. 2. 2; 2. 3. 1; 2. 3. 2; 2. 4; 2. 5. 1. 1; 2. 6; 3. 1. 3; 3. 2. 1; 3. 2. 2; 4. 13; 5. 1
summary 2. 3. 4. 2; 2. 6; 3. 2. 2; 6. 4; 7. 1
superscript 3. 3. 3; 5. 16. 1
    use of 7. 2. 2
survey 2. 1. 3; 2. 3. 5. 1–2; 4. 5
table
    of contents 3. 1; 3. 1. 6
    placement of 5. 11. 5
    relation of 5. 11. 2
tense 2. 3. 4. 2; 4. 5; 4. 8
thesis 1. 2; 2. 7. 1; 3. 2. 1; 5. 11. 2
    formulating 1. 2; 2. 4
    statement 2. 4; 2. 5; 2. 6; 3. 1. 2; 3. 2. 1. 2; 4. 13
    working 2. 4
title
    capitalized 5. 9. 1
    in quotation marks 5. 9. 3; 7. 3. 6. 3; 7. 3. 7. 5; 7. 3. 8. 3; 8. 1. 4
    underlined (italicized) 5. 9. 5
    without underlining or quotation marks 5. 9. 4
tone 2. 3. 4. 2; 2. 4; 4. 2
topic 1. 1; 1. 2; 2. 1; 2. 1. 1; 2. 1. 2; 2. 1. 4; 2. 2. 1; 2. 2. 1. 2; 2. 2. 1. 4–6; 2. 2. 2; 2. 3. 1; 2. 3. 4; 2. 3. 4. 2; 2. 4; 2. 6; 3. 2. 1. 1; 7. 1. 3. 9; 9. 1. 3. 1
    broad 2. 1. 2. 1; 2. 1. 2. 2
    narrow 2. 1. 2. 1; 2. 1. 2. 2
    sentence 2. 5. 1. 3; 4. 10; 4. 13
unbiased language 4. 12
underlining 5. 3; 5. 6; 5. 9. 2; 5. 9. 4; 5. 9. 5; 8. 2
voice 4. 3
    active 4. 7
    passive 4. 7

Index

square bracket 6.7 ; 6.12
subject 1.1 ; 1.2 ; 2.1 ; 1.1 ; 2.1.1-2 ; 2.2.1.1 ; 2.2.1.3 ; 2.2.1.5-6 ;
   2.2.2 ; 2.3.1 ; 2.3.2 ; 2.4 ; 2.5.1.1.2.a ; 3.1.3 ; 3.2.1 ; 3.2.2 ; 4.13 ;
   5.1
summary 2.8 ; 4.2 ; 2.6 ; 3.2 ; 6.4 ; 7.1
superscript 3.3 ; 5.16.1
use of 7.2.2
survey 2.1.3 ; 2.3 ; 5.1-2 ; 4.5
table
   of contents 3.1 ; 3.1.6
   placement of 5.11.5
   relation of 5.11.2
tense 2.3.4.2 ; 4.5 ; 4.8
thesis 1.2 ; 2.2.8 ; 3.2.1 ; 5.11.2
   formulating 1.2 ; 2.2
statement 2.4 ; 2.5 ; 2.6 ; 3.1.2 ; 3.2.1.2 ; 4.13
working 2.4
title
   capitalized 3.9.1
   in quotation marks 5.9.3 ; 7.3.6.3 ; 7.3.7.2 ; 7.3.8 ; 8.1.4
   underlined (italicized) 5.9.3
   without underlining or quotation marks 5.9.4
tone 2.3.1.2 ; 2.4 ; 4.2
topic 1.1 ; 1.2 ; 2.1.1 ; 2.1.1.2 ; 2.2.1.4 ; 2.2.1 ; 2.2.1.1 ; 2.2.1.4-6 ; 2.2.1.7 ;
   2.3.1 ; 2.3.4 ; 2.3.1.2 ; 2.4 ; 2.9 ; 2.11 ; 3.2 ; 10.5 ; 9.3.1
broad 2.1.2 ; 1.2 ; 1.2.2
narrow 2.1.1.2 ; 2.1.2.2
sentence 2.5.1.1 ; 4.10 ; 4.13
unbiased language 4.12
underlining 5.2 ; 5.6 ; 5.9.2 ; 5.9.4 ; 5.9.5 ; 8.2
voice 4.7
   active 4.7
   passive 4.7